c.1

SIMON FRASER UNIVERSITY LIBRARY

Unless recalled, all materials
due on last date stamped

Remembering the Crusades

RETHINKING THEORY
Stephen G. Nichols and Victor E. Taylor, *Series Editors*

Remembering the Crusades

Myth, Image, and Identity

Edited by
NICHOLAS PAUL
and SUZANNE YEAGER

The Johns Hopkins University Press
Baltimore

The Johns Hopkins University Press
2715 North Charles Street
Baltimore, Maryland 21218-4363
www.press.jhu.edu

Library of Congress Cataloging-in-Publication Data

Remembering the crusades : myth, image, and identity / Nicholas Paul and Suzanne Yeager,
editors.
      p. cm. — (Rethinking theory)
Includes bibliographical references and index.
ISBN-13: 978-1-4214-0425-7 (hdbk.: alk. paper)
ISBN-10: 1-4214-0425-7 (hdbk.: alk. paper)
1. Crusades — First, 1096–1099. 2. Crusades — First, 1096–1099 — Historiography.
3. Crusades — First, 1096–1099 — In literature. 4. Crusades — Influence. I. Paul, Nicholas,
1977– II. Yeager, Suzanne M.
D161.2.R46   2012
956'.014 — dc23   2011026161

A catalog record for this book is available from the British Library.

*Special discounts are available for bulk purchases of this book. For more information,
please contact Special Sales at 410-516-6936 or specialsales@press.jhu.edu.*

CONTENTS

ACKNOWLEDGMENTS

This volume is the fruit of two felicitous meetings, both made possible by the wonderfully collegial atmosphere of the Center for Medieval Studies at Fordham University. The first was between the two editors, who wondered whether they might find some common ground between their own research — crusade and family memory, on the one hand, and crusade and memory in the medieval imaginary, on the other. To further explore the larger question of the crusades within medieval conceptualizations of the past, we the editors organized a larger meeting, an international three-day conference held at Fordham in March 2008. The event received an enormously positive response, encouraging us to put together this volume of essays, some of which grew out of papers given at the conference.

In addition to our contributors, whose hard work and patience we hope has at last been rewarded, we are grateful to the many people who supported us in the preparation of this volume. The anonymous reader for the Johns Hopkins University Press provided us with invaluable advice on shaping and editing the project. We also deeply appreciate Professor Stephen Nichols's enthusiasm for our study and thank editors Trevor Lipscombe, Matt McAdam, Kara Reiter, Linda Forlifer, and Barbara Lamb at the Press for helping us bring the volume to completion.

At every step along the way in realizing this project, Maryanne Kowaleski shared her friendship and advice, and she provided indispensable comments on our introduction. We also benefited from the advice and encouragement of Suzanne Conklin Akbari, Geraldine Heng, Jonathan Riley-Smith, Caroline Smith, and Kathryn A. Smith.

For their help in staging the conference that inspired this collection, we thank the director of Medieval Studies, Maryanne Kowaleski; Dean Nancy Busch of the Graduate School of Arts and Sciences; the dedicated group of graduate students who assisted in running the event; and of course all of the conference participants who contributed so richly to the conversation about crusade and memory. We hope that this volume continues to enrich the discussions that were begun at that meeting.

Finally, we are grateful to our families for their patient support as we finished work on this volume. Caroline Paul and Ieuan Williams will no doubt be glad to see this project finally completed so that we can now get to work making happy memories with Graeme James Yeager Williams and Anthea Jean Paul, who both appeared slightly in advance of the publication.

Remembering the Crusades

Introduction

Crusading and the Work of Memory, Past and Present

NICHOLAS PAUL *and* SUZANNE YEAGER

$\mathfrak{I}$N LATE NOVEMBER OF 1097 the Picard nobleman Anselm of Ribemont composed a letter to Archbishop Manasses of Reims, informing
him of the progress of the armies of the First Crusade, recently arrived
before the city of Antioch in northern Syria.[1] Anselm had been among
those men and women who answered the call issued by Pope Urban II in
1095 to take up arms and march to the East to defend the Eastern Church
and free the city of Jerusalem and other holy places from the perceived
tyranny of Muslim rule. In his letter, Anselm related how the crusaders
captured the city of Nicaea and then marched across Asia Minor. But he
prefaced his narrative and descriptions with a special plea: "I pray however that you and the canons of the mother church of Reims, my lords and
fathers, should remember us (*ut memores nostri sitis*), not only me and
those who labour in this place in the service of the Lord, but also those of
the army of the Lord who have fallen or rest in peace."[2] Anselm emphasized his plea by naming some of his fallen companions, urging his friend
and "everyone whom this letter reaches" to pray for the dead, and assur-
ing them that these men had not died in vain because of their victorious
conquest of many cities and castles.[3]

Anselm's letter can be seen as the nexus of several commemorative
processes. By asking a scribe to record his account of battles, sieges, suffering, and hope, Anselm was creating one of the earliest written memorials
of the crusading experience. But the letter itself was also a call for commemoration, an instrument with which he hoped to interleave the experiences of the crusaders with the thoughts and commemorative prayers of
the canons of Reims. Once letters like those that Anselm sent had been
received, read aloud, and recopied, as texts in circulation they also became

monuments; the space they occupied in manuscripts, like the one written at the Priory of Saint-Martin-des-Champs in Paris containing Anselm's letter, became the platform around which communities could construct their own collective understandings of what had happened to the army of Christians in the past and in distant lands. These written records were thus part of the architecture around which the collective memory of crusade was constructed.[4]

Anselm and his companions must have known, on some level, that their undertaking and experiences represented something extraordinary not only in their own lifetimes but also in what they saw as the fulfilment of the divine plan of salvation history. Indeed, judging only from the enormous textual response that it generated, the First Crusade was one of the most resonant events in medieval European history.[5] The subsequent crusading campaigns to the Holy Land, Iberia, and the Baltic and against enemies of the church within Europe were no less resonant, either for participants or for those communities — Christian, Jewish, Muslim, and pagan in both Europe and the Near East — that were affected by them. The varied ways in which these events were recalled and interpreted through the lenses of local history or broader conceptions of the sacred or mythic past, as well as when and where they were invoked and contested, had far-reaching implications for all these communities. As the contributions to this volume show, the crusades became a central element in the discourses of identity for individuals, institutions, and communities.

What Do We Mean by "Crusades"?

Medieval people had no consistent term of reference for the series of Christian religious wars that we call "crusades," and modern scholars have debated both the geographic and chronological scopes of historical experiences that should be associated with this essentially postmedieval label.[6] Attempts to define a crusade have led some historians to privilege the place of Jerusalem and to deem as crusades only those expeditions directed toward its conquest or defense. Others focus on the psychological impulse in the minds of common participants, often said to be steeped in eschatological fears and expectations; such scholars are inclined to include in their definition popular movements, such as the so-called Children's Crusade of 1212 and the *pastoreux,* or Shepherds' Crusades, which were neither sanctioned nor supported by the papacy. Yet others would include all forms of religious violence waged by Christians during the Middle Ages. Perhaps the most widely accepted approach, at least among historians of the crusades, is what is known as the "pluralist" school of crusade history, whose adherents would count as "crusades" all those military undertakings understood to have been penitential in nature (like or even *as* pilgrimages), sanctioned by central ecclesiastical authorities, and whose participants often engaged in the particular rite of taking the cross and the crusader's vow.[7] More recent scholarship has also explored what might be called "virtual" or "affective" crusading, whereby in prayer or contemplation or through vicarious suffering, even those not directly involved in crusading warfare might be seen to have shared in the experience of crusading.[8]

How individuals and communities perceived the past has not, until very recently, been considered relevant to how we should understand the contours and evolution of the crusading movement. It is not difficult to see, however, that all crusading projects, whether they were directed toward the conquest or defense of the Holy Sepulchre in Jerusalem or to some other objective in another theater of war, were generated and sustained in large part through reference to shared sacred, historical, and mythic pasts. Accounts of Urban II's announcement of the first crusading project at the council of Clermont in 1095 and narratives of the expedition written by participants focus heavily on the sacred geography of the Holy Land, invoking the places associated with Christ's passion, the central narrative in medieval Christian cultural memory.[9]

While the invocation of sacred memory and the call to follow "in the footsteps of Christ" would continue throughout the early history of the crusades,[10] this particular commemorative discourse was joined, after the conquest of Jerusalem by the First Crusade in 1099, by exhortations to new waves of crusaders to look back on the achievements of earlier crusaders and follow in *their* footsteps (*vestigia inhaerere* or *vestigia subsaequere*).[11] When Pope Eugenius III issued his call for the Second Crusade in 1145, for instance, he explicitly invoked the rewards that had been offered by Pope Urban II in 1095 and the glory and accomplishments of those who had accepted the challenge.[12] The First Crusade was also the touchstone of those who, like the bishops and magnates of eastern Saxony who composed the "Magdeburg charter" of 1107–8 and archbishop Diego

Gelmirez of Compostela in Galicia in 1124, sought to transform local conflicts into penitential crusading wars.[13] By the middle of the twelfth century, the First Crusade was memorialized not only in Latin chronicles but also in vernacular literature, architecture, artworks, and liturgy.

In addition to the sacred memory of the Gospels, which linked the crusaders to Christ, and the historical memory of the First Crusade, which gave cohesion and purpose to their efforts, it is possible to identify other, sometimes mythic, pasts, which were closely interwoven with memories of the crusades. Most prominent among these are the proto-crusade images and legends associated with the sack of Jerusalem by Titus and Vespasian in the first century,[14] the conquest of Jerusalem by Heraclius in the sixth century,[15] and the legendary pilgrimages and wars of Charlemagne in the late eighth and early ninth centuries.[16] The knowledge that Charlemagne, who in fact fought limited and inconclusive campaigns in northeastern Iberia, was considered in the twelfth century to have been the leader of a massively successful war of crusading conquest in Spain has provided the basis for major reevaluations of the growth of the Iberian Peninsula as a theater of crusading conflict.[17] Into this maelstrom of sacred, historical, and mythical pasts, men and women brought the memories of their own experiences and those of their families and local communities. In the years before his death in 1317, for instance, an individual like John of Joinville would pass on his personal recollections of what he had experienced on crusade with King Louis IX of France in Egypt some sixty years before as well as the memory of his ancestors who had fought, and in some cases died, on crusades to the Holy Land for generations.[18]

In terms of both the institutional development of the movement itself and the experiences and mentalities of the individuals who were involved, therefore, the perception and interpretation of the past are of paramount importance to our understanding of the crusades and their place in the medieval world. But the memory of the crusades also transcended the world of crusaders and crusading institutions, to become a part of confessional, national, and now global conceptions of the past.[19] In Europe, having served as a topic for debate and a weapon of war in the Reformation contests between Protestants and Catholics, and then as an example par excellence for Enlightenment thinkers of what they saw as the dangerous results of fanaticism and the gross arrogance and abuses of the Church, the crusades emerged, in the nineteenth century, as a focal point for romantic nationalism.[20] In the 1830s, for instance, King Louis Philippe of France sponsored the creation of the Salles des Croisades at the palace of Versailles, a gallery of rooms dedicated explicitly to the commemoration of certain crusading events. The popularity of this romantic project resulted in a campaign of forgery on the part of French aristocrats who wished to have their coats of arms represented alongside those of the famous crusading heroes (among them Anselm of Ribemont), who were by then seen as heroes of the French nation.[21] Likewise, in the twenty-first century, the word *crusade* continues to be invoked to make political and ethical statements, and the images and associations it conjures in the collective memory are deployed to impugn some causes and extol others.[22]

Over the past three decades, both the study of the crusades and the study of the operation of memory in the medieval world have seen remarkable growth and development. In this volume we aim to demonstrate the potential advantages to the study of the crusades offered by approaches and methods that are sensitive to discourses of commemoration and representation. We have brought together scholarly work from different areas of medieval studies to discuss how individual crusaders or the events of the crusades were memorialized (or suppressed) by contemporary observers and subsequent generations in texts and artworks; to examine the negotiation and production of crusading images and memories; and to explore the role of these images and memories in shaping both the crusading movement itself and the identities of communities directly or indirectly affected by the crusades. This work cannot hope to encompass all approaches and sources currently available. In the chapters offered here, however, we hope to encourage further investigations of the ways in which medieval people from many societies, places, and faiths deployed memories of crusade to describe and aid their communities, situate themselves relative to others, perceive their ancestors in a certain light, and commemorate themselves and their ideals for posterity.

Memory in Modern Theory and Medieval Practice

The concept of memory, as it is now applied across the humanities and social sciences, is used to describe a wide variety of processes whereby individuals, communities, and whole societies make present what has been rendered absent to them by forces of distance, trauma, or time.[23] Among these processes are the mnemonic mechanisms by which we as individuals actively seek to recall, reconstruct, and re-create the past. Some of the approaches included in this volume consider the "autobiographical" processes through which a person's life experiences from early childhood are understood and arranged in light of powerful social and psychological influences, attitudes, beliefs, and desires. Contributors also examine the "communicative memory" that arises from everyday contacts and discourses and the "cultural memory" associated with persistent rites, images, and other cultural configurations.

That remembering is fundamentally a social process and therefore provides a useful vector for inquiry into society and culture was first observed by Maurice Halbwachs, a student of Emile Durkheim. In his 1925 work *Les Cadres sociaux de la mémoire*,[24] Halbwachs demonstrated that collective memory, a concept he distinguished from history, is sustained by social contexts, that what is remembered serves the needs of the remembering group, and that the memory's endurance is often determined by that group's social power. Halbwachs's later work has particular significance to the study of the crusades, as his only major case study of the operation of collective memory, *La topographie légendaire des évangiles en terre sainte*, focused on the role of pilgrims and crusaders in the creation of Christian pilgrim typologies in the Holy Land.[25] In *La topographie*, Halbwachs not only demonstrated the utility of the concept of social memory for the study of ancient and medieval societies but also suggested the potentially important links among memory, religion, culture, and notions of sacred space.

Halbwachs's call for the application of the concept of collective memory to the study of past societies did not gain much attention until the late 1980s and early 1990s, when it was rediscovered by a new generation of scholars, most notably the French historian Pierre Nora and Egyptologists Jan Assmann and Aleida Assmann.[26] As new studies of memory proliferated, the concept of collective memory was subject to significant revisions, especially by medievalists, who have demonstrated both the centrality of commemoration to medieval culture and the distinctive nature of medieval mnemonic practice.[27] In *Social Memory* (1992), for instance, Chris Wickham (a medievalist) and James Fentress challenged Halbwachs's sharp distinction between history and memory, arguing that, although the authors of medieval historical texts often worked their material within the constraints of particular historical genres or theological conceptions of historical practice, their works are still essentially a collection of "usable pasts," through which the social memory of author and audience may be accessed.[28] Where Wickham and Fentress stressed the social utility and malleability of the past as it was drawn upon by a chronicler like Gregory of Tours or by Icelandic saga poets, Patrick Geary emphasized the "burden" of commemoration, particularly in memorializing the dead, and the challenge it posed to eleventh-century lay and religious communities, for whom memory was at once "essential and impossible."[29] Geary also insisted that memory was "gender specific," a point that has subsequently been explored in great depth in the work of Elisabeth van Houts.[30] The same monastic communities that, for Geary, labored under the weight of their commemorative responsibilities were also, as Amy Remensnyder has shown, engaged in processes of "imaginative memory," which competitively reconfigured the narratives of their foundation.[31]

Responding to the flood of works applying the study of social memory to various periods and cultures, and anticipating what one historian despairs of as the inherent "vagueness" of the study of social or collective memory,[32] Jeffrey K. Olick and Joyce Robbins have insisted on a set of rudimentary principles for what they call the "historical sociology of mnemonic practice."[33] According to their proviso, research in this area must be conducted with the understanding (1) that memory is "the central medium through which identities are constructed," (2) that different periods of history produce distinct mnemonic processes and cultures of memory, and (3) that ideas about the past are inherently manifold and competitive.

Before we turn to the contributions in this volume, it is worth considering how each of these three principles might be brought to bear as we consider the crusades from the point of view of commemorative cultures and mnemonic practices. To begin, if one considers memory as the medium of identity formation, then scholarly explorations of crusade as "identity machine" become productive for many reasons. With their potent admixture of violence, suffering, distance, sacred ritual, and cross-cultural encounters, the crusades created a dynamic framework for the development and performance of medieval identities. The past decade has been rich with theoretical studies of medieval identity, emphasizing its constructed nature and its close relationship with culturally specific, collective, medieval recollections of the past.[34] While countless elements come to bear in relating social identity, the ways in which the events of the crusades were recalled or commemorated have been shown to influence a sense of religious identity, exploring, for instance, what it meant to be Christian, Jewish, or Muslim or, in more local contexts, what it meant to be English,[35] a French king,[36] a member of a Jewish community in a Rhineland town,[37] or a nobleman aspiring to chivalry.[38] Recent scholarship has also drawn attention to the place of the crusades in the discourse of medieval gender identity, exploring how gender was defined during the crusades, examining the designations of crusading as a male space, addressing the experiences of women who went on crusade, and establishing the roles of women, particularly women rulers, in the societies established on the crusading frontiers.[39]

The crusades also brought about entirely new modes of social identity. While they helped to shape the identities of existing communities, the military campaigns fought by crusaders and their opponents resulted in the establishment not only of the new social and legal category of the "crusader" (the *crucesignatus* of thirteenth-century canon lawyers) but of whole new frontier societies as well. Forged by conquest and colonization, these hybrid societies may have possessed their own mnemonic culture, which in turn could shape notions of the past among communities far from the frontier.[40] It was in Jerusalem, for instance, that a liturgy celebrating the conquest of the city by the crusaders in 1099 was first celebrated. By the mid-twelfth century, however, there is evidence that this liturgy was also being celebrated in the West.[41] A much better-known transfer of knowledge about the past was made in the form of Archbishop William of Tyre's Latin history of the crusader conquest and rule over Jerusalem. Translated into Old French before 1223, it became one of the standard narratives of crusading events in medieval and early modern Europe and received its first printing in Middle English in 1481.[42]

In commemorating the crusades, religion was often inextricable from various identities shaped by locality, gender, race, class, and other factors created from within or perceived from without a specific society. Studies of the formation of religious identities in the Middle Ages have suggested that crusades, along with other encounters, played a significant role in the formation of images of the religious Other and the related process through which ideas of race were constructed.[43] The vocabulary used to describe the societies involved in crusading, such as *East* and *West*, *Christian* and

Muslim, Sunni and *Shi'a,* among many others, varied according to context. Many contributors to this volume use these terms to offer a construction that they will later prove is much more complex and rich than these classifications allow. This exploration of the ways crusade was remembered works against the perception of the crusades as a social monolith complete with totalizing ideas about different sects of Christianity, Islam, Judaism, and other religions and reveals more individualized portraits of the encounters among the different cultures of the Baltic, Byzantium, Europe, the Levant, and North Africa. These speak to a more complicated picture of interaction, one that involved a multiplicity of experiences during the crusades. As the studies presented here show, societal constructions of religion, race, and other signs of community were continually made and unmade, imagined, recollected, and disseminated over the course of centuries, as memories of the crusades were passed down over generations.

The dynamic nature of these constructions owes much not only to the societal impact of the events, places, and people associated with the crusades but also to the proximity of these elements to the commemorators. Such events, places, and people were often separated by great distances in space and time from the medieval European communities who commemorated them in narratives, artworks, and liturgies. As noted above, medieval mnemonic processes shaped identity, and yet, at the same time, these processes were themselves bounded by time and place. Understanding the commemorative processes through which the crusades were evoked by these communities therefore requires sensitivity to medieval mnemonic practices and cultures. Through the works of Augustine, medieval Christians inherited from their classical forebears the tradition of *ars memoria,*[44] a philosophy of the mind that understood memory not only as a mental system for the storage and retrieval of information but also, as Mary Carruthers demonstrated in her classic study, *The Book of Memory* (1990), as the key to invention and a necessary component in imagination.[45] In the Augustinian tradition of *memoria,* the act of remembering — itself the result of a combining of recollected objects in the chambers of the mind with objects from the present — could shape new forms and result in nuanced memories. The Augustinian idea of *memoria* was integral to medieval intellectual discourses and to the medieval use of texts, but it was also, in the words of Patrick Geary, "a key organizing principle . . . in every aspect of medieval life."[46]

The medieval West was littered with objects that could be used to evoke the crusading past. Communities that contributed participants to Eastern crusades could often point to relics in their possession that had traveled back from the crusading frontier.[47] In Iberia, memories of crusading victories were associated with the banners crusaders carried in battle and the tombs of crusading heroes.[48] A critical tool for remembering in crusading contexts was the sacred geography of the Holy Land, where particular shrines and relics and even the city of Jerusalem itself could act as mnemonic devices for the storage and evocation of narratives.[49] In the West, images invoking the crusading past were depicted in stained glass,[50] wall paintings,[51] and figural sculpture.[52] For Muslims living in the Near East, memories of the efforts to repel the crusaders and reconquer the holy places in Jerusalem were often literally inscribed in the form of commemorative poetry on the surfaces of buildings, some of which were architecturally altered in the wake of conquest to act as memorial monuments.[53]

This reclaiming of contested sites through memorial verse and architecture reminds us that, in addition to their importance in the construction of identity and their association with distinct commemorative cultures, crusading texts and objects corresponded to views of the past that varied between and even within communities and that were often openly competitive with one another. Although it hardly needs to be said that perceptions of the crusading past varied greatly among Christians, Muslims, and Jews, precious little evidence remains of occasions when these memories were openly disputed across cultural lines.[54] Within each community of faith, however, we find abundant evidence of the multiplicity and contestation of crusading memories. For Christians, the opportunities for distinction in chivalric glory and pious service associated with crusading fueled the competitive claims about the crusading past. Even the relatively low-ranking noble families of Amboise in the Touraine and Ardres in Flanders would proudly preserve their own accounts of their ancestors' deeds at the siege of Antioch in 1097–98.[55] A writer in the service of the latter family excoriated the storytellers who did not include the name of the illustrious lord of Ardres in their tales of the crusade. Similarly, in thirteenth-century England, memories of the embarrassing defeat of the Seventh Crusade at the battle of Mansourah in Egypt were gradually subsumed into the memory of a heroic English martyr, William Longespée, whose glorious death redeemed the English contribution to an otherwise French debacle.[56]

The Organization of This Book

To bring sustained focus to these complex interactions between crusade and memory, we have grouped the book's eleven chapters into three parts: "Remembrance and Response," "Sites and Structures: Cities, Buildings, and Bodies," and "Institutional Memory and Community Identity." Through these three critical lenses, we hope to show how certain communities and individuals responded to the cultural, existential, and intellectual challenges posed by crusading warfare and ideology, the place of crusading memories in real and imagined geographies, and the role of the crusading past in shaping collective and institutional identity. In the process of grouping these essays into categories for the purposes of publication, we recognized the many areas of overlap and countless points of contact among these studies; these topics and subsequent treatments made a multitude of other headings possible. For this project, however, we selected a framework that we think shows each work most productively: in multidisciplinary conversation with its adjacent chapters.

REMEMBRANCE AND RESPONSE

The alchemical fusion of piety and violence that occurred at the moment crusades were preached, the great mobilization of resources and participants they required, and the desperate military conflicts that ensued forced contemporary Jewish, Muslim, and Christian observers living in their aftermath to fundamentally reevaluate their perspectives on themselves and each other. The first section of our book, "Remembrance and Response," explores the reactions of writers from three religious traditions to the changes recently wrought upon their communities by the advent of religious violence. In their essays, Christine Chism, Chaviva Levin, and Jay Rubenstein demonstrate how memories of strained coexistence, violent massacres, and triumphant victory acted as the foundation for narratives of wonder and loss, strategies of future survival, and the anticipation of imminent apocalypse.

In "Memory, Wonder, and Desire in the Travels of Ibn Jubayr and Ibn Battuta," Christine Chism considers two narratives composed in the aftermath of crusading conquest and Muslim reconquest by the medieval Muslim travelers Ibn Jubayr and Ibn Battuta. The account of the first traveler, Ibn Jubayr, records his experiences in the Levant in the four-year period before the battle of Hattin, when "the Franks" still occupied the lands they had conquered during and after the First Crusade. Chism contrasts Ibn Jubayr's work with Ibn Battuta's *Travels*, written circa 1355, in which the author and his scribe remembered their movements through the same landscape after the effective end of crusading operations in the region. By comparing two accounts otherwise separated by time and standpoint, Chism uncovers interactions between the Muslim traveler and local Muslim and Christian communities he encountered. Importantly, memories of these interactions are not consistently marked by animosity; rather, they evoke a range of responses, including wonder, desire, and longing. This variety of commemorative responses in turn suggests a complex range of attitudes between opponents on either side of the city walls and contested zones that marked the crusading frontier.

Like the two Muslim accounts of travel through the crusading frontier, R. Ephraim of Bonn's narrative of the massacre of Rhineland Jews following the preaching of the Second Crusade is not primarily ideological in nature. Instead, as Chaviva Levin shows, Ephraim's account, the *Sefer Zekhira*, was focused on strategies for the survival of his community. This sets the *Sefer Zekhira* apart from the narrative accounts of the massacres that followed the preaching of the First Crusade forty years earlier. While these earlier works focus on the martyrs who "sanctified God's name," or killed themselves rather than be killed or forcibly baptized by the crusaders, Levin shows how Ephraim of Bonn preferred to minimize martyrdom and concentrate instead on how it was possible to "sanctify God's name" through survival. Levin's essay is not only about medieval memories but also about how modern Ashkenazik perceptions of the medieval past have preferred to universalize the earlier experience of anti-Jewish violence at the time of the First Crusade, seeing only the ideology of martyrdom. Like Chism, Levin highlights the variety of possible pathways for narrative commemoration.

Living in the aftermath neither of an altered geography nor of a devastated community, but of the triumphant conquest of Jerusalem by the crusaders in 1099, the Frankish canon Lambert of Saint-Omer nonetheless looked back at a crusade and imagined an apocalypse. As Jay Rubenstein demonstrates, the challenge that the First Crusade posed to an intellectual like Lambert was how to integrate memories of the recent triumph within the normative framework of salvation history. Especially challenging was the problem of where to place the crusade within the Six Ages of the world as established by Augustine. Remarkably, as Rubenstein shows, the effect of the crusade and the subsequent establishment of a new Latin Kingdom of Jerusalem upon Western Christians was so great that to Lambert they were not simply events in history but the end of history itself. By working with a series of biblical and popular prophecies, along with Augustinian historiography, Lambert created an interpretation of the First Crusade in which the Franks, in enacting the campaign, were fulfilling the will of God and helping to bring about the Last Judgment.

SITES AND STRUCTURES:
CITIES, BUILDINGS, AND BODIES

How crusading memories were mapped onto space and place had the potential to affect the memories themselves and their sites of commemoration. Like those that precede them, the chapters in the second section of our book are also concerned with commemorative responses to the crusades, but they add focus on how locations and structures were memorialized and, in some cases, altered because of events and ideas associated with the crusades. The first two essays, by Jerrilynn Dodds and Jaroslav Folda, demonstrate this in literal fashion, remarking on the passing on of vestigial forms in architecture and illustrated manuscripts. Suzanne Conklin Akbari and David Morris, in turn, show how this process occurred textually, offering approaches to literature that suggest a unique crusade poetic. All four chapters also demonstrate the centrality of the city of Jerusalem, the contested sacred space at the center of crusading conflicts of the Near East, to the configuration of crusading memory.

Dodds's essay, "Remembering the Crusades in the Fabric of Buildings," examines the use of banded arches in Romanesque churches and situates these decorative features in relation to their earlier use in the early Islamic architecture of the city of Jerusalem. The presence of banded arches in Romanesque churches has long been of interest to art historians. But while these dark and light alternating arches have traditionally been associated with the Great Mosque at Cordoba, Dodds suggests that they may refer directly and specifically to the architecture of Jerusalem. The great monuments of Romanesque style that use banded arches — Ste. Madeleine at Vezelay, Notre Dame at Le Puy, and Notre Dame du Port at Clermont — are all linked through their close association with the First and Second Crusades. Thus in their use of the banded arch the great Romanesque churches refer directly to the buildings co-opted by the Frankish crusaders. In this way, a late antique decorative technique used first by Muslims to mark their rule over Jerusalem became the means by which crusaders marked the memory of their crusading conquests.

The visual echoes of Jerusalem embedded in the Romanesque ecclesiastical architecture of the West bear out once again the monumental significance of the First Crusade in the Western European imagination. As the fate of the Latin Kingdom established by the crusaders in 1099 grew increasingly desperate over the course of the later twelfth and thirteenth centuries, however, and memories of the crusading past were necessarily renegotiated, the visual and performative evocations of this past were in some cases revised. In "Commemorating the Fall of Jerusalem: Remembering the First Crusade in Text, Liturgy, and Image," Jaroslav Folda tracks the visual representations of the conquest of Jerusalem by the crusaders in illuminated manuscripts of the continuations of William of Tyre's enormously popular *History of Outremer*. Folda notes how the later fall of Jerusalem to Saladin in 1187 and successive changes in rulership of the city necessitated a different Christian approach toward remembering the notable event of the Fall of Jerusalem to the Franks in 1099. Subsequent commemorations of Jerusalem, especially those after the failure of Louis IX to regain the Holy City in his Crusade of 1249–50, changed to a lament. Folda explores the impact of these changing commemorations on the illustrations of the First Crusade that appear in the manuscripts of the *History of Outremer*, many of which were done post-1250. By examining which crusading scenes illuminators chose to depict before and after 1291, Folda finds that positive memories of the First Crusade remained important, even when Jerusalem was in Muslim hands and the crusader states were under attack.

Memories of the First Crusade were certainly not the only models of siege warfare to inspire later medieval crusading. Images of crusade were themselves inspired by many works, from classical stories of Troy to Josephan accounts of Jerusalem's fall, to name only a few. Like Folda's description of the fate of the holy city, Suzanne Conklin Akbari's chapter shows an interest in the question of how medieval writers portrayed the position and use of fallen cities, although her essay suggests a very specific type of siege poetic at work in later crusading literature. In her chapter, "Erasing the Body: History and Memory in Medieval Siege Poetry," Akbari demonstrates how siege poetry stands out among Middle English texts by virtue of its preoccupation with "immanence," that is, what Akbari calls "the sense that a time of violent resolution is close at hand." Here, the city's inevitable fall will result in the dispersal of all it contains, whether goods, persons, or some ephemeral quality. In examining the textual images of the city besieged, she focuses on two Middle English poems, both entitled *The Siege of Jerusalem* but deriving from different traditions. One recounts the fall of the city in the eleventh century according to the account of crusade historian William of Tyre, and the other describes the demise of that city in the first century to Titus and Vespasian. Akbari places these violent falls of the city first in context with then-abundant Troy literature, and then in contrast with later, crusade literatures centered on Jerusalem. Through these dual lenses she observes that siege writing uses a shared mode, or "narrative shorthand," to encapsulate information about historical change. In assessing these works together, she finds that as a textual sign, the city under siege becomes a site of memory and of forgetting, both the end of a nation and the beginning of a new cycle of imperial might. Correspondingly, the body that serves as the microcosm of the city is suspended: destined to be destroyed in the climactic resolution of the siege but permanently remembered in the ongoing cycle of *translatio imperii*. In this chapter, Akbari examines texts from antiquity to the twelfth century, including the *Aeneid* and the *Roman de Troie;* this discussion sets the foundation for the siege of Jerusalem's conformity to the Troy model, as seen in such texts as the *Roman de Thebes*. In contrast, she explores siege literature drawn from imaginative crusade writings, such as the *Sege of Melayne* and the related, later *Capystranus*. Within all these siege-related texts, images of the city, along with those of the male body and the tomb, make visible significant discontinuities between one period of time and another. Through analysis of these structures, Akbari shows how narrations of siege allowed premodern writers to make sense of historical change and to embody the fallen city, establishing its significance for past, present, and future audiences.

Like Dodds, Folda, and Akbari, who write of the transformation of fallen cities and the changes in perceptions and roles of cities brought about by crusading, David Morris describes a variable typology of femininity applied to Jerusalem, the prized city of the early crusades. Morris shows how changes in perception of the city as a feminine figure varied depending on the fortunes of the Christian crusaders. In "The Servile Mother: Jerusalem as Woman in the Era of the Crusades," Morris explores how the image of Jerusalem as a slave woman in distress evolved over the course of the twelfth century. Borrowing from biblical exegetical typologies and applying them to crusading, Pope Urban II and others referred to the city variably as slave woman, as a woman violated by the infidel, or as mother; these expressions allowed expanded family relationships involving the holy city, including, as Morris puts it, "God as cuckold, Muslims as adulterous paramours, and crusaders as Jerusalem's revenge-minded sons." In this study, Morris locates a striking departure from traditional biblical exegesis and argues convincingly that these adapted images of a crusade-battered city owed much to the discourse of the Investiture Contest, in which reformers used the language of gender and subjugation to describe the perceived oppression of the Roman Church by lay authorities. For Morris, as well as Akbari, the production of Jerusalem as a literary trope in the crusades drew extensively from other medieval models of femininity and masculinity in order to commemorate ideas of that city's importance, to suggest an urgent need to protect it, and to establish its pivotal place in crusading memory. In this portion of the volume, enduring memories of Jerusalem and its inhabitants — whether through banded arches, liturgy, manuscripts, or early typologies — were portrayed as essential for the success of all those who remembered crusade.

INSTITUTIONAL MEMORY AND COMMUNITY IDENTITY

The concern over the influence of the crusading past on the present and future is not visible only in the contexts of individual and communal survival and salvation mentioned here, nor seen solely in the important place of Jerusalem; the preservation and use of crusading memory is also observed in the everyday context of medieval and present-day self-fashioning. The third and final part of the book demonstrates how institutions, such as polities, religious sects, and orders, adapted memories of crusading events and people to reflect a particular view of the past helpful to perpetuating the community's self-image. In "Institutional Memory and Community Identity," Mohamed El-Moctar begins the discussion with his chapter, "Saladin in Sunni and Shi'a Memories." Present-day views of crusading individuals owe much to mythologies begun in the past, and yet, as El-Moctar shows, some currently held notions about the crusades and its leaders are relatively new creations generated by the political exigencies of the twentieth and twenty-first centuries. El-Moctar explores the depictions of Saladin by medieval Muslim historians and finds that the writers' Sunni or Shi'a affiliations had little impact on their depictions of Saladin; he was portrayed variably by both sides, and there was no strict boundary be-tween Sunni and Shi'a regarding the good reputation of Saladin. In con-trast, El-Moctar observes that many of today's Sunni Muslims idealize the sultan as a figure whose piety and courage unified Islam, while more recent Shi'a Muslim writings portray him otherwise, as "selfish adventurer" and destroyer of the Shi'a Fatimid Empire. In tracing the development of such polarized views of Saladin, El-Moctar looks to the multiplicity of experi-ences recorded in the medieval Levant by different Islamic groups and revises the position of present-day historians who may assume that sec-tarian divisions decided the sultan's reputation in the medieval period.

The use of crusade imagery to portray crusading figures in support of varying political powers and jurisdictions has been observed across time, in many medieval sources; this book offers a study of the sack of Constantinople during the Fourth Crusade as another excellent example. Here, David M. Perry considers the transformation of another figure who, like Saladin, held a role in crusade and whose images were altered over time by political expedience. In his chapter, "Paul the Martyr and Vene-tian Memories of the Fourth Crusade," Perry follows the career of St. Paul the Martyr, telling the story of how the saint's posthumous reputation was adapted over time to bolster the rising role of Venice and the concurrent fall of Constantinople in the Fourth Crusade. An examination of the story of relic theft told by the anonymous clerical author from the Venetian monastery of San Giorgio Maggiore in the circa 1220 *Translatio corporis beatissimi Pauli martyris de Constantinopoli Venetias* revises contempo-rary views of Latin failures in the East by creating new traditions about the saint, who died in 351 C.E. This particular *translatio* involves Constantinople in its plan in such a way as to remember a new history of the crusade, portraying the Fourth Crusaders as victors because, as the writer explains, in diverting the crusade to Constantinople, they had punished the Greeks, thereby enacting God's will. Here, Perry convincingly suggests that the narrative of the Fourth Crusade itself is reified as a type of *furta sacra* story later used to justify the sack of Constantinople and the dispersal of its treasures.

Like saints and generals whose depictions have been adapted to comment on and, in some cases, justify crusade, so, too, institutions managed the public perceptions of their pasts while carefully cultivating their own corporate memories of crusading involvement. In "Aspects of Hospitaller and Templar Memory," Jonathan Riley-Smith moves the focus of the volume's third section from institutional memories of individuals to remembrances of larger groups. This chapter explores the effect of traumatic events upon the memories of the crusading military orders of the Knights Templar and the Hospital of St. John of Jerusalem. By comparing narratives that surfaced at times of crisis for the orders — after the capture of Jerusalem by Saladin in 1187 or during the suppression of the Templars by Philip IV of France in the first decade of the fourteenth century — Riley-Smith uncovers the orders' varying strategies for dealing with traumatic memory and treating information received under duress. Through this investigation, Riley-Smith notes several key differences between the stories about the foundation of the orders and their function and finds that these discrepancies reveal tensions and disagreements that existed between different members of the institutions. Competing narratives about Gerard, the founder of the Hospitallers, for example, may have been circulating within the Hospitaller community as early as the 1160s, and they reflected differing opinions about whether the order should have engaged in military activities. In finding an institution-wide adoption of specific legends that substantiated these opinions, Riley-Smith shows the necessity of dynamic, changing, and even competing narratives in order to preserve the life of an institution.

Related closely to Riley-Smith's essay on the role of memory in the life of the military orders, Laura Whatley's chapter examines one of the military order's efforts to substantiate its authority through visual signs. In "Visual Self-fashioning and the Seals of the Knights Hospitaller in England," Whatley situates medieval seals as "highly mobile and intrinsically visual artifacts embodying individual and communal identity, sometimes providing the most complete record of a group's structure and self-image." The visual culture of the Order of the Hospital of St. John of Jerusalem in England was largely eradicated during the Reformation, making the seals all the more important. Whatley shows that these little-studied Hospitaller seals in England not only provide information about the order's attitude to the crusades and its international connections to the continent and the Latin East but also suggest that the Hospitallers in England, far removed from the Holy Land, relied on the seals to import their legitimacy as both a military and a religious order and to reaffirm their utility and authority. As a concrete example of the mobilization of crusade memory from event to artifact, Whatley's seals, like the various texts, objects, and architectural features discussed in this volume, offer a snapshot of crusading memories.

Representing a sampling of diverse cultural groupings, religious affiliations, and time periods, the chapters in this volume seek to provide standpoints from which to observe a multiplicity of memorial strategies responding to, managing, and producing crusading experiences. It is our hope that these chapters, considered together, will contribute to a view of the crusades that involved complex, dynamic commemorative responses on the part of those affected by them; we also hope to show the processes of medieval memorialization in action, attesting to the important role of memory-making in defining political, cultural, and religious expectations and in allowing individuals and entire groups to shape how both they, and the crusades, would be remembered.

Notes

1. "Epistola I, Anselmi Ribodimonte ad Manassem archiepiscopum Remorum," in *Die Kreuzzugsbriefe aus den Jahren 1088–1100*, ed. Heinrich Hagenmeyer (Innsbruck: Wagnerische Universitäts-Buchhandlung, 1901), 144–46.

2. "Precor etiam uos et canonicos sanctae matris ecclesiae Remensis, patres et dominos meos, ut memores nostri sitis, nec solummodo mei uel eorum, qui in seruitio Dei adhuc desudant, sed et illorum, qui de exercitu Domini armis corruerunt aut in pace quieuerunt" (ibid., 144).

3. "In certainty, we have acquired two hundred cities and castles for the Lord" (ibid., 145).

4. Paris, Bibliothèque Mazarine, MS 1710. Another of Anselm's letters, however, was copied as far away as Catalonia in the twelfth century. See José Martínez Gázquez, "'Aciebus ordinatis' en la Epist. II A. de Ribodemonte ad M. Archiep. Remorum del manuscrito 944 de la Biblioteca de Cataluña," *Medievalia* 9 (1990): 161–67.

5. For the resonance of particular historical events, such as wars or earthquakes, and collective memory, see James Pennebaker and Becky Banasik, "On the Creation and Maintenance of Collective Memories: History as Social Psychology," in *Collective Memory of Political Events: Social Psychological Perspectives,* ed. James Pennebaker, Dario Paez, and Bernard Rimé (Mahwah, NJ: Lawrence Erlbaum, 1997), 3–20. The concept is explored in a medieval context, using the Norman conquest of Anglo-Saxon England as the central example, by Elisabeth M. C. van Houts, *Memory and Gender in Medieval Europe: 900–1200,* Explorations in Medieval Culture and Society (Basingstoke, UK: Macmillan, 1999), 123–42.

6. For the variety of terminology, see Giles Constable, "The Historiography of the Crusades," in Constable, *Crusaders and Crusading in the Twelfth Century* (Burlington, VT: Ashgate, 2008), 18; Jonathan Riley-Smith, *What Were the Crusades?,* 4th ed. (San Francisco: Ignatius Press, 2009), 2.

7. For the foregoing definitions, see Constable, "The Historiography of the Crusades," 17–20, and Norman Housley, *Contesting the Crusades* (Oxford: Blackwell, 2006), 1–23. For a full description of the "pluralist" position, see Riley-Smith, *What Were the Crusades?,* passim.

8. See, e.g., Anne E. Lester, "A Shared Imitation: Cistercian Convents and Crusader Families in Thirteenth-Century Champagne," *Journal of Medieval History* 36, no. 4 (2009): 353–70; Suzanne M. Yeager, "*The Siege of Jerusalem* and Biblical Exegesis: Writing about Romans in Fourteenth-Century England," *Chaucer Review* 39, no. 1 (2004); 70–102; and Yeager, *Jerusalem in Medieval Narrative* (Cambridge: Cambridge University Press, 2008), ch. 4.

9. The accounts of Urban's sermon are collected and translated in Edward Peters, *The First Crusade: The Chronicle of Fulcher of Chartes and Other Source Materials,* 2nd ed. (Philadelphia: University of Pennsylvania Press, 1998), 25–37.

10. For the expression, see William Purkis, *Crusading Spirituality in the Holy Land and Iberia, c. 1095–c. 1187* (Woodbridge, UK: Boydell Press, 2008), 40–41, and passim for the concept more generally.

11. For an early use of the expression, see the 1137 letter of the knight William Grassegals to King Louis VII of France in Jay Rubenstein, "Putting History to Use: Three Crusade Chronicles in Context," *Viator* 35 (2004): 134.

12. Jonathan Phillips, *The Second Crusade: Extending the Frontiers of Christendom* (New Haven: Yale University Press, 2008), 37–60 and 280–82.

13. See Giles Constable, "Early Crusading in Eastern Germany: The Magdeburg Charter of 1107/8," in Constable, *Crusaders and Crusading,* 211.

14. Yeager, *Jerusalem in Medieval Narrative,* 78–107; Suzanne Conklin Akbari, "Placing the Jews in Late Medieval Literature," in *Orientalism and the Jews,* ed. Derek Penslar and Ivan Kalmar (Hanover, NH: University Press of New England, 2005), 32–50; and Malcolm Hebron, *The Medieval Siege: Theme and Image in Middle English Romance* (Oxford: Clarendon Press, 1997), 123.

15. Gustav Kühnel, "Heracles and the Crusaders: Tracing the Path of a Royal Motif," in *France and the Holy Land: Frankish Culture at the End of the Crusades,* ed. Daniel Weiss and Lisa Mahoney (Baltimore: Johns Hopkins University Press, 2004), 63–76.

16. Purkis, *Crusading Spirituality,* 150–65, and Jace Stuckey, "Charlemagne as Crusader? Memory, Propaganda, and the Many Uses of Charlemagne's Expedition to Spain," in *The Legend of Charlemagne in the Middle Ages: Power, Faith, and Crusade,* ed. Matthew Gabriele and Jace Stuckey (New York: Palgrave Macmillan, 2008), 137–52.

17. Purkis, *Crusading Spirituality,* 150–65, and Nikolas Jaspert, "Historiografía y legitimación carolingia: El monasterio de Ripoll, el Pseudo-Turpín y los condes de Barcelona," in *El Pseudo-Turpín: Lazo entre el culto jacobeo y el culto de Carlomagno. Actas del VI Congreso Internacional de Estudios Jacobeos,* ed. Klaus Herbers (Santiago de Compostela: Xerencia de Promoción do Camiño de Santiago, 2003), 297–315.

18. Caroline Smith, *Crusading in the Age of Joinville* (Burlington, VT: Ashgate, 2006), 87–93.

19. Jacques Le Goff, *History and Memory,* trans. Steven Rendall and Elizabeth Claman (New York: Columbia University Press, 1991), 97.

20. Constable, "The Historiography of the Crusades," 11–16, and Ronnie Ellenblum, *Crusader Castles and Modern Histories* (Cambridge: Cambridge University Press, 2007), 12–17.

21. David Abulafia, "Invented Italians in the Courtois Forgeries," in *Crusade and Settlement: Papers Read at the First Conference of the Society for the Study of the Crusades and the Latin East and Presented to R. C. Smail,* ed. Peter W. Edbury (Cardiff: University College Cardiff 1975), 135–47; Elizabeth Siberry, *New Crusaders: Images of the Crusades in the Nineteenth and Early Twentieth Centuries* (Aldershot, UK: Ashgate, 2000), 51–52 and 169–70; and Adam Knobler, "Holy Wars, Empires, and the Portability of the Past: The Modern Uses of Medieval Crusades," *Comparative Studies in Society and History* 48, no. 2 (2006): 293–325.

22. Christopher Tyerman, "Conclusion: Crusading Our Contemporary," in *Fighting for Christendom: Holy War and the Crusades* (Oxford: Oxford Univer-

sity Press, 2004), 190–210; Jonathan Riley-Smith, "Islam and the Crusades in History and Imagination, 1 November 1898–11 September 2001," *Crusades* 2 (2003): 151–67; Gary Dickson, *The Children's Crusade: Medieval History and Modern Mythistory* (New York: Palgrave Macmillan, 2008); and Jonathan Phillips, *Holy Warriors: A Modern History of the Crusades* (New York: Random House, 2009), 308–44.

23. Recent overviews of the literature can be found in Bill Niven, "Review Article: On the Use of 'Collective Memory,' " *German History* 26, no. 3 (2008): 427–36; Jeffrey K. Olick and Joyce Robbins, "Social Memory Studies: From 'Collective Memory' to the Historical Sociology of Mnemonic Practices," *Annual Review of Sociology* 24 (1998): 105–40, esp. 106–26; and Alan Kirk, "Social and Cultural Memory," in *Memory, Tradition, and Text: Uses of the Past in Early Christianity,* ed. Alan Kirk and Tom Thatcher (Leiden: Brill, 2005), 1–24. See also Jeffrey K. Olick, " 'Collective Memory': A Memoir and Prospect," *Memory Studies* 1 (2008): 23–29. For the use of memory by medievalists in particular, see Michael Borgolte, "*Memoria:* Bilan intermédiaire d'un projét de recherché sur le Moyen Age," and "*Memoria:* A propos d'un objet d'histoire en Allemagne," in *Les tendances actuelles de l'histoire du moyen age,* ed. Jean-Claude Schmitt and Otto Gerhard Oexle (Paris, 2002), 53–70 and 105–26.

24. Maurice Halbwachs, *Les cadres sociaux de la mémoire* (Paris: Presses Universitaires de France, 1952); originally published as *Les travaux de l'aneé sociologique* (Paris: F. Alcan, 1925). Jan Assmann argues that, although he was probably drawing on the work of Halbwachs, the art historian Aby Warburg should be seen as a co-originator of the theory of collective memory. See Jan Assmann, "Collective Memory and Cultural Identity," in *New German Critique* 65 (1995): 125.

25. Maurice Halbwachs, *La topographie légendaire des évangiles en Terre Sainte* (Paris: Presses Universitaires de France, 1941).

26. Pierre Nora, ed., *Les lieux de mémoire,* 7 vols. (Paris: Gallimard, 1984–92); Jan Assmann, Aleida Assmann, and Christof Hardmeier, eds., *Schrift und Gedächtnis: Beitrage zur Archäologie der literarischen Kommunikation* (Munich: W. Fink 1983); and Jan Assmann, *Die kulturelle Gedächtnis: Schrift, Erinnerung, und politische Identität in frühen Hochkulturen* (Munich: C. H. Beck, 1992).

27. As Jacques Le Goff (*History and Memory*) pointed out, two books dedicated to questions of a *mentalité* (if not a *mémoire*) *collective* were raised by Robert Folz's book on the myth of Charlemagne, *Le souvenir et la légende de Charlemagne dans l'empire germanique médiévale* (Paris: Les Belles Lettres, 1950), and by George Duby, with reference to the battle of Bouvines, *La dimanche de Bouvines: 27 Juillet, 1214* (Paris: Gallimard, 1973).

28. Chris Wickham and James Fentress, *Social Memory* (Oxford: Blackwell, 1992), 144–72.

29. Patrick Geary, *Phantoms of Remembrance: Memory and Oblivion at the End of the First Millennium* (Princeton: Princeton University Press, 1994).

30. Van Houts, *Memory and Gender in Medieval Europe,* passim, and van Houts, ed., *Medieval Memories: Men, Women, and the Past in Europe: 700–1300* (Harlow, UK: Longman, 2001).

31. Amy Remensnyder, *Remembering Kings Past: Monastic Foundation Legends in Medieval Southern France* (Ithaca: Cornell University Press, 1995), and Remensnyder, "Legendary Treasure at Conques: Reliquaries and Imaginative Memory," *Speculum* 71 (1996): 884–906.

32. Niven, "On the Use of 'Collective Memory,'" 436.

33. Olick and Robbins, "Social Memory Studies," 122–34.

34. Our use of the "identity machine" is inspired by Jeffrey Jerome Cohen (*Medieval Identity Machines* [Minneapolis: University of Minnesota Press, 2003], xiii), who drew upon the "desiring machines" of Gilles Deleuze and Felix Guattari.

35. Yeager, *Jerusalem in Medieval Narrative,* 48–77.

36. Cecilia Gaposchkin, *The Making of Saint Louis: Kingship, Sanctity, and Crusade in the Later Middle Ages* (Ithaca: Cornell University Press, 2008).

37. Robert Chazan, *In the Year 1096: The First Crusade and the Jews* (Philadelphia: Jewish Publication Society, 1996).

38. Maurice Keen, *Chivalry* (New Haven: Yale University Press, 1996).

39. See, e.g., Hans Eberhard Mayer, "Studies in the History of Queen Melisende of Jerusalem," *Dumbarton Oaks Papers* 26 (1972): 93–182; Glenn Burger and Steven F. Kruger, eds., *Queering the Middle Ages* (Minneapolis: University of Minnesota Press, 2001), 104–6; Susan Edington and Sarah Lambert, *Gendering the Crusades* (New York: Columbia University Press, 2001); and Christoph T. Maier, "The Roles of Women in the Crusade Movement: A Survey," *Journal of Medieval History* 30, no. 1 (2004): 61–82.

40. Homi K. Bhabha, *The Location of Culture* (New York: Routledge, 1994), and Stephen Greenblatt, ed., *New World Encounters* (Berkeley: University of California Press, 1993).

41. Amnon Linder, "The Liturgy of the Liberation of Jerusalem," *Medieval Studies* 52 (1990): 110–31, and Sylvia Schein, *Gateway to the Heavenly City: Crusader Jerusalem and the Catholic West (1099–1187)* (Aldershot, UK: Ashgate, 2005), 29–31.

42. Peter W. Edbury and John Gordon Rowe, *William of Tyre, Historian of the Latin East* (Cambridge: Cambridge University Press, 1988), 3–5, and Dana Cushing, ed., *A Middle English Chronicle of the First Crusade: The Caxton "Eracles"* (Lewiston, NY: Mellen Press, 2001).

43. See, e.g., Suzanne Conklin Akbari, *Idols in the East: European Represen-tations of Islam and the Orient, 1100–1450* (Ithaca: Cornell University Press, 2009); Robert Chazan, *Fashioning Jewish Identity in Medieval Western Christen-dom* (Cambridge: Cambridge University Press, 2004); W. J. van Bekkum and Paul M. Cobb, eds., *Strategies of Medieval Communal Identity: Judaism, Christianity, Islam* (Belgium: Peeters, 2004); and John V. Tolan, *Saracens: Islam in the Medieval European Imagination* (New York: Columbia University Press, 2002).

44. Frances Yates, *The Art of Memory* (Chicago: University of Chicago Press, 1966).

45. Mary Carruthers, *The Book of Memory: A Study of Memory in Medieval Culture* (Cambridge: Cambridge University Press, 1990), and Carruthers, *The Medieval Craft of Thought* (Cambridge: Cambridge University Press, 1998). See also Beryl Rowland's response to Carruthers in "The Artificial Memory, Chaucer, and Modern Scholars," *Poetica* 37 (1993): 1–14.

46. Geary, *Phantoms of Remembrance,* 18.

47. For relics taken to the West after the First Crusade, see Jonathan Riley-Smith, *The First Crusade and the Idea of Crusading* (Philadelphia: University of Pennsylvania Press, 1986), 122–23. While a number of examples can be found among the list of True Cross relics collected by Anatole Frolow (*La relique de la Vraie Croix: Recherches sur la développement d'un culte* [Paris: Institut français d'études byzantines, 1961]), the greatest single collection of examples is still Paul Riant's study of the materials taken from Constantinople after the Fourth Cru-sade, *Exuviae sacrae Constantinopolitanae,* 2 vols. (Geneva, 1877–78; rept. Paris: Comité des travaux historiques et scientifiques, 2004).

48. Joseph O'Callaghan, *Reconquest and Crusade in Medieval Spain* (Phila-delphia: University of Pennsylvania Press, 2003), 190–93.

49. Yeager, *Jerusalem in Medieval Narrative,* 115–16.

50. Elizabeth A. R. Brown and Michael W. Cothren, "The Twelfth-Century Crusading Window of Saint Denis: *Praeteritorum enim recordatio futurorum est exhibitio,*" *Journal of the Warburg and Courtauld Institutes* 49 (1986): 1–40.

51. Martine Meuwese, "Antioch and the Crusaders in Western Art," in *East and West in the Medieval Mediterranean: Antioch from the Byzantine Reconquest until the End of the Crusader Principality,* ed. Krijnie N. Ciggaar and David M. Metcalfe (Leuven: Peeters, 2006), 351–54.

52. Nurith Kenaan-Kedar, "The Significance of a Twelfth-Century Sculptural Group: Le retour du croisé," in *Dei gesta per Francos: Etudes dediées à Jean Richard,* ed. Michel Balard, Benjamin Kedar, and Jonathan Riley-Smith (Alder-shot, UK: Ashgate, 2001), 29–45.

53. Carole Hillenbrand, *The Crusades: Islamic Perspectives* (New York: Rout-ledge, 2000), 111–60.

54. For the juxtaposition of Jewish crusade memory with Christian sacred history, see Eva Haverkamp, "Martyrs in Rivalry: The 1096 Jewish Martyrs and the Thebean Legion," *Jewish History* 23, no. 4 (2009): 319–42.

55. Nicholas Paul, "Crusade, Memory, and Regional Politics in Twelfth-Century Amboise," *Journal of Medieval History* 31, no. 2 (2005): 127–41. For complaints about the "singer of the Song of Antioch," see Lambert of Ardres, *The History of the Counts of Guines and Lords of Ardres,* trans. Leah Shopkow (Philadelphia: University of Pennsylvania Press, 2001), 165 and 240n468.

56. Simon Lloyd, "William Longespee: The Making of an English Crusading Hero," pt. 1, *Nottingham Medieval Studies* 35 (1991): 41–69, and pt. 2, *Nottingham Medieval Studies* 36 (1992): 79–125.

Part One

Remembrance and Response

CHAPTER ONE

Memory, Wonder, and Desire in the Travels of Ibn Jubayr and Ibn Battuta

CHRISTINE CHISM

EMORIES ARE NOT RECONSTRUCTIVE but creative, concocted through flexible chains of association, pointing forward and backward in time in ways that are haphazard, proleptic, not fully in control. Memory simultaneously creates its subject, the rememberer, and its object, the past, which exist in a given form only as long as the process of memory continues. Memories are processes, yielding utterly and invisibly to constant re-creation — and their energy depends on intimacy — an urgency and implication within the events described that more institutionalized genres of past-making, such as formal history, often strain to keep at a distance. It is this intimacy of memory — in particular, the moments of wonder, amazement, and desire that arrest and re-create the rememberer — that I want to track in this chapter, as they emerge in the two Muslim travelers' accounts, Ibn Jubayr's *Account of the Events That Befell upon Certain Journeys* (1183–85) and Ibn Battuta's *Travels* (ca. 1355).[1]

Ananya Jahanar Kabir and Deanne Williams have usefully refocused attention to wonder in cultural encounter, by treating it not as a trope calculated to mystify the other and render it up for consumption and delectation, but rather as a trope that rivets attention and thus conduces to the questioning of cultural paradigms.[2] The accounts of Ibn Jubayr and Ibn Battuta are structured by moments of wonder and amazement; they draw on the Arabic genre of *'aja'ib* ("wonder-tale"), a variety of literary *adab* (polite literature for instruction and enjoyment).[3] However, what happens at moments of wonder in these texts goes beyond generic obligation. The moments of wonder, I argue, open out to culture-crossing fantasies and desires that complicate the more paradigm-building functions of cultural memory.[4] They suggest other modes of relationship between Christian and Muslim cultures, centered in bodily encounters that reach across cultural and religious distance to acknowledge the hauntings, losses, and desires incurred by centuries of crusading warfare. These memorial texts, driven by wonder, make history intimate in strikingly unpredictable ways.

Each of these accounts by Muslim travelers complicates assumptions about the significance of the crusades as the working out of ongoing ideological rifts between the various sects of medieval Christians and Muslims. These accounts yield flashes not just of interreligious opposition but also of indifference, amicable coexistence, pragmatic and sustainable mutual profiteering, and even longing and desire, as they stage and restage the travelers' astonishments at the unique local arrangements to be found while treading the history-worn landscapes of the medieval Levant at the height of twelfth-century crusading warfare and of the Levant after the Mamluk reconquest. By attending to the way wonder and desire complicate the travelers' narratives, we can begin to dismantle the crusades as a cultural monolith: the substantiating origin of an opposition between East and West, Islam and Christianity, past and present that is rendered mythical and inescapable through its construction. We can resubject the specter of crusade as implacable intercultural warfare—which has done and is doing so much sinister ideological work—to the uncertainties of remembered experience from which it was abstracted and mythologized, and thus work to render the mythologies themselves less certain. Even more interestingly, we can see the strains and errant desires in compensation for which the mythologies are generated, and begin to unpack the mythologies themselves not as immemorial cultural truths but rather as historically specific narratives of desire and fear.

Chronicle and 'Aja'ib: Genres of Memory

The travel account of the twelfth-century medieval Muslim traveler Ibn Jubayr purports to be travel notes, written while on the road either daily or at frequent intervals.[5] It is organized by the months of the Islamic lunar calendar as a chronicle: at its outset it roots itself with a prayer for safety, a date, and a location: "The writing of this chronicle was begun on Friday, the 30th of the month of Shawwal, 578 AH (25th of Feb. 1183) at sea, opposite Jabal Shulayr [Sierra Nevada]. May God with His favour grant us safety" (Ibn Jubayr, 27). At the time of writing, the traveler was already well on the road, having set out from Granada three weeks before. The intervals between the dates given for the journey's events and the dates of their recording dimensionalize the journey, allowing it to emerge as both fixed and dynamic. Ibn Jubayr's chronicle creates memory as a recapitulation of a journey still ongoing, the traveler himself uncertain of return. Conjured event, written account, and traveler's recollection are continually lagging, catching up, looping with one another, in counterpoint to the orderly procession of Islamic months that organizes its itinerary. As the narrator continually recollects his journey, he simultaneously constitutes himself as perpetually vulnerable and performs a defense against that vulnerability. In the process, he gives us a vivid, personalized tracing of the intercrusade Levant, which has the certainty of event and the excitement of romance, as he suffers delays, shipwrecks, the fear of robbery, sudden rescues, the passing of Muslim armies laden with Christian spoils and prisoners; in sum, he memorializes the strangely orderly chaos of the Levant during Saladin's conquests in the four years prior to the Third Crusade.[6]

The second narrative I am treating constitutes a very different act of memory and a different literary genre.[7] In contrast to Ibn Jubayr's, the *Rihla* of Ibn Battuta disdains temporal organization—in fact, the dates it haphazardly interpolates are frequently inaccurate or impossible, and even its itinerary is sometimes dubious. Ibn Battuta's 1355 account, like that of Marco Polo, purports to be dictated from memory after the return home from a twenty-nine-year journey, at the behest of Abu 'Inan Faris, the Sultan of Fez:

> A gracious command prescribed that [Ibn Battuta] should dictate an account of the cities which he had seen on his journeys, of the interesting events which had clung in his memory . . . [and that] the humble servant Muhammad ibn Juzayy should assemble that which [he] had dictated on these subjects into a compilation that should comprehend what was of profit in them and ensure the full attainment of their objects, giving care to the pruning and polishing of its language and applying himself to its clarification and adaptation to the taste [of readers], that they might find enjoyment in these curiosities.
> (Ibn Battuta, 1:6)

Like Rusticello romancing Marco Polo, Ibn Juzayy was not a passive scribe; he abbreviates Ibn Battuta, interpolates poetry and philosophy, and cribs liberally from Ibn Jubayr's own previous account.[8]

Ibn Juzayy's recollection of noteworthy events structures the postcrusade Levant as a series of memorial delectations. Like Ibn Jubayr's account, it seems to reach after both historic certainty and literary artifice; it is arranged formally as a series of short chapters labeled alternately *dhikrs* ("accounts," "recollections") and *hikayat* ("tales," "anecdotes"). Ibn Battuta's account is associative and anecdotal; it simultaneously pillages other texts and claims eyewitness authority. It clings conservatively to prelaid patterns of tourism,[9] even as it savors "present and moving" moments that capture the exotic everyday. Where Ibn Jubayr's account impressed audiences, including the great historian Ibn Khaldun, and made a literary reputation for him, Ibn Battuta's was received with skepticism.

This is partly because, where Ibn Jubayr shapes a chronicle, Ibn Battuta and Ibn Juzayy deliver an *'aja'ib,* an account of the miraculous. The medieval Arab travel writer of *'aja'ib* has taken on a duty to recreate the world as an unfolding course of marvels. This in itself undercuts the idea of memory as reconstitutive and offers instead a confectional memory, tempting, teasing, and provoking the appetites of its audience. Where Ibn Jubayr's chronicular looping of narrative and event to create memory would seem to attest to its eyewitness authenticity and exciting vividness, Ibn Battuta's twenty-nine-year memory extravaganza holds itself up for retrospective aesthetic appreciation.[10]

Yet, Ibn Battuta's *'aja'ib* is not as different from Ibn Jubayr's chronicle as it seems. They actually share an emphasis on wonder and the unknown because what is strange and unexpected is what sticks in the memory. When what is being remembered is something so complex, traumatic, and protracted as the crusades, the narrative becomes a moving lens for encounters that are difficult to fit into overarching patterns. In both Ibn Battuta and Ibn Jubayr, the narrators are continually placed in uncanny positions, improvising and obliterating boundaries between self and other, friend and stranger, Muslim and Christian. Battle lines are rendered palpable but often in astonishingly exceptional ways — after all, it is the marvelous and exceptional that strikes to alertness and become remarkable, not the banalities of hatred as usual. These travel narratives remember the crusades in palpitations of the traveler's heart, unpredictably, and conduce readers to their historical complexity, as encounters both of estrangement and connection.

By bracketing the crusades between these two centuries-distant accounts, we can glimpse the crusades' tactical multiplicity, their weird detachment from much of the civil life in the region at the time, their capacity to provoke not only war and hate but also seduction, attraction, business as usual, incredulity, and even reverence. The rest of this chapter traces these moments of memorial amazement in order to extricate and investigate the alterity of crusade not as cultural mythology but as a complex, subjective experience, in which memory (his own and other's) can transform the traveler himself into something entirely unexpected — a subject desiring across enemy lines, or the treasured relic of an alien religion.

Invisible Borders: Ibn Jubayr in the Levant

The world of the crusade-period Levant was highly stratified between and within cultural and confessional microregions. Recent archaeological and historical investigations by Ronnie Ellenblum and Adrian J. Boas have challenged previously dominant historiographies;[11] Ellenblum paints a picture of Eastern cultural *convivenca* between acculturated Franks, regional Christians, and Muslims,[12] whereas Boas stresses confessional sequestration and enmity, yielding a picture of suddenly urbanized Frankish crusaders clinging to cities and fortresses.[13] Ellenblum's accounts yield a much more complex picture of Frankish rural settlement predominantly within already Christian areas, where cultural separations were complicated by mercantile and political relationships that could tactically shift and be worked to various ends at different times. Ellenblum demonstrates patterns of Frankish settlement that generally maintain the patterns of Christian and Muslim customary relationships in the region.[14] Frankish settlers tended to settle in towns and regions where Christian practice was already dominant, while maintaining heterogeneous and tactical relationships with the different Christian, Muslim, and Seljuk Turkish denizens and foreign potentates. The picture is one of confessional microclimates, networked locally within confessions, more warily between confessions, but also remotely to sometimes polarized alignments of mercantile power and armed political influence in Damascus, Egypt, Asia Minor, the Mediterranean, and the West. Throughout the region, sociocultural separations were tactically maintained to preserve norms of guarded relationship. This historical picture of guarded detente is underscored but also complicated by currents of wonder and desire in Ibn Jubayr's intercrusade account.

Virtually the moment he enters into the contested landscapes of Palestine, Ibn Jubayr is taken aback by the capacity of Levantine customs to sequester and contain interreligious conflict, while simultaneously giving it safe zones to play out in modulated ways. On the eve of the Third Crusade, while Saladin was mounting the abortive siege of Kerak (Ibn Jubayr, 313–15),[15] Ibn Jubayr communicates the wonder of finding that the most powerful boundaries between warring religionists are not the walls and ditches of besieged cities but rather those that the militants improvise themselves, by custom, usage, and tradition, a constant cultural reinscription of memory. Ibn Jubayr is mesmerized by the efficacy of these notional boundaries and obsessively notes their permutations.

> One of the astonishing things that is talked of is that though the fires of discord burn between the two parties, Muslim and Christian, two armies of them may meet and dispose themselves in battle array, and yet Muslim and Christian travelers will come and go between them without interference. In this connection we saw . . . the departure of Saladin with all the Muslims troops to lay siege to the fortress of Kerak. . . . This Sultan invested it, and put it to sore straits, and long the siege lasted, but still the caravans passed successively from Egypt to Damascus, going through the lands of the Franks without impediment from them. In the same way the Muslims continuously journeyed from Damascus to Acre (through Frankish territory), and likewise not one of the Christian merchants was stopped and hindered (in Muslim territories). . . . The soldiers engage themselves in their war, while the people are at peace and the world goes to him who conquers. . . . May God by His favor exalt the word of Islam. (300–301)

Ibn Jubayr describes how all of the region's militants preserve the value of the region by detaching their wars both from civil life and trade. He sees this isolation as a deliberate and unnatural strategy, a "usage of war of the people of these lands" (301) and one that extends cooperatively across enemy lines. Ibn Jubayr's astonishment is sharpened by a sense of his own vulnerability as a Muslim traveler along the road from Damascus to Acre. He knows that he is traveling in danger of reprisals. This sense of vulnerability cuts across narrative triumphalism to render Muslim and Christian experiences of war more commensurate. Later, Ibn Jubayr describes the trains of Christian and Jewish prisoners and booty being conveyed to Damascus after Saladin's raid on Nablus, and he prays for Saladin's victory: "May God assist him, and in His power and glory, cause it to fall to him" (314). Yet Ibn Jubayr also reminds the reader how much is at stake for him on maintaining the separation between military disputes and civil life: "We ourselves went forth to Frankish lands at a time when Frankish prisoners were entering Muslim lands. Let this be evidence enough to you of the temperateness of the policy of Saladin" (314).

When Ibn Jubayr abandons descriptions of crusade and countercrusade for descriptions of Levantine civil life, he continues to highlight his wonder at the extent to which peace was safeguarded by notional and memorial boundaries. On the way to Banyas, Ibn Jubayr notes two such boundaries in quick succession. The first is a tree on the Banyas road called "The Tree of Measure": "It was the boundary on this road between security and danger, by reason of some Frankish brigands who prowl and rob thereon. He whom they seize on the Muslim side, be it by the length of the arms or a span, they capture; but he whom they seize on the Frankish size at a like distance, they release. This is a pact they faithfully observe and is one of the most pleasing and singular conventions of the Franks" (Ibn Jubayr, 315). The tree of measure shows that even Frankish brigands are capable of allowing an arbitrary but customary location to take precedence over religious aversions. The second boundary Ibn Jubayr notes is in the Christian-controlled valley below Banyas: "The cultivation of the vale is divided between the Franks and the Muslims, and in it there is a boundary known as 'The Boundary of Dividing.' They apportion the crops equally, and their animals are mingled together, yet no wrong takes place between them because of it" (315). This boundary lacks even a physical barrier, and the animals mingle across it, and yet peaceful and equitable exchange on both sides are guarded by their recognition of it.

Perhaps it is because Ibn Jubayr continually highlights his astonishment at how notional are customary boundaries that mediate Levantine coexistence that his subsequent observations of the Christians and their customs begin to cross more dangerous lines. His descriptions of the Christian principalities of Acre, Tyre, and Tiberias begin to display a new sense of vulnerability. In these territories, military attack from Christians is less dangerous than seduction by them. At first the narrator displaces this vulnerability onto the Muslims of the region, as when he describes the Muslim inhabitants in the Christian-ruled countryside around Tibnin:

> Our way lay through continuous farms and ordered settlements, whose inhabitants were all Muslims, living comfortably with the Franks. God protect us from such temptation (*fitna*). They surrender half their crops to the Franks at harvest time, and pay as well a poll-tax of one dinar and five qirat for each person. Other than that, they are not interfered with, save for a light tax on the fruits of trees. Their houses and all their effects are left to their full possession. . . . But their [the Muslims']
> hearts have been seduced, for they observe how unlike them in ease and comfort are their brethren in the Muslim regions under their (Muslim) governors. . . . The Muslim community bewails the injustice of a land-lord of its own [faith], and applauds the conduct of its opponent and enemy, the Frankish landlord, and is accustomed to justice from him.
> (Ibn Jubayr, 316–17)

Here Ibn Jubayr uses the common trope of praising an enemy's virtue to provoke internal social reform, but the language of temptation, seduction, and danger is noteworthy; the Arabic word *fitna,* which he repeats in the account, has primary connotations of attraction, seduction, and charm and secondary ones of dissension and disorder.[16] And, interestingly, what is most dangerous, most seductive here, is Christian good management. Ibn Jubayr includes himself in a prayer of preservation from it.

Later on, the language of attraction and seduction loses its displacement and begins to touch the traveler himself more intimately and anxiously. In Tyre he describes a Christian wedding procession:

> All the Christians, men and women, had assembled, and were formed in two lines at the bride's door. Trumpets, flutes, and all the musical instruments, were played until she proudly emerged between two men who held her right and left as through they were her kindred. She was most elegantly garbed in a beautiful dress from which trailed, according to their traditional style, a long train of golden silk. On her head she

wore a gold diadem covered by a net of woven gold, and on her breast
was a like arrangement. Proud she was in her ornaments and dress,
walking with little steps of half a span, like a dove, or in the manner of
a wisp of cloud . . . We thus were given the chance of seeing this alluring
sight, from the seducement of which God preserve us. (Ibn Jubayr,
320–321)

This pyrotechnic set piece not only vividly expresses the narrator's sense of
enticement and danger (*fitna* is used again) but also conveys it to the
reader. It uses poetic metaphor to draw us in, reading like an Arabic
ghazal (love poem), lushly figural and evocative.[17] "God protect us from
the seducement of the sight."

So clear is the allure in this passage, it is not surprising that Ibn Jubayr,
as though in compensation, immediately conjures a vision of the misery of
Muslims living under the rule of non-Muslims. The following passage is
even more passionately rhetorical, as though the fearful discourse could
counterbalance the previous beguilement:

There can be no excuse in the eyes of God for a Muslim to stay in any
infidel country, save when passing through it, while the way lies clear
in Muslim lands. They will face pains and terrors . . . there is also the
absence of cleanliness, the mixing with the pigs, and all the other prohibited matters too numerous to be related or enumerated. Beware,
beware of entering their lands. May God Most High grant His beneficent indulgence for this sin into which (our) feet have slipped, but his
forgiveness is not given save after accepting our penitence. . . . Among
the misfortunes that one who visits their land will see are the Muslim
prisoners walking in shackles and put to painful labor like slaves. In
like condition are the Muslim women prisoners, their legs in iron rings.
Hearts are rent for them, but compassion avails them nothing. (Ibn
Jubayr, 321–22)[18]

On the eve of Ibn Jubayr's journey to Norman Sicily, this passage admon-
ishes an all too errant memory as a "slipping" of the traveler's feet toward
frightening assimilations. It invokes imagined miseries to offset immediate
allures and restores the grand narrative of Muslim-Christian enmity. It
denies the experiences that the traveler has just undergone and disciplines
him (and his audience) in religious truism. And it effects its discipline as

palpably as it can, through the conjured bodies of captive, expatriate co-religionists: beset by stenches and chains. The processions of shackled Muslim women replace the heart-stopping Christian bride.

A culminating incident describes an encounter with a Maghribi Muslim convert to Christianity whom "the devil had increasingly seduced and incited . . . until he renounced the faith of Islam, turned unbeliever, and became a Christian in the time of our stay in Tyre" (Ibn Jubayr, 323). It happens right before the narrator's eyes and there is more than a touch of "there but for the grace of God," in his frantic prayer: "We beg the Great and Glorious God to confirm us in the true word in this world and the next, allowing us not to deviate from the pure faith and letting us, in his grace and Mercy, die Muslims" (323–24).

In the next leg of the journey — the description of Christian-ruled Sicily — the traveler's vertigo intensifies further as he circles between the ambivalent memories he constructs, the compensatory mythologies he is moved to conjure, and an astonished third space where inadmissible desires for connection can flash into visibility and recede. Here, the traveler is at his most vulnerable; he is actually shipwrecked in the straits of Messina (Ibn Jubayr, 336–37). The owners of entrepreneurial rescue boats have their payment demands met not by the destitute castaways but by William II of Sicily himself (337). William hears that there are needy Muslims on board and takes pity on them, preventing them from being robbed and sold into servitude. This is unnerving for the traveler; he carefully gives thanks to God rather than to William, but he underscores his astonishment at having been the recipient of such extraordinary mercy.

The subsequent account of Sicilian culture is overshadowed by the traveler's curiosity about William II's uncanny intercultural regime, where Christian "filth" abounds, but "the Muslims live beside them with their property and farms [and] the Christians treat [them] well and 'have taken them to themselves as friends' (Qur'an XX, 41)" (Ibn Jubayr, 339) — although they are taxed and thus prevented from full prosperity. He paints an initial picture of the Arabic-speaking William as a friend and patron to Muslims, under whose reign, nonetheless, Muslims still live in fear: an interesting way to skirt the cognitive dissonance of Christian good management. Once again, women move to the fore to do ideological work:

> The handmaidens and concubines in his palace are all Muslims. One of
> the strangest things told us . . . was that the Frankish Christian women
> who came to his palace became Muslims, converted by these hand-
> maidens. All this they kept secret from their King. Of the good works of
> these handmaidens there are astonishing stories. It was told to us that
> when a terrifying earthquake shook the island, this polytheist [William]
> in alarm ranged around his palace, and heard nothing but cries to God
> and his Prophet from his women and pages. At sight of him, they were
> overcome with confusion, but he said to them: "Let each invoke the
> God he worships and those that have faith shall be comforted." (340)

This account directs both desire and fear toward an ecumenical fantasy:
the idea that humans could simply express their separate beliefs with
immunity and leave it to God to sort out the faithful from the unfaithful.
The earthquake reduces king and handmaidens to the same terrified level,
yet the king's comforting of his outed crypto-Muslim maidservants has the
power of a benediction.

Later on, the traveler retrenches, once more shoring up the boundaries
between confessions by making clear that the greatest threat to Muslim faith is not Christian enmity but Christian friendliness: "We traveled
along a road. . . . Groups of Christians that met us themselves uttered the
first greetings, and treated us with courtesy. We observed in their attitude
and insinuating address towards the Muslims that which would offer
temptation to ignorant souls. May God, in his power and beauty, preserve
from seducement the people of Muhammad" (Ibn Jubayr, 345). Open
friendliness and courtesy are swiftly reframed as "insinuation" and seduction. Yet there can be no seduction without desire, and the inadmissible
fantasy of beneficent Christian rule continues to entice.

> One of the strangest examples of seducement into waywardness that
> we witnessed happened as we left the castle, when one of the Chris-
> tians seated at the gate said to us: "Look to what you have with you,
> pilgrims, lest the officials of the Customs descend on you." He thought,
> of course, that we carried merchandise liable to customs duty. But an-
> other Christian replied to him saying, "How strange you are. Can they
> enter into the King's protections and yet fear? I should hope for them
> nothing but thousands of *rubayyat*.[19] Go in peace, you have nothing

to fear." Overwhelmed with surprise at what we had seen and heard, we departed. (347)

Is it possible to unpick here in whom the "seduction into waywardness" inheres? Is it the first Christian, who warns of punitive taxation and who actually is misleading the Muslim travelers because he does not know they are pilgrims, or is it the second Christian, who alienates his co-religionist ("How strange you are") to reassure the Muslims that the king's protection renders fear unthinkable and enormous rewards imaginable? The narrator uses the response of surprise here to leave the question suspended.

This suspension is the last, most ambiguous reward of tracking astonishment through each encounter. The traveler's surprise, vividly conveyed to the reader, temporarily paralyzes enculturated ideological reflexes. It arrests the reader, even if briefly, in a fantasy space where different acts of connection and desire can be imagined: the coexistence of Christian and Muslim in the Levant and in Sicily, admiration for the gorgeous Christian bride, William's rescue of desperate Muslim castaways, his comforting of the terrified crypto-Muslim handmaidens, and a safety devoid of fear to Muslim pilgrims. The William who emerges from Ibn Jubayr's account is astonishing, threatening, and desired because he comforts Muslims in need, rewarding rather than punishing difference.

Ultimately, however, the same pause of astonishment that allows these fantasies of connection to emerge also makes them inconsequential. Surprise, by definition, is exceptional. The traveler continually moves on, reconstructing the old mythologies, only to freeze and shatter them in new astonishments. In sum, Ibn Jubayr's narrative of the Levant is an exercise in dynamic memory, continually restitching itself. The sense of immediacy and vulnerability within this recollection draws attention to the narrator's wonder and desire in a Mediterranean landscape in which religious absolutisms cannot even begin to encompass the strangeness of everyday experience.

"Something there is that doesn't love a wall"

By contrast, Ibn Battuta, writing almost two hundred years later, constructs a very different landscape of memory. His Levant is emphatically postcrusade, melancholically postcolonial, laid open for tourism and pilgrimage. The scars of crusade are palpable everywhere, but the dangers and intimacies of Ibn Jubayr's intercrusade Levant have evaporated. Traversing its itinerary, Ibn Battuta's text revisits Ibn Jubayr's in an uncanny palimpsest upon which a great hand has smeared away half the landscape. The fortress of Ascalon and the mosque of 'Umar are in ruins, though there is a wonderful red column remaining there that returned to its place after marauding Christians tried to carry it off (Ibn Battuta, 1:81). Tiberias is a ghost town (1:84); Tripoli had just been rebuilt (1: 88–90). The busy, stinking city of Acre, whose Christian filthiness Ibn Jubayr had lamented at length (318–19, 323–24), in Ibn Battuta flashes by in ruins in a single sentence (1:83). Tyre is an uninhabited ruin also — no more weddings there (1:83–84). Even in ruins, however, Tyre remains impregnable. In a curious act of memorial plagiarism, the narrator conjures from the past a description of its former fortifications and chained harbor, in a passage arguably borrowed from Ibn Jubayr. The effect is as though the unassailable city could be transported from the twelfth to the fourteenth century to haunt its own wreckage. The overriding atmosphere of the entire region is a posttraumatic subsidence from political and economic entrepôt to placid regional backwater — an outpost of the Mamluk Sultanate of Egypt. The traveler circulates not with any sense of danger, but freely, as a tourist, taking in the lesser sites before hitting Damascus.

The most startling change to Ibn Battuta's Levant is the openness of the cities, the wearing down of walls, fortifications, and buildings by war and the restoration of Muslim sovereignty. Jerusalem is naked because Saladin and his successors destroyed the walls to prevent Christians from fortifying themselves within it once more (Ibn Battuta, 1:77–78). Antioch's ferociously solid wall had been pulled down by Baybars (al Malik al-Zahir) (1:103). All over the Levant, the boundaries between protected interiors have become too costly to maintain. This dis-immurement enforces a psychogeographical detente. Potential combatants are forced to improvise; parties cannot dig in; travelers may be hospitably or hostilely received, but there cannot be any last-ditch retreats or extended sieges within a landscape so shorn of ditches or fortresses. The regional administrators have effectively shifted the rules by which a besieged few can protect themselves from superior forces and retain local power. It is both a canny response to crusader tactics and a canny management of the region's intercultural draw on pilgrims from many faiths.

This belated postcrusade landscape takes us far from Ibn Jubayr's intercrusade account of carefully superintended and culturally performed boundaries. Ibn Jubayr's walls were comforting, even if notional. If maintained, they separated regional inhabitants from their other-faith neighbors, guarded against conversion, and immersed enmity in the customary interactions of neighbors who are firmly enough separated by confession that physical proximity remains unthreatening. It is when the walls become permeable, identities convertible, desires errant, that Ibn Jubayr's rich dialectics of desire and fear begin to play. In Ibn Battuta, by contrast, the leveling of physical barriers deactivates cultural and religious differences, forces them into mutual negotiations that preserve the demilitarized and Islamized balance of power. There is no sense of seductive difference to spur more astonishing recollections.

It is when Ibn Battuta leaves Muslim territory that his narrative begins to resonate with the kind of vulnerability and desire that characterizes Ibn Jubayr's. In the account of a visit to Constantinople after its conquest in 1204 by armies of Frankish crusaders and during its rule by the Latin emperors who were their descendants, walls and doorways once more become sites for negotiating fear and desire (Ibn Battuta, 2:504–14). Ibn Battuta's Constantinople is a city of well-guarded divisions, riven by the Golden Horn. One quarter of the city, Istanbul, contains the palaces of the emperor, the nobles, and the majority of the city population. Its gated markets are closed at night, and its magnificent churches include the Hagia Sophia (2:506–10). The other quarter, Galata, houses the remains of the Frankish regime that conquered Constantinople during the Fourth Crusade and comprises a magnificent harbor and a polyglot of international traders: Genoese, Venetians, Romans, and French. Their buildings and churches, Ibn Battuta adds slightingly, are dirty and inferior (2:509).

Ibn Battuta underscores the ceaseless border checks that he must undergo to move within and about the city. At the gates of the palace, "we found . . . about a hundred men, who had an officer of theirs with them on top of a platform, and I heard them saying *Sarakinu, Sarakinu,* which means Muslims. They would not let us enter, and when the members of the khatun's party told them that we had come in her suite, they answered, 'They cannot enter except by permission,' so we stayed by the gate" (Ibn Battuta, 1:504). The emperor's permission obtained, Ibn Battuta and his retinue are assigned a house near the imperial palace, which they do not dare leave for three days, even though permission for them to move about the city has been given and proclaimed in all the bazaars. They are granted an audience with the emperor on the fourth day; and Ibn Battuta describes the process of slowly penetrating the emperor's layers of security with a mounting sense of terror. They pass through five increasingly guarded gateways; at the fourth, all of them are searched for weapons; though they are assured that this is something all incomers, noble, common, foreign, and domestic must undergo. Ibn Battuta is conducted to the final gate between four men, who lead him by the sleeves into the emperor's receiving hall. By this time he is so unnerved that the emperor invites him to be seated, "so that [his] apprehension might be calmed" (Ibn Battuta, 2:506). After he collects himself, the emperor beckons him forward and invites him to sit before him, but the traveler fearfully refuses the familiarity. A Jewish interpreter translates between them as the emperor asks him about the shrines he has visited in Jerusalem, the Sacred Rock, the cradle of Jesus, and the Church of the Holy Sepulchre, as well as the many other cities and shrines he has visited in Egypt, Damascus, and Iraq. Pleased with his answers, the emperor gifts him with a robe of honor and assigns him a horse, bridle, local guide, and ceremonial umbrella. In this regalia, Ibn Battuta is paraded under guard in the marketplaces of the city to ensure his recognition as being under the emperor's protection. Ibn Battuta comments that this custom is normalized to safeguard "Turks who come from the [neighboring and allied] territories of Uzbek so that the people may not molest them" (2:506). It suggests the guarded porousness of the boundaries between adjunct Byzantine and Mongol regimes.

During the traveler's meanderings within the city, the same sense of semipermeable boundary obtains. Yet what is striking about Ibn Battuta is his persistent desire to trespass. What Ibn Jubayr resists as seduction, Ibn Battuta courts as wonder and knowledge. There are some doors the Muslim traveler will not pass because they are guarded by crosses, to which all passers must prostrate themselves. Thus the traveler never visits Hagia Sofia. However, he enters its outer court and gathers descriptions of what is inside, securing the eyes of others to see what he might not. In the same vein, while many scholars think that the entire visit to Constantinople is fabricated or lifted from other narratives, we might ask why Ibn Battuta is driven to include it, even contrafactually, beyond a completist wish to outdo all previous travel narratives. I would argue that the encountering of cultural difference becomes desirable in Ibn Battuta in a way that does not threaten him as a Muslim but rather reconstitutes him while expanding his knowledge of the Muslim world and its border zones. As a result, Islam itself emerges as more flexional and polymorphic, less a line to be fearful of crossing than a field of mysteries that it is profitable to explore. In the process, both the traveler and his confession are transformed, and these transformations do not seduce and betray but rather dramatize a marvelous capacity for endurance amid change.

The transformational payoff for daring to bypass boundaries and recognize the shared spaces that both Islam and Christianity hold dear in memory emerges in the traveler's final encounters with Christian religious practice within the city. Ibn Battuta is fascinated by Christian monasticism: he visits a monastery, which he carefully explains is "what a *zawiya* [religious house] is among Muslims" (Ibn Battuta, 2:511), and listens raptly as a young man reads the gospel to an audience of nuns "in the most beautiful voice I have ever heard" (2:511–12). One day, as he is following his Greek guide around the city, he meets an ascetic and monk whom he is told is Andronicus II, the former emperor.[20]

> When the Greek [guide] saluted him the king asked about me, then stopped and said to the Greek (who knew the Arabic tongue) "Say to this Saracen (meaning Muslim) 'I clasp the hand which has entered Jerusalem and the foot which has walked within the Dome of the Rock and the great church called Qumama [the Holy Sepulchre] and Bethlehem,' " and he put his hand upon my feet and passed it over his face. I was amazed at their belief in the merits of one who, though not of their religion, had entered these places. He then took me by the hand and as I walked with him asked me about Jerusalem and the Christians living there. (2:512–13)

As he pauses in astonishment under the monk's touch upon his hand and feet, the traveler is transformed abruptly and powerfully into a mediator of the lost and cherished places of the Holy Land to those who mourn them. The monk/emperor interpellates the body of the stranger and enemy as a relic of the shrines that he had visited, reverently or disbelievingly, as he circulated through the Holy Land, mostly on his way to somewhere else. Ibn Jubayr describes similar episodes, but they are intrareligious—as when the crypto-Muslims of Norman Sicily beg him for any relics he might have brought from Mecca and Medina, or when crowds of people meet returning pilgrims and vie to feed them, to touch through their bodies the shrines they have visited. By contrast Ibn Battuta extends Ibn Jubayr's sacred mediations across religious lines. The lost holy spaces come memorially to inhabit the body of the Muslim traveler himself, and are smeared, with the dust of the roads he has taken, upon the face of the Christian stranger. The Christian still ends up dirty, but what a bizarre turn for the stereotype of Christian filth to take.

This encounter bespeaks the production of a space of possibility that transcends differences in religious practice, conjuring the lost and absent ground into tangibility through the body of an enemy marked as *Sarakinu*. It transforms a barrier into a door. Like the astonished pauses in Ibn Jubayr, it is brief and inconsequential. Yet it becomes, however briefly, the center of the narrative's desires — to encounter strangeness in ever more expansive and indefatigable detours. Ibn Battuta's astonishment shows why travel itself is such a powerful mode of knowledge and memory: because it is risky, dynamic, transformative. The traveler puts himself in the service of reimaginable geographies in ways that even he himself cannot predict or comprehend. Effectively both Ibn Battuta and Ibn Jubayr dramatize what we might call an extension of an "observer effect" intrinsic to travel narrative: by which the observer and describer of a place comes to change (and, at least here, to be changed by) the phenomena he observes.[21] The world emerges through the incessant transformations of the traveler, who makes claims on it, maneuvers for greater access and profit, and is amazed by the moments in which he is caught off guard and made to interpret the world in ways he could not predict. What becomes most wonderful is not what is seen but what the observant, urbane, fearful, proficient Muslim traveler may — without warning — become.

The differences between Ibn Jubayr and Ibn Battuta bespeak the way memory performs differently across a two-hundred-year traumatic divide. The aftermath of the crusades was indubitably a fiercer separation between the rival confessions. At the same time, such individual subjective encounters gesture at a hidden, unpredictable, and deeply unnerving history of intercultural influence, desire, and mutual learning. Politically, the Franks of the First and Second Crusades modeled to Nur ad-Din and Saladin the urgency of Muslim intrareligious unity and instigated the countercrusades, which successfully united and militarized the disparate Seljuk and Arab sultanates. Culturally, the often uncomfortable intercalation of Muslim, Christian, and Jewish devotion at Levantine shrines illuminates the astonishing intimacy of Ibn Battuta's encounter with the emperor/monk of Constantinople. Recollecting such wonders in these accounts can enrich our study of the unpredictable ways the crusades resonated to those who traversed their divided landscapes.

Notes

1. I am using the following English translations and Arabic editions: Ibn Battuta, *The Travels of Ibn Battuta, A.D. 1325–1354*, vols. 1–4, trans. H. A. R. Gibb (New Delhi: Munshiram Manoharlal, 2004); Ibn Battuta, *Rihlat Ibn Battuta* (Beirut: Dar al-Nafa'is, 1997); Ibn Jubayr, *The Travels of Ibn Jubayr*, trans. R. J. C. Broadhurst (London: Jonathan Cape, 1952); and Ibn Jubayr, *Rihlat Ibn Jubayr* (Beirut: Dar al-Kitab al-Lubanani, n.d.). Translations and page numbers are Gibb's and Broadhurst's except where otherwise noted. For Ibn Battuta, because Gibb's translation sometimes takes liberties, I have checked the Arabic edition and consulted Ross E. Dunn, *The Adventures of Ibn Battuta, a Muslim Traveler of the Fourteenth Century* (Berkeley: University of California Press, 2005), and L. P. Harvey, *Ibn Battuta* (London: I. B. Tauris, 2007).

2. Ananya Jahanara Kabir and Deanne Williams, eds., *Postcolonial Approaches to the European Middle Ages: Translating Cultures* (Cambridge: Cambridge University Press, 2005), 8.

3. Roger Allen associates *adab* with cultural and intellectual enrichment and education (221); *'aja'ib* is a subtype of *adab,* which, in his view, substantiates the listener's status quo: "The exotic and unbelievable . . . were presumably intended to amaze and even terrify, and in so doing, to underscore for the audience the pleasing security of its own existence" (240). For these two travel narratives, I believe wonder functions differently; see Roger Allen, *The Arabic Literary Heritage: The Development of Its Genres and Criticism* (Cambridge: Cambridge University Press, 1998).

4. The nurturing of cultural memory in corporeal rituals, visual culture, and textual record does effective and sometimes terrifying social work; commemorations gradually inflect and create the ideologies and doxa that fabricate a convincing social reality. See, e.g., Miri Rubin, *Gentile Tales: The Narrative Assault on Late Medieval Jews* (Philadelphia: University of Pennsylvania Press, 2004), and

Paul Connerton, *How Societies Remember* (Cambridge: Cambridge University Press, 1989).

5. Carole Hillenbrand cautions against a too-literal recourse to Ibn Jubayr in *The Crusades: Islamic Perspectives* (New York: Routledge, 2000), 262–63.

6. For an excellent general introduction to the Crusades, see Jonathan Riley-Smith, *The Crusades: A History,* 2nd ed. (New Haven: Yale University Press, 2005); for a social history of Latin Levantine society and institutions, see Joshua Prawer, *Crusader Institutions* (Oxford: Oxford University Press, 1980); for Mamluk social organization, see Ira Marvin Lapidus, *Muslim Cities in the Later Middle Ages* (Cambridge, MA: Harvard University Press, 1967); for Arabic writings on the Crusades and countercrusades, see Fransceso Gabrieli, *Arab Historians of the Crusades,* trans. E. J. Costello (Berkeley: University of California Press, 1969).

7. See Roxanne L. Euben, *Journeys to the Other Shore* (Princeton: Princeton University Press, 2006), 63–85, for a brilliant discussion of the interweaving of familiarity and alterity in Ibn Battuta.

8. Jennifer R. Goodman situates Marco Polo's narrative within romance conventions in *Chivalry and Exploration: 1298–1630* (Woodbridge, UK: Boydell Press, 1998), 83–103. Ross E. Dunn offers a very useful ongoing assessment of Ibn Battuta's narrative, outlining manuscripts and translations (1–12), situating events in larger historical contexts, and assaying particular incidents for historicity: Dunn, *The Adventures of Ibn Battuta.*

9. Ian Richard Netton, "Tourist *Adab* and Cairene Architecture: The Medieval Paradigm of Ibn Jubayr and Ibn Battutah," in *The Literary Heritage of Classical Islam,* ed. Mustansir Mir and Jarl E. Fossum (Princeton: Darwin Press, 1993), 274–84.

10. It is not, of course, without somewhat unconvincing attestations of complete trustworthiness; Ibn Juzayy writes: "I have related all the anecdotes and historical narratives which he related, without applying myself to investigate their truthfulness or to test them, since he himself has adopted the soundest methods of authenticating those of them that are wholly acceptable, and has disclaimed responsibility for the rest of them by expressions which give warning to that effect" (Ibn Battuta, 1:7).

11. The historiographical intervention is sketched in Ronnie Ellenblum, *Frankish Rural Settlement in the Latin Kingdom of Jerusalem* (Cambridge: Cambridge University Press, 1998), and elaborated more fully in Ellenblum, *Crusader Castles and Modern Histories* (Cambridge: Cambridge University Press, 2007). Boas synthesizes Ellenblum's and Prawer's approaches and applies them to an overview of Frankish material culture that reveals its complex regional boundary lines: Adrian J. Boas, *Crusader Archaeology: The Material Culture of the Latin East*

(London: Routledge, 1999). Benvenisti integrates Ibn Jubayr as a source through-out his earlier 1970 study and yields a similarly complex picture: Meron Benvenisti, *The Crusaders in the Holy Land* (New York: Macmillan, 1970).

12. E. G. Rey, *Essai sur la domination français en Syrie Durant le moyen âge* (Paris: Thunot, 1866); L. Madelin, "La Syrie franque," *Revue des deux mondes,* 6th ser., 38 (1916): 314–58; E. Duncalf, "Some Influences of Oriental Environ-ment in the Kingdom of Jerusalem," *Annual Report of the American Historical Association for the Year 1914* (Washington: Government Printing Office, 1914); and Renée Grousset, *Histoire des croisades et de royaume de Jérusalem,* 3 vols. (Paris: Plon, 1934–36).

13. R. C. Smail, *Crusading Warfare 1097–1193: A Contribution to Medieval Military History* (Cambridge: Cambridge University Press, 1956), and Joshua Prawer, *Crusader Institutions* (Oxford, Oxford University Press, 1980), esp. 102–42 and 201–14.

14. Ellenblum, *Frankish Rural Settlement,* 214–21.

15. The crusader fortress of Kerak was a danger point for Muslim pilgrims at this time (1183–84). It dominated a major pilgrimage route between Damascus and land routes toward the holy cities of the Hijaz, Mecca, and Medina and thus endangered the performance of one of the five pillars of the Muslim faith. At this period, Kerak was also in the charge of one of the most immoderate of the crusader leaders, Reynauld of Chatillon (Arnât of al-Kurak in Arabic chronicles). From it, he launched raids on Muslim pilgrims and merchants. He had made even more of a name for himself in 1182 by actually mounting a ship into the Red Sea itself to threaten the Hijaz directly: Hillenbrand, *The Crusades,* 291–93. The Muslim chronicler Ibn al-Athîr describes the siege of Kerak (115–19), Reynauld's capture at the battle of Hattîn (121–23), and his summary execution at Saladin's hand (124): Gabrieli, *Arab Historians.*

16. Edward William Lane, *An Arabic-English Lexicon* (Beirut: Librairie du Liban, 1968), and Albert de Biberstein Kazimirski, *Dictionnaire arabe français* (Beirut: Librairie du Liban, 1860).

17. Allen usefully describes the genre of *ghazal* and offers a range of translated examplars: *The Arabic Literary Heritage* (172–87).

18. Hillenbrand usefully describes the major tropes of anti-Frankish invective as structures based on purity and contamination, suggesting that such stereotypes of filth and infection intensified during the crusades: *The Crusades,* 257–327. Ibn Jubayr indulges in such tropes freely when he describes the stench of Acre and compares the Franks to pigs. I suggest that they often intensify in his narrative virtually in compensation for some of seductive inter-relationships gestured to-ward in the moments of amazement I am describing.

19. A *rubayyat* is a quarter of a dinar; three dinars was the equivalent of a

Mamluk junior soldier's monthly salary. Thousands of *rubbayat* is therefore a large sum of money.

20. Dunn points out that the man Ibn Battuta encounters could not have been the former emperor Andronicus II, who was forced to abdicate by his son Andronicus III and did in fact retire to a monastery, because Andronicus II was dead by February of 1332, and Ibn Battuta set out for the city either on 5 July 1332 or 14 June 1334 (it is very difficult to date this part of the narrative at all) and could not have arrived there before Andronicus's death. Dunn speculates that Ibn Battuta either did not catch his interlocutor's name correctly or was misled by the palace guide; see *The Adventures of Ibn Battuta*, 170–72.

21. The observer effect in quantum physics is the effect that the act of looking itself exerts on the particles being observed; at least one photon has to strike whatever is being observed in order for it to be seen, and at the quantum level, the addition of even a photon to the system matters. The observer effect has also been adapted to psychology to describe the way human behavior changes once the actor knows he is being observed. I am extending it even further to suggest that the observer is also affected by what he is observing because, especially in Ibn Battuta's case here, he is being observed right back by Andronicus II in ways he cannot guess.

CHAPTER TWO

Constructing Memories of Martyrdom

Contrasting Portrayals of Martyrdom in the Hebrew Narratives of the First and Second Crusade

CHAVIVA LEVIN

HE MEDIEVAL EUROPEAN IDEOLOGY of crusade appears, at first blush, to have little, if anything, to say about medieval Jews. And yet, when European Christians set out on crusade, Ashkenazic (or Northern European) Jewish communities were invariably caught up in their wake. In both the First Crusade (1096–99) and the Second Crusade (1146–48), the two focal points of this chapter, renegade Christian preachers fomented anti-Jewish hostility with the result that the Jews of Rhineland Germany were attacked not only as a consequence of increased upheaval attendant on the crusading expedition but also in the name of crusade.[1] When confronted by crusaders with the alternatives of conversion and death, many (though by no means all) Ashkenazic Jews opted to die as Jews rather than to live as Christians.

Each of these attacks, or series of attacks, and the Jewish responses to them, was commemorated by Jews in historical narratives composed in Hebrew some time later. The narratives of each of these crusades evince a different attitude toward the Jewish response of martyrdom. This study examines the differing constructions of martyrdom and seeks the rationales that underlie those contrasting portrayals in these Hebrew narratives of crusade.

For the experience of Rhineland Jews during the First Crusade, three narrative texts have survived: the shorter account, known as the "Mainz Anonymous," so named for its focus on Mainz; the longer "Solomon bar Samson" account; and a third record, composed by R. Eliezer bar Natan ("Raban"), which is distinguished by its use of the more innovative literary genre of narrative alongside and interspersed with the more traditional genre of liturgical poetry.[2]

The experiences of Jews during the Second Crusade were recorded only in a single narrative, the *Sefer Zekhira* of R. Ephraim of Bonn, a nephew of Raban.[3] There are many affinities between the two episodes of anti-Jewish violence and the narratives they engendered, and R. Ephraim of Bonn's text, like that of his uncle, uses two genres, poetry and prose.[4] One translator of these texts has gone so far as to claim that "although the *Sefer Zekhira* of Ephraim of Bonn deals with the Second Crusade, in style and attitude it remains in the tradition of the three earlier [First Crusade] chronicles. . . . Above all, the document shows us that during the Second Crusade, the Jews of Germany viewed the persecutions, understood their roles, and greeted their agonies in the same spirit as had their forebears during the First Crusade."[5] For most readers of these texts, that "spirit" is exemplified by the Jewish response of martyrdom when confronted by crusaders with the alternatives of conversion to Christianity or death.

A closer look, however, reveals significantly different attitudes toward Jewish martyrdom in the narratives of the Second Crusade from those of the First. The First Crusade narratives highlight and valorize the willingness to be killed or to kill oneself and one's children rather than convert to Christianity,[6] or what has been termed *activist martyrdom*.[7] The portrayal of Jewish martyrdom in the First Crusade narratives alongside liturgical poetry composed to memorialize the Jewish martyrs of that crusade contribute significantly to the production of an Ashkenazic self-image in which activist martyrdom becomes a hallmark of Ashkenazic identity.[8]

Sefer Zekhira, Ephraim of Bonn's Hebrew Second Crusade narrative, by contrast, evinces a different response to Jewish martyrdom.[9] Whereas the earlier narratives celebrate Jewish willingness to die for the faith, this text minimizes the depiction of martyrdom and instead foregrounds the effective strategies for Jewish survival employed during this crusade.

Martyrdom in the Hebrew Narratives of the First Crusade

The Hebrew First Crusade narratives recount multiple Jewish responses to the crusader attacks of 1096, showing that these responses ranged from efforts at political negotiation, to attempts at flight, to fighting back against the attackers, to death at the hands of crusaders.[10] One of the most striking aspects of these narratives, though, is their depiction of Jewish sacrificial martyrdom, which is the most distinctive attribute of the texts.[11] They are replete with arresting portrayals not only of Rhineland Jews allowing themselves to be killed rather than submit to conversion to Christianity (the traditional Jewish interpretation of martyrdom) but also of Jews killing themselves and their children to preclude such forcible conversion.[12]

The authors or editors of those texts render potentially horrifying episodes of parents killing their children as praiseworthy, situating these martyrs within the contours of a long Jewish tradition of martyrdom and sacrifice in witness of God.[13] They mobilize the imagery of the sacrificial cult of the Temple in Jerusalem in their portrayals of Jewish martyrs and present Jewish suicide, or self-martyrdom, and even parental killing of children to avoid forcible conversion to Christianity in robustly positive terms. Drawing on images of Temple sacrifice and on the reenactment of *Akedat Yitzhak,* the Binding of Isaac, as well as on earlier Jewish biblical and Talmudic martyr figures such as Daniel, Hananiah, Mishael and Azarya, Rabbi Akiba, and Hannah and her seven sons, the First Crusade narratives laud the martyrs' behaviors and present them as models to be emulated.[14]

As historians of the medieval Jewish experience have assimilated contemporary thinking about medieval writing about the past, fruitful new perspectives have been brought to bear on these narratives, and contemporary readers of these texts have questioned the extent to which these portrayals reflect what actually happened in 1096. Approaching these texts as responses to the anxieties and needs of their mid-twelfth-century authors and editors, scholars have raised the possibility that the narratives themselves reflect doubt about the martyrs' course of action, thereby validating the lack of martyrdom on the part of the survivor-editors of the texts.[15] Even with these new perspectives, though, there is overall agreement that one of the significant goals of these Hebrew First Crusade narratives is to justify the unprecedented Jewish response of suicide and sacrifice of children by means of highlighting, valorizing, and celebrating those actions.

Whether or not these narratives accurately represent Jewish patterns of behavior in 1096, their portrayal of the Jews of Ashkenaz as preferring martyrdom, even sacrificial martyrdom, to conversion or death at the hands of Christians had a significant impact on both the medieval Ashkenazic self-image and on the perception of the Jews of medieval Ashkenaz on the part of modern historians. This sense of self is exemplified in the response of R. Meir of Rothenburg, a thirteenth-century German Jewish scholar, to the excruciatingly poignant question of what penance should be performed by a father who had killed his children in the course of attack by Christians but whose attempt at killing himself had failed. The Rabbi's response, that no penance was necessary because the father had acted in accordance with the by-this-time established tradition of Ashkenazic Jews, reflects the integration of the ideal of sacrificial martyrdom into the Ashkenazic self-image.[16] Modern historians of the medieval Jewish experience, meanwhile, have also constructed a dichotomy between the paradigmatic Ashkenazic martyrs and their Sephardic, or Spanish brethren, who were viewed as more likely to convert to Christianity when confronted with persecution.[17] The impact of the Hebrew First Crusade narratives' valorization of martyrdom on the character and perception of the Jews of medieval Ashkenaz, then, has been both deep and abiding.

Martyrdom as Portrayed in *Sefer Zekhira*

Sefer Zekhira has been the subject of far less scholarly attention and scrutiny than the First Crusade narratives have been, and, as noted previously, readers of this text and its portrayal of martyrdom have situated it within the tradition of those earlier narratives. Recent readers of *Sefer Zekhira* have focused on the contrast between the reality of the Second Crusade, in which Jews were far more effectively protected from outbreaks of violence, and on Ephraim of Bonn's effort to conform to the tradition initiated by the earlier accounts. Thus, Shmuel Shepkaru writes:

> Ephraim reported the developments of the Second Crusade in the style
> of his Ashkenazic predecessor, yet a sense of better protection for the
> Jews is conveyed this time around. . . . Even more significant is the fact
> that none of these martyrs took their own lives or the lives of others.
> Based on the language and metaphors of our documents, and, especially, the poetry of the period, however, these two facts may be forgot-

ten. Following the First Crusade style and symbols of the *aqedah* and *qorbanot,* these twelfth century documents aspire to match the heroic behavior and magnitude of the First Crusade.[18]

Simha Goldin adopts a similar interpretation of this text:

> [Ephraim of Bonn] is very much aware that he is continuing the tradition of writing and commemoration of the Jews of past generations. . . . Both the content and form of his writing are clearly influenced by his relative, Rabbi Eliezer bar Nathan [Raban]. He too places more emphasis on the motif of death for *Kiddush Hashem* than on anything else. . . . The connection between the events of the First and Second Crusades also clarifies the common message: the need to keep the faith at any price — "death for sanctification of God's Name." Even if the First Crusade's picture of forced conversion no longer fits, Rabbi Ephraim focused his stories again and again on confrontations between crusaders and Jews and on the religious violence wreaked on them. That is to say, he stressed the centrality of Jewish death as martyrs, as a reaction to Christian attempts to convert them by force. . . . In reaction to [Christian] religious intensity, Rabbi Ephraim bar Yaakov stressed their willingness to die for sanctification of God's name by using . . . First Crusade motifs . . . : the *Akeda* of Isaac, Rabbi Akiba, the theme of sacrifice, and the *midrashim* about the reception of martyrs into Heaven. There is no doubt that he had either these or similar sources before him.[19]

Though Shepkaru and Goldin differ in their assessment of the religious intensity of the anti-Jewish attacks of the Second Crusade as presented in *Sefer Zekhira,* both concur that, in its use of language and images, Ephraim of Bonn's account hews to the traditions of First Crusade portrayals of Jewish martyrdom even as those fail to represent or conform to the realities of the Jewish experience during the Second Crusade.

Careful consideration of *Sefer Zekhira,* however, suggests that, despite the structural similarities to the earlier narratives, and especially to that of Raban, Ephraim's portrayal of martyrdom differs from that of the First Crusade texts in significant ways. I contend that *Sefer Zekhira* minimizes the portrayal of Jewish martyrdom, focusing instead on strategies for Jewish survival and on Jewish assertiveness in the face of Christian provocation.[20] Unlike the First Crusade narrative depictions valorizing and celebrating Jewish martyrs and martyrdom as models to be emulated, for *Sefer Zekhira,* episodes of martyrdom, or loss of Jewish life, are shown not as models to be emulated but as representing a failure on the part of those who died to adhere to the effective protocol for Jewish safety.[21] Ephraim of Bonn's depictions of Jewish martyrdom during the Second Crusade emphasize that those who were killed failed to flee to or to remain within the safe confines of a fortress or, at minimum, to stay in their secure homes and not travel on unprotected roads between established residences.[22]

This message is adumbrated in *Sefer Zekhira*'s report of encounters between Jews and crusaders in Germany in 1146, in which each description of a Jewish martyrdom or death accentuates the reality that the victim did not conform to Ephraim's prescribed policy. Thus, R. Simon the Pious of Trier's martyrdom was occasioned by his travel between Cologne, where he had arrived on his return from England, and Trier, his final destination.[23] Mina of Speyer was attacked and mutilated, though not killed, when she left the city.[24] Abraham and Samuel, two "handsome lads" who lived in a [village] at the foot of the mountain atop which the fortress of Wolkenburg was situated, were killed because they were "beguiled by their youth" to ascend the mountain to check on Jewish affairs in the fortress.[25] R. Isaac b. Joel HaLevi and Judah of Mainz met their deaths while making wine at the time of the grape harvest, presumably in fields outside the city, where they were left vulnerable to attack.[26] Alexandri son of Moses, Abraham son of Samuel, and Kalonymus son of Mordecai, residents of Bachrach who had fled to fortress of Stahleck, were attacked and killed when they descended from the fortress to attend to their affairs in their hometown at the foot of the mountain.[27] In *Sefer Zekhira*'s portrayal, leaving the confines of the fortress in which the community had sought refuge or leaving the confines of the communal enclave in the city places an individual in a position of grave danger.

The lesson is reiterated on a communal level in Ephraim's depiction of the anti-Jewish attacks of 1147. His portrayal suggests that the danger posed not only by crusaders but also by the general upheaval that followed in the wake of the crusade had intensified, so flight to a fortress had by this point become the sole effective strategy. *Sefer Zekhira* bemoans the community of Wurzburg's choice to remain in Wurzburg even after all other communities had fled to fortresses: "On the twenty-second day of the month of Adar, the evildoers attacked the community of Wurzburg, for all the other communities had already fled to the rocks and fortresses. The inhabitants of Wurzburg had anticipated living in tranquility, but instead endured distress and destruction. Woe, Woe, Woe."[28] In Ephraim of Bonn's depiction, the ill-advised decision of the Wurzburg community to remain in Wurzburg resulted in the community's being subjected to a libelous accusation of having killed a Christian, whose dead body had been discovered in the river, and twenty-two Wurzburg Jews were consequently killed.

Sefer Zekhira and Its Objectives

In order to understand this narrative's portrayal of martyrdom, it is first necessary to apprehend the purpose and nature of the text; only then is it possible to consider the role played by the depiction of martyrdom as it relates to advancing the author's agenda. Ephraim's focus on strategies for Jewish survival in preparation for the coming storm leads to his minimizing depictions of martyrdom. For Ephraim, episodes in which Jews are killed, no matter how steadfastly they may have adhered to their faith, are cautionary tales *not* to be imitated. In *Sefer Zekhira*, martyrdom is accentuated only when accompanied by additional forms or modes of Jewish resistance. *Sefer Zekhira* celebrates the details of martyrdom principally when the martyr succeeds in perpetrating acts of overt defiance prior to his death or when the death of the martyred Jew would be worthy of note under any circumstance by virtue of his prominence, as in the case of R. Peter, student of the great Tosafists R. Samuel ben Meir (Rashbam) and Rabbi Jacob ben Meir (Rabbenu Tam). Thus, R. Samuel b. Isaac of Worms is lauded for injuring three of the Christians who fatally wounded him, and the text highlights that Kalonymus b. Mordechai managed to leave a visible glob of spit on a crucifix before he was killed.[29] By the same token, although Ephraim of Bonn acknowledges the martyrdom of the "humble and modest, venerable and pleasant" scholar R. Isaac son of R. Elyakim, along with twenty others, in his portrayal of the attack on the Wurzburg community, the account centers on those who survived. It reports that Simon son of Isaac, "an accomplished student," sustained twenty injuries, yet managed to survive for a full year.[30]

The focal point of *Sefer Zekhira*'s depiction of the attack on Wurzburg, to which Ephraim devotes eight of the eighteen lines recounting all that transpired there, is the successful escape of R. Simon b. Isaac's sister. Brought into a church to be forcibly baptized, she instead sanctified God's name by spitting on what the narrative's Jewish author terms "the abomination" (Heb. תיעוב), likely again a crucifix.[31] After being attacked with "stones and fists," she successfully feigned death despite repeated efforts to determine whether or not she was alive. Finally, under cover of night, she was rescued by a gentile laundress who successfully spirited her out of the church. *Sefer Zekhira*'s use of the description "*kiddesha et ha-shem*," "she sanctified God's name," in this instance is striking: the term is typically used of those who forfeit their lives in martyrdom, but this woman did not suffer martyrdom; rather, she survived. For Ephraim of Bonn, this was a successful instance of sanctification of God's name in that the protagonist was able to sanctify God's name by spitting on the crucifix *and* surviving.[32]

It is worthy of note that even those instances of martyrdom (or other *Kiddush Hashem*) accompanied by resistance reflect less than optimal circumstances. Had the Jews of Wurzburg fled to a fortress, or had R. Samuel ben Isaac of Worms *not* been traveling between cities, or R. Kalonymus b. Mordechai *not* left the safety of the fortress, none of these "defiant" martyrs would have found himself in harm's way. While *Sefer Zekhira*'s narrative may celebrate resistant, as opposed to passive (or even "activist," or self-inflicted), martyrdom, Jewish survival remains, for the work's author, the primary objective toward which Jewish actions should be directed.

Martyrdom in Prose and Poetry

Ephraim does not, however, completely repudiate the Ashkenazic tradition of martyrdom. Instead, he utilizes the liturgical poetry that is embedded in his text to memorialize the martyrs of the Second Crusade.[33] Ephraim's portrayal of the martyrs differs from the portrayal in the earlier narratives in that he does not fully endorse martyrdom, but he nevertheless seeks to memorialize the martyrs and expresses the hope that God will avenge their deaths. This tendency to relegate the martyrs to the poetic sections of the text finds extreme expression in *Sefer Zekhira*'s portrayal of the experiences at Bachrach, הם ("*Ham*"), סולי ("*Sully*"), and קרנטן ("*Carentan*"), though the identity of these three communities remains unclear.[34] Whereas the poetic lament for a community typically follows the prose account in *Sefer Zekhira*, in the rendering of the experiences of the community of Bachrach the pattern is reversed, with the liturgical poem, or *piyyut*, preceding the narrative. The *piyyut* mourns the death of those who were killed: "God's wrath was vented on them, causing the blood of the pious to be shed . . . may the right hand of God sustain them, giving them refuge beneath the tree of life."[35] The narrative that immediately follows, by contrast, reports that some Jews saved themselves by submitting to baptism, but then immediately fled and returned to Judaism. It would seem that, even as he eulogizes Bachrach's dead, Ephraim of Bonn suggests that, in the absence of alternatives, temporary conversion to Christianity was a potentially effective technique for saving Jewish lives. This represents a remarkable contrast to the Hebrew First Crusade narratives, which minimize their portrayal of Jews who converted to Christianity publicly while remaining faithful Jews to the extent that they could in order to exalt the ideal of sacrificial martyrdom.[36]

Ephraim's stance becomes increasingly unmistakable in *Sefer Zekhira*'s treatment of the episode at "*Ham*." The narrative tersely states only that 150 people were killed. The accompanying poem, however, suggests that at "*Ham*" parents slaughtered (or were prepared to slaughter) their children to avoid conversion in a manner reminiscent of that depicted in the Hebrew narratives of the First Crusade: "How great is their merit! For they have bound their sacrifices and prepared their offerings, Like Isaac their father."[37]

As we have seen, the binding, or sacrifice, of Isaac served as a significant symbolic model in the depictions of the killing of children by parents in the Hebrew narratives of the First Crusade. Ashkenazic readings of the *Akedah* (liturgical poem describing the Binding of Isaac) often asserted that Abraham had indeed sacrificed Isaac, and that Isaac was subsequently revived—a reading that predates the First Crusade but that gained currency in its wake.[38] That Ephraim of Bonn was familiar with this reading is evident from his own *Akedah*:

> He made haste, he pinned him down with his knees, He made his two
>   arms strong.
> With steady hands he slaughtered him according to the rite,
> *Full right was the slaughter.*

Down upon him fell the resurrecting dew, and he revived. (The father)
seized him (then) to slaughter him once more. Scripture, bear
witness! Well-grounded is the fact:
And the Lord called Abraham, even a second time from heaven.[39]

When Ephraim of Bonn draws upon the imagery of the Sacrifice of Isaac in
his *piyyut* about "*Ham,*" he evokes the (by that time familiar) Ashkenazic
image of parents slaughtering their children. Where the Hebrew First
Crusade narratives elaborate on that motif, however, *Sefer Zekhira* down-
plays it; where the First Crusade texts portray these sacrificial martyrdoms
as models to be valorized and emulated, *Sefer Zekhira* pays homage to
such martyrdom and to the need to memorialize and venerate the martyrs
only in its poetic sections, while the prose depiction is astonishingly brief
and unemotional, virtually uninformative.[40]

Similarities between the Hebrew Narratives of the First and Second Crusades

These disparate renderings of martyrdom bring to the fore the issue of the
interplay between medieval narrative accounts of the past, the events they
depict, and the contemporaneous needs of the author and his audience.
These differences are to some degree shaped by the divergent outcomes of
the anti-Jewish attacks. In 1096, Rhineland Jewish communities were
decimated, but in 1146, those communities were by and large able to craft
effective strategies for survival.[41] I suggest, though, that these varied depictions are more significantly conditioned by the particular agendas and
needs of the authors of the earlier and later narratives. It should come as
little surprise that the contrasting realities of the First and Second Crusades engendered different responses, that their respective narratives were
constructed in response to dissimilar stimuli, and that those narratives
differ fundamentally in kind.

In his 1973 article on this text, Robert Chazan convincingly argued, on
the basis of the text's report of developments in the Middle East, that *Sefer
Zekhira* was composed in the 1170s, probably in the late 1170s. Considering the work as a response to the needs of the author's present, rather
than as reflecting a desire to record the past for posterity, Chazan posited
that it was the anticipation of the impending Third Crusade that impelled

Ephraim to write his account of the Second Crusade. Chazan sees the impetus as Ephraim's fear that "a new Crusade might evoke some of the severe anti-Jewish animus of its predecessors" and that "a recapitulation of earlier instances of courage and steadfastness would have profound value" in the newly heightened atmosphere.[42] I question, however, whether it is primarily a message of "courage and steadfastness" that Ephraim attempts to impart to his contemporary audience, and suggest instead that the primary goal animating this work is to serve as a blueprint for effective Jewish strategies for survival in the face of the anti-Jewish attacks that were by this point expected in the wake of Christian calls to crusade. *Sefer Zekhira,* then, adopts a radically different vantage point from that assumed by the First Crusade narratives. Where those narratives were stimulated by, among other possibilities, a need to justify and valorize activist martyrdoms and explain God's apparent abandonment of the holy Jewish communities of the Rhineland, as well as a desire to assuage the guilt of the survivors, *Sefer Zekhira* celebrates God's protection of those same Jewish communities from a potential recurrence of a similar catastrophe. This posture is evident from the narrative's outset, as the text's prose section opens: "Let this be recorded for later generations to praise and magnify Almighty God."[43] This first section, in which Ephraim draws on motifs from the biblical Book of Esther, sets the scene by describing Radulph's anti-Jewish preaching and Bernard of Clairvaux's efforts to protect Jews, ends: "Blessed is the Redeemer and Savior, blessed be His Name!"[44] Ephraim constructs the experiences of Rhineland Jews during the Second Crusade using the model of the Esther narrative, that is, as a narrative of catastrophe averted, and seeks to convey to his audience the strategies that that contributed to this successful outcome.[45]

Martyrdom, then, does not occupy the central role in *Sefer Zekhira* that it does in the earlier narratives, nor is it similarly lauded. The relative absence of portrayals of sacrificial martyrdom in *Sefer Zekhira* is a product both of the greater success in protecting Jews and the concomitant reduced need for Jewish martyrdom during the Second Crusade and of the different objectives of the authors of the First Crusade narratives and of Ephraim of Bonn. As has become a commonplace in the study of medieval texts about the past, these Hebrew narratives of crusade represent the construction of memories of the events that stand behind the texts in order to advance authorial goals reflecting the needs of the author's present.

There can be no question that the realities that underlie these narratives have a significant impact on the narrative construction, but the narratives' authors clearly sculpt their depiction of the past in the service of their overarching goal. The First Crusade narratives seek theological understanding of the destruction of Rhineland Jewish communities and attempt to valorize and justify martyrdom, particularly "activist" or "sacrificial" martyrdom. As a result, such martyrdoms are the hallmark of these texts. *Sefer Zekhira* advances the significantly different objectives of portraying successful strategies for saving Jewish lives and highlighting Jewish aggressiveness and defiance in the face of Christian provocation. The relative effectiveness of the strategies employed by Rhineland Jewish communities during the Second Crusade, in sharp contrast with the experiences of the earlier crusade, enable the narrative's author to assume a different perspective and to adopt different goals, but those goals also influence the author's overall portrayal and, especially, his depiction of martyrdom. *Sefer Zekhira* portrays less martyrdom than the First Crusade narratives do not only because there were fewer martyrs but also because depictions of loss of Jewish life, especially in the absence of some form of anti-Christian defiance, run counter to the narrative's goals. Martyrdom, refracted through the lens adopted by this text, becomes a failure rather than an ideal.

Perceptions of Ashkenazic attitudes toward martyrdom have been dominated by the images of First Crusade martyrdom exemplified in the Hebrew narratives of that crusade. As I have attempted to show, however, the authors of the Hebrew narratives of crusade constructed divergent portrayals of martyrdom, which conformed to and served the larger aims of their respective works, suggesting that the construction of Jewish memories of crusade and of martyrdom during crusade is more complex than has heretofore been acknowledged.

Notes

1. For an examination of how these massacres have been treated in the historiography of the First Crusade, see Benjamin Z. Kedar, "Crusade Historians and the Massacres of 1096," *Jewish History* 12 (1998): 11–31.

2. The texts of the Hebrew narratives of the First Crusade have been published in Adolf Neubauer and Moritz Stern, eds., *Hebräische Berichte über die Judenver-*

folgungen während der Kreuzzüge (Berlin: L. Simion, 1892); in Abraham Habermann, ed., *Sefer Gezerot Ashkenaz ve-Tsarfat* (Jerusalem: n.p., 1945); and in Eva Haverkamp, ed., *Hebräische Berichte über die Judenverfolgungen während des ersten Kreuzzugs* (Hanover: Hahnsche Buchhandlung, 2005). On the anthologizing of narratives of persecution, see David N. Myers, "*Mehabevin et ha-tsarot*: Crusade Memories and Modern Jewish Martyrologies," *Jewish History* 13 (1999): 49–64. English translations of the three narratives appear in *The Jews and the Crusaders: The Hebrew Narratives of the First and Second Crusades*, ed. and trans. Shlomo Eidelberg (Madison: University of Wisconsin Press, 1977). Translations of the "Mainz Anonymous" and "Solomon bar Samson" narratives (designated "Short" and "Long," respectively) appear in Robert Chazan, *European Jewry and the First Crusade* (Berkeley: University of California Press, 1987), 225–97. Synoptic translations of the three narratives appear in Lena Roos, *"God Wants It!": The Ideology of Martyrdom in the Hebrew Crusade Chronicles and Its Jewish and Christian Background* (Turnhout: Brepols, 2006), A1–A125. Recent discussions of the relationship between the three narratives include Anna Sapir Abulafia, "The Interrelationship between the Hebrew Chronicles on the First Crusade," *Journal of Semitic Studies* 27 (1982): 221–39; Chazan, *European Jewry*, 40–45; Chazan, *God, Humanity, and History: The Hebrew First Crusade Narratives* (Berkeley: University of California Press, 2000), 19–27 and 217–22; and Roos, *"God Wants It!*," 11–16.

3. The text of *Sefer Zekhira* has been published in Neubauer and Stern, *Hebräische Berichte*, in Habermann, *Sefer Gezerot*, and in Habermann, ed., *Sefer Zekhirah: Selihot ve-Kinot* (Jerusalem, 1970). An English translation appears in Eidelberg, *The Jews and the Crusaders*.

4. There are four manuscript copies of *Sefer Zekhira*; each of these follows a copy of the First Crusade narrative of Raban. Perhaps because Ephraim was Raban's nephew, or as a result of the practically identical endings of the two texts, or on account of the structural similarities between the two in their shared use of prose and poetry, or because, by contrast with the other First Crusade narratives, for each of which only a single manuscript copy has survived, the combination of prose and poetry conformed more closely to the more familiar liturgical models of commemoration. Gerson D. Cohen, "The Hebrew Crusade Chronicles and the Ashkenazic Tradition," in Minḥah le-Naḥum: *Biblical and Other Studies Presented to Nahum M. Sarna in Honour of His 70th Birthday*, ed. Marc Brettler and Michael Fishbane (Sheffield: JSOT Press, 1993), 36–53, emphasizes the liturgical character of the narratives. Yosef Hayim Yerushalmi, *Zakhor: Jewish History and Jewish Memory* (rpt., Seattle: University of Washington Press, 1996), 37–50, emphasizes the innovative nature of the prose narratives and claims that the innovation did not have staying power. With respect to the Raban narrative, Chazan

notes that the poetic sections lack the specificity of the prose depictions. He writes, in *God, Humanity, and History:* "On the one hand, this generic lamentation is surprising, given the prose setting into which it is inserted. At the same time, it is precisely this prose setting that permits the generic lamentation since the facts . . . have been provided in the framing narrative" (110). The relationship between the prose and poetic sections of *Sefer Zekhira* is addressed below.

5. Eidelberg, *The Jews and the Crusaders,* 9.

6. I treat these three narratives as reflecting a unified approach to martyrdom, though there are, of course, multiple voices and perspectives represented in these narratives, as explored by Chazan, *God, Humanity, and History,* 29–111, and by Roos, *"God Wants It!,"* 262–65. Roos contends that the ideology of active martyrdom is strongest in the Solomon bar Samson narrative, which she views as the latest of the three, and suggests that the "strengthening of the ideological content [i.e., depiction of active martyrdom] of [the Solomon bar Samson narrative] corresponds to a weakening of the conviction that acts of active martyrdom were permitted or recommended on the part of the general populace" (65). Readers of the narrative concur, however, that valorization of the Jewish martyrs as heroes is a theme common to the three narratives. As Jeremy Cohen has noted: "Unquestionably the most striking aspect of the 1096 persecutions and their Hebrew chronicles is the slaughter of Ashkenazic Jews by their own hands. . . . The three Hebrew chronicles of the Crusade and most subsequent Jewish memories have considered such martyrdom awe-inspiring, the ultimate expression of religious self sacrifice"; see his *Sanctifying the Name of God: Jewish Martyrs and Jewish Memories of the First Crusade* (Philadelphia: University of Pennsylvania Press, 2004), 13.

7. The Hebrew term is *Kiddush ha-Shem,* or sanctification of the divine name. Other designations of the martyrdom depicted in these narratives include "active martyrdom," "self-wrought *Kiddush ha-Shem,*" "self-inflicted martyrdom," "sacrificial martyrdom," and "self-sacrificial martyrdom."

8. The Hebrew First Crusade narratives and the martyrdoms they depict have generated a voluminous literature, which cannot be enumerated here. Helpful starting points and recent studies include Chazan, *European Jewry;* Chazan, *God, Humanity, and History;* Yom Tov Assis, Jeremy Cohen, Aharon Kedar, Ora Limor, and Michael Toch, eds., *Facing the Cross: The Persecutions of 1096 in History and Historiography* [in Hebrew] (Jerusalem: Magnes Press, 2000); Cohen, *Sanctifying the Name of God;* Shmuel Shepkaru, *Jewish Martyrs in the Pagan and Christian Worlds* (Cambridge: Cambridge University Press, 2006); Roos, *"God Wants It!";* and Simha Goldin, *The Ways of Jewish Martyrdom* (Turnhout: Brepols, 2008). Though representing barely the tip of the iceberg, these books should aid the reader who wishes to begin to approach these texts. My objective here is to introduce these well-studied narratives and their portrayal of Jewish martyrdom to the

unfamiliar reader to contrast their depictions of martyrdom with that of Ephraim of Bonn's *Sefer Zekhira*. On the impact of First Crusade martyrdom on Ashkenazic identity, see below.

9. While the Hebrew First Crusade narratives have received considerable scholarly consideration, far less attention has been paid to *Sefer Zekhira*. Works treating this narrative (or aspects of the narrative) include: Robert Chazan, "R. Ephraim of Bonn's *Sefer Zechirah*," *Revue des Etudes Juives* 132 (1973): 119–26; Shoshanna Gershenzon and Jane Rachel Litman, "The Bloody 'Hands of Compassionate Women': Portrayals of Heroic Women in the Hebrew Crusade Chronicles," in *Crisis and Reaction: The Hero in Jewish History*, ed. Menachem Mor, Studies in Jewish Civilization 6 (Omaha, NB: Creighton University Press, 1995), 73–91; Ivan Marcus, "Jews and Christians Imagining the Other in Medieval Europe," *Prooftexts* 15 (1995): 209–26; and Susan L. Einbinder, "Jewish Women Martyrs: Changing Models of Representation," *Exemplaria* 12 (2000): 105–227. Shmuel Shepkaru's *Jewish Martyrs in the Pagan and Christian Worlds* and Simha Goldin's *Ways of Jewish Martyrdom* are recent works on Jewish martyrdom that begin to consider and contextualize the portrayal of martyrdom in *Sefer Zekhira*.

10. See Chazan, *European Jewry*, 85–136.

11. See, e.g., Jeremy Cohen's comment above, n6.

12. On the innovative character of this martyrdom, see Chazan, *European Jewry*, 105–36; Haym Soloveitchik, "Religious Law and Change: The Medieval Ashkenazic Example," *Association for Jewish Studies Review* 12 (1987): 205–21; and Soloveitchik, "Halakhah, Hermeneutics, and Martyrdom in Medieval Ashkenaz, *Jewish Quarterly Review* 94 (2004): 77–108 and 278–99.

13. For recent works on pre-Crusade Jewish martyrdom, see Daniel Boyarin, *Dying for God: Martyrdom and the Making of Christianity and Judaism* (Stanford: Stanford University Press, 1999); Abraham Gross, *Spirituality and Law: Courting Martyrdom in Christianity and Judaism* (Lanham, MD: University Press of America, 2005); Shepkaru, *Jewish Martyrs*, 6–106; and Goldin, *The Ways of Jewish Martyrdom*, 47–82.

14. On these images see Alan L. Mintz, *Hurban: Responses to Catastrophe in Hebrew Literature* (New York: Columbia University Press, 1984), 84–108; Shalom Spiegel, *The Last Trial: On the Legends and Lore of the Command to Abraham to Offer Isaac as a Sacrifice; The Akedah*, translated from the Hebrew with an Introduction by Judah Goldin (Philadelphia: Jewish Publication Society, 1967); Gerson D. Cohen, "The Story of Hannah and Her Seven Sons in Hebrew Literature," in Cohen, *Studies in the Variety of Rabbinic Cultures* (Philadelphia: Jewish Publication Society, 1991), 39–60; Louis Finkelstein, "The Ten Martyrs," in *Essays and Studies in Memory of Linda R. Miller,* ed. Israel Davidson (New York: Jewish Theological Seminary, 1938); as well as the discussions in Chazan, *Euro-*

pean Jewry; Shepkaru, *Jewish Martyrs*; Goldin, *The Ways of Jewish Martyrdom*; and Roos, *"God Wants It!."*

15. Examples include Ivan Marcus, "From Politics to Martyrdom: Shifting Paradigms in the Hebrew Narratives of the 1096 Crusade Riots," *Prooftexts* 2 (1982): 40–52; David J. Malkiel, "Vestiges of Conflict in the Hebrew Crusade Chronicles," *Journal of Jewish Studies* 52 (2001): 323–40; Israel Jacob Yuval, *Two Nations in Your Womb: Perceptions of Jews and Christians in Late Antiquity and the Middle Ages* (Berkeley: University of California Press, 2006), 135–204; and Cohen, *Sanctifying the Name of God*. By contrast, Robert Chazan has been a leading proponent of the claim that the First Crusade narratives reliably depict patterns, if not specifics, of Jewish behavior in 1096.

16. See the discussion of this *responsum* and its import in Soloveitchik, "Religious Law and Change," 209–10, and in David Berger, "Jacob Katz on Jews and Christians in the Middle Ages," in *The Pride of Jacob: Essays on Jacob Katz and His Work,* ed. Jay M. Harris (Cambridge, MA: Harvard University Center for Jewish Studies, 2002), 48–50. A similar expression of the centrality of martyrdom to medieval Ashkenazic identity is reflected in a Tosafist discussion of the possibility that Jewish law might not demand martyrdom under certain conditions (*Tosafot Avodah Zarah,* 54a, s.v. *ha be-tzina*), cited by Jacob Katz, *Exclusiveness and Tolerance: Studies in Jewish-Gentile Relations in Medieval and Modern Times* (Oxford: Oxford University Press, 1961), 83–84, and Berger, "Jacob Katz," 47. In Berger's formulation: "The tosafists remark that the ordinary processes of halakhic reasoning appear to yield the conclusion that it is permissible to commit idolatry under threat of death provided that the act does not take place in the presence of ten Jews. *Tosafot* does not merely reject this position. Rather, we are witness, at least initially, to what Katz properly describes as an extraordinary phenomenon — a cri de coeur instead of an argument. 'God forbid that we should rule in a case of idolatry that one should transgress rather than die.'"

17. Gerson D. Cohen, "Messianic Postures of Ashkenazim and Sephardim," in *Studies of the Leo Baeck Institute,* ed. Max Kreutzberger (New York: F. Ungar, 1967), 117–56. This characterization has been challenged from both directions. As noted previously, scholars of the Ashkenazic experience have begun to locate expressions of doubt and reluctance to become martyrs even in the First Crusade narratives, and they have also highlighted the experience of volitional conversion on the part of the Jews of Ashkenaz. This trend is exemplified now in David Malkiel, *Reconstructing Ashkenaz: The Human Face of Franco-German Jewry, 1000–1250* (Stanford: Stanford University Press, 2008). By the same token, recent studies such as Miriam Bodian, *Dying in the Law of Moses: Crypto-Jewish Martyrdom in the Iberian World* (Bloomington: Indiana University Press, 2007), have focused on martyrdom, rather than conversion, in the experience of Spanish Jews.

While these advance a more nuanced understanding of the histories of these Jewish communities, the sense of the centrality of martyrdom to the Ashkenazic self-image continues to prevail, whether or not it accurately reflects the medieval Ashkenazic experience.

18. Shepkaru, *Jewish Martyrs*, 219–20.

19. Goldin, *The Ways of Jewish Martyrdom*, 183–84.

20. Robert Chazan, "Ephraim of Bonn's *Sefer Zechirah*," 120, observed that "Ephraim sees [a] key to Jewish safety in the decision to seek refuge in well-fortified citadels and has suggested that one of the impulses animating Ephraim in his composition of the text sometime in the 1170's was his fear of the impending Third Crusade and his desire to provide a record of earlier Jewish behavior." Chazan emphasizes the "recapitulation of earlier instances of courage and stead-fastness" on the part of Jews confronted with "the stark choice flowing from Christian violence," and he reads the text as "a powerful evocation of earlier self-sacrifice and a significant addition to the Ashkenazic library of martyrdom litera-ture" (125–26). I argue that it is not martyrdom but effective flight to safety that Ephraim portrays as the model for emulation.

21. Roos, *"God Wants It!,"* 265, recently noted that "the only extant chronicle which tells of the persecutions of these communities during the Second Crusade in 1146–1148 mentions merely one case of suicide and no case of Jews killing each other, as a response to persecutions." This assessment is accurate for the narrative portions of the text, although, as we shall see, one of the poetic segments does allude to parents killing children in the manner of the First Crusade narratives. Roos adduces this as support for her claim that, "paradoxically, a strengthening of the ideological content [i.e. the portrayals of active martyrdom] of [the Solomon bar Samson narrative] corresponds to a weakening of the conviction that acts of active martyrdom were permitted or recommended on the part of the general populace." Roos's reading is unconvincing for multiple reasons. First, she claims that a single phenomenon, the weakening of the commitment to active martyr-dom, engendered opposing results—a highlighting of such martyrdom in one narrative and its absence from another. Additionally, her presentation assumes that *Sefer Zekhira* represents an unmediated reflection of the presence or absence of activist martyrdom during the Second Crusade, without entertaining the pos-sibility that there is a paucity of such depictions for other reasons, including authorial agenda. A conclusion about a weakening of the Ashkenazic commitment to martyrdom in general and active martyrdom in particular must take in account the gamut of Ashkenazic literature, including legal literature, codes, commen-taries, *responsa,* and liturgical poetry, rather than relying on two narratives of crusade alone.

22. Shepkaru, *Jewish Martyrs*, 216–18, also observes that "assaults usually

took place on roads between major centers," "riding out the storm in a shelter appears to have been a successful Jewish method of defense," and "the advice to ride out the storm in shelters is clear."

23. Habermann, *Sefer Gezerot,* 116, and Eidelberg, *Jews and the Crusaders,* 122–23.

24. Habermann, *Sefer Gezerot,* 116, and Eidelberg, *Jews and the Crusaders,* 123.

25. Habermann, *Sefer Gezerot,* 117, and Eidelberg, *Jews and the Crusaders,* 124.

26. Habermann, *Sefer Gezerot,* 117, and Eidelberg, *Jews and the Crusaders,* 124–25.

27. Habermann, *Sefer Gezerot,* 118, and Eidelberg, *Jews and the Crusaders,* 125.

28. Translation adapted from Eidelberg, *Jews and the Crusaders,* 127. Eidelberg does not include the lament ("woe, woe, woe") that appears in the Hebrew original.

29. Habermann, *Sefer Gezerot,* 118, and Eidelberg, *Jews and the Crusaders,* 125. This episode is treated in Elliott S. Horowitz, "The Jews and the Cross in the Middle Ages: Towards a Reappraisal," in *Philosemitism, Antisemitism, and "the Jews": Perspectives from the Middle Ages to the Twentieth Century,* ed. Tony Kushner and Nadia Valman (Aldershot, UK: Ashgate, 2004), 115–17.

30. Habermann, *Sefer Gezerot,* 119, and Eidelberg, *Jews and the Crusaders,* 127.

31. On this episode, see Horowitz, "The Jews and the Cross," 115–17. On the medieval Jewish use of derogatory terminology for Christians and Christian sacred objects, see Katz, *Exclusiveness and Tolerance,* 89–90, and Anna Sapir Abulafia, "Invective against Christianity in the Hebrew Chronicles of the First Crusade," in *Crusade and Settlement,* ed. Peter W. Edbury (Cardiff: University College Cardiff Press, 1985), 66–72; and for this term in particular, see Horowitz, "The Jews and the Cross," 114–17.

32. Shepkaru, *Jewish Martyrs,* 219–20, sees the use of the description of this woman as having sanctified God's name as a "development of the phrase *qiddush ha-shem.* Although Shimon bar Isaac's sister survived her brush with coerced baptism, Ephraim describes her as 'sanctifying the [Divine] Name.' Rejecting Christianity alone qualified as martyrdom." I suggest that this does not reflect the paucity or inadequacy of martyrdom during the Second Crusade but Ephraim's valuation of Jewish survival over death, even as a martyr.

33. The relationship between the prose and poetic segments of *Sefer Zekhira* demands further investigation.

34. See Eidelberg, *Jews and the Crusaders,* 175–76n43, for a survey of the various opinions as to the locations of the places.

35. Habermann, *Sefer Gezerot,* 118; Eidelberg, *Jews and the Crusaders,* 126–

27. Though the prose depiction does not specify that the baptized Jews were from Bachrach, the flow of the text suggests that they were.

36. Roos, *"God Wants It!,"* 18–21 recently suggested that the objective of the First Crusade narratives was not to encourage martyrdom but rather to encourage "proper modes of behaviour when pressured by the Christian majority, above all to avoid wholehearted and permanent conversion to Christianity." Most readers of these texts have noted the focus on martyrdom and the minimization of conversion, even if temporary (though such converts are not vilified in the narratives). It seems to me that, while the First Crusade narratives are sympathetic in their portrayal of those who accept baptism to save their lives, baptism is not a preferred choice in these narratives.

37. Habermann, *Sefer Gezerot,* 120, and Eidelberg, *Jews and the Crusaders,* 128–29.

38. For the history of the idea that Isaac was slaughtered at the Akedah, see Goldin's translation of *The Akedah* in Spiegel, *The Last Trial,* and Jeremy Cohen, *Christ Killers: The Jews and the Passion, from the Bible to the Big Screen* (Oxford: Oxford University Press, 2007), 38–44.

39. Translation in Spiegel, *The Last Trial,* 148–49.

40. Shepkaru, *Jewish Martyrs,* 221, offers a different reading. He notices the contrast and concludes: "Quite significant is Ephraim's use of the First Crusade authors' style to report incidents that he clearly knew little about. . . . The sketchiness of Ephraim's report hinders us from drawing solid conclusions regarding the behavior of the casualties. What can be said with more certainty is that the literary style of the First Crusade Hebrew narratives continues to dominate Ephraim's eulogy." He assumes that the prose reports of what transpired in the communities of *"Ham," "Sully,"* and *"Carentan"* reflect Ephraim's lack of information and that the poem represents his imaginative use of First Crusade models to fill that gap. In my reading, these reflect editorial choices by the author to advance the goals of his composition.

41. I do not advance the claim that 1096 was a turning point or "watershed" event for the Jews of medieval Christendom. The largely effective protection of Jews against crusader attacks during the Second Crusade is adduced as evidence against viewing the First Crusade as such a turning point for Northern European Jewry. See Chazan, *European Jewry,* 197–209.

42. Chazan, "R. Ephraim of Bonn's *Sefer Zechirah,*" 125–26.

43. Eidelberg, *Jews and Crusaders,* 121.

44. Ibid., 122.

45. By contrast, in the First Crusade narratives, echoes of the biblical Book of Lamentations predominate.

CHAPTER THREE

Lambert of Saint-Omer and the Apocalyptic First Crusade

JAY RUBENSTEIN

AROUND THE YEAR 1112, Lambert, a canon of the Church of Saint-Omer, began an eight-year process of writing everything that he had ever learned into a book. He called it the *Liber floridus* to indicate the diversity of its contents, gathered, he says, "from the heavenly meadow."[1] Its texts and illustrations, preserved in an autograph manuscript at the University of Ghent, together provide an encyclopedic, or at least a wide-ranging reference tool suitable for classroom use in the early twelfth-century cathedral school. Such a diversity of material is not always easy to navigate. Lambert arranged his book associatively, which is to say that he put one text beside another when they reminded him of each other, sometimes rearranging them again when new connections suggested themselves.[2] Despite this somewhat labyrinthine organizational system, one theme does appear to permeate the text, recurring again and again in often surprising places: the story of the First Crusade.[3]

Lambert mentions the crusade, for example, in the captions for his famous drawing of the mystical Palm Tree, surrounding its trunk with brief, annalistic descriptions of the expedition and short lists of the first Frankish kings and patriarchs of Jerusalem.[4] He discusses it more directly in several short chronicles, including his own original work, "The Years of Our Lord, the Sixth Age."[5] He sacralized the campaign in his liturgical calendar, where he lists among saints' days the anniversaries of key battles. One of the longest texts in the *Liber floridus* is an abridged version of a crusade chronicle usually attributed to Bartolphe de Nangis, itself an abbreviation of the history by Fulcher of Chartres.[6] In the middle of that chronicle, Lambert added a map of Jerusalem and a portrait of the Holy Sepulchre; original map and portrait now lost from his *Liber*, their likenesses included in a later copy preserved at Leiden.[7] In a book about everything, the First Crusade occupies a position of remarkable importance.

It is not difficult to surmise the reasons why. Lambert's intellectual peers recognized the crusade as a moment of unprecedented importance, and they wrote about it often. But Lambert had more personal reasons to ponder the crusade. His count, Robert of Flanders, had been one of the heroes of the crusade and had died in 1111, just one year before Lambert began work on the *Liber floridus*. It is likely that Lambert would have witnessed Robert returning from the Holy Land in 1101, caught up in the glow of victory, he and his entourage all carrying palm fronds gathered at the River Jordan. But, above all, Lambert had had direct contact with the crusade's most famous hero. For on 30 March 1106, in the Church of Saint-Omer, Bohemond of Taranto, disinherited son of Robert Guiscard, now ruler of Antioch, had preached a new crusade-sermon, itself an event Lambert memorialized in his book's liturgical calendar.[8] Other scholars have speculated about Bohemond's possible role in encouraging Frankish historians to rewrite the *Gesta Francorum* and in the process to produce the theologically infused second generation of crusade narratives.[9] But the only important historian whom we can speak of with near certainty as having heard Bohemond preach was Lambert of Saint-Omer. And Lambert wrote a book not just about the crusade, but rather, about everything.

Like all crusade writers, Lambert attempted to draw lessons from Jerusalem's conquest, and like many, he found it to be a fundamentally eschatological, even apocalyptic, story.[10] Lambert did not engage in millenarian speculations or set a specific date for the probable denouement of history, as some had done a century earlier, around the year 1000, and as followers of Joachim of Fiore would do a century later, fixing their sights on 1260 as the probable year of Antichrist.[11] A failure to set a specific date, however, does not make Lambert's ideas any less revolutionary than Joachim's. For he seems not to have asked, "Is the world about to end?" He wondered instead, "Has the Apocalypse started?" or, more radically, "Has the world already ended?"

Lambert may have seen the crusade as an event inseparable from apocalyptic speculations, but few modern historians share his conviction. In recent years only Jean Flori has made a forceful and persistent case on behalf of an apocalyptic crusade.[12] Flori's work in turn grows out of the earlier scholarship of Paul Alphandéry and Alphonse Dupront, who saw the crusade narrative as interwoven with millenarian and apocalyptic themes.[13] According to such a model, the crusaders expected Christ to appear immediately upon Jerusalem's conquest, there to inaugurate a 1,000-year period of peace and earthly justice. These ideas, however, have stood outside the mainstream of crusade historiography, which instead emphasizes the more conventional themes in medieval piety: the desire to go on pilgrimage and the need to perform penance.[14] Peter the Hermit appears to have preached some sort of apocalyptic message, but the painstaking scholarship of Heinrich Hagenmeyer long ago diminished the Hermit's reputation as a source for crusader thought.[15]

Apocalypticism, however, was fundamental to crusade thought, inherent in the very idea of a crusade and woven throughout all the narratives. As historians we tend not to recognize it because we do not ask the same question as did our medieval counterparts—How did the conquest of Jerusalem fit into the grand story of salvation? We have also perhaps attributed too much influence to St. Augustine, who famously forbade any attempt to calculate apocalyptic chronologies in his monumental work *The City of God*.[16] To presume that one injunction from Augustine could successfully shut down for eight centuries speculation about when the world might end borders on naïveté.[17] One need only point toward the popularity throughout the Middle Ages of the "Revelations of Pseudo-Methodius," an unapologetically millenarian text, to see how vibrant the millenarian tradition was within Europe's intellectual classes.[18] The intersection of these ideas—apocalyptic, historical, and political—appears plainly, even schematically, in the texts and diagrams of the *Liber floridus*. Out of a mixture of Augustinian theology, biblical exegesis, chronological calculation, and popular prophecy, Lambert created a compelling vision of history and current events, suggesting that Jerusalem's conquest in 1099 had inaugurated humanity's finest hour and its last days.

The key points of his thought are contained in two diagrams (figs. 3.1 and 3.4). The crucial one, figure 3.1, contains an overview of history according to the famous Six Ages model. It consists of a large circle whose center contains a red and blue face identified as *mundus,* surrounded by six roughly equal semicircles, each representing an age of history and listing the key events from that age. Lambert's divisions are conventional. The First Age runs from Adam to Noah; the Second Age from Noah to

FIGURE 3.1. The Six Ages of the World until King Godfrey. Ghent, Universiteitsbibliotheek Gent, MS 92, fol. 20v. Photograph courtesy of Ghent University Archive.

TABLE 3.1   Lambert's Six Ages of History

First Age: Adam to Noah	2,242 years
Second Age: Noah to Abraham	942 years
Third Age: Abraham to David	973 years
Fourth Age: David to the Babylonian Captivity	512 years
Fifth Age: Babylonian Captivity to Christ/Augustus	548 years
Sixth Age: Christ to the Conquest of Jerusalem	1,099 years

Abraham; the Third from Abraham to David's coronation as king; the Fourth from David to the Babylonian Captivity; the fifth from the Babylonian Captivity to Christ/Augustus; and the sixth Age from Christ to the conquest of Jerusalem. A sort of ribbon runs around each section and within each part of the ribbon is a brief statement of how long the age beneath it lasted (see table 3.1). The first two numbers are fairly authoritative, with most early universal histories agreeing on them.[19] The sources for the next three ages are less obvious. Lambert does not appear to have chosen them for millenarian purposes, that is, he does not wish to demonstrate that the world will end in the year of creation 6000. Based on the figures given here, that year would have passed in 783.

What connects this diagram in figure 3.1 to the First Crusade is its title: "The Ages of the World until King Godfrey." It is a surprising decision to stop the summary of history not with current events (if Lambert were writing in 1112, the year 1111 and the death of Count Robert of Flanders might have been a viable endpoint) but rather with an event that was by this time about fifteen years in the past.[20] To quote the entire summary of the Sixth Age: "Augustus, Christ, apostles, evangelists, martyrs, confessors, virgins. In the year of the Lord 1099, in the seventh indiction, Duke Godfrey took Jerusalem." The chronology in the ribbon reads, "In the Sixth Age, to the capture of Jerusalem, 1099 years."[21] It raises an obvious question: Has the Sixth Age already ended? Or, did the Seventh Age—the Age that parallels the seventh day of creation, when God rested—begin in 1099 with Godfrey's coronation in Jerusalem?

Any twelfth-century reader would have sensed this question, especially upon turning one page back in the manuscript, to folio 19v, where a similar diagram appears (fig. 3.2), labeled "The Order of the Chief Ruling Kingdoms."[22] Again, Lambert has divided his circle into six sections, with a circular spot in the middle labeled "Ages of the World" and with titles

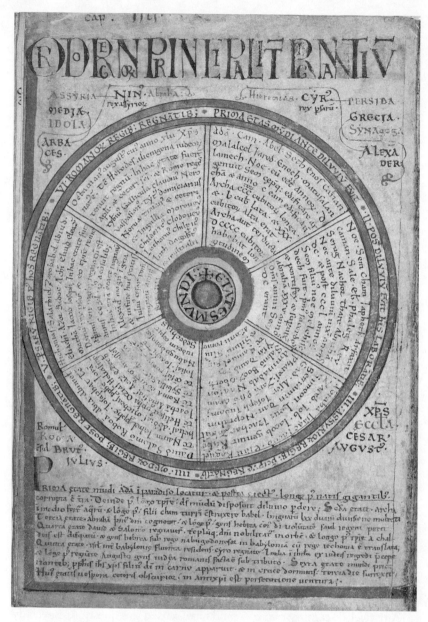

FIGURE 3.2. The order of the chief ruling kingdoms. Ghent, Universiteitsbibliotheek Gent, MS 92 fol. 19v. Photograph courtesy of Ghent University Archive.

for each age running around the circle's outer edge. The First Age he simply calls "time before the flood." The Second was "time of labor after the flood." The Third Age marked the ascendancy of the Assyrian kings, followed in the Fourth by the Median kings, the Fifth by the Persian kings, and then finally, in the Sixth Age, Roman kings ruled the world. This diagram makes clear what the other implies. After the first two ages, each era ended with the appearance of a new empire.

Then, by turning forward one page, a reader would see that something similar had happened after 1,099 years in the Sixth Age, and in Jerusalem no less. Unlike the other empires, whose authority had gradually shifted to the west, in the direction of the setting sun, the new kings returned east, to the very center of the earth. Might the kingdom of Jerusalem be a new world empire? Lambert does not say as much. But the monk Guibert of Nogent does, in a poem in his 1108 crusade chronicle.

> This city, often made plunder to kings,
> Had known complete and utter destruction;
> O, city, by this blessed conquest,
> You deservedly ought to rule.
> You should draw to you Christian kingdoms,
> And you will see the glories of this world come here
> And give thanks to you, as their mother.[23]

Lambert's diagrams express a similar idea. Godfrey's elevation was an epochal moment in human history: a new empire and a new era.

The same concept — of the crusade as the capstone to history — appears on the very first page of the *Liber floridus,* where we find a breathtaking overview of human events. Lambert does not begin, as one would expect, with Adam and Eve but with the incident that provided structure to Augustine's *City of God:* "Cain, the first son of Adam, founded the first city, which he called Effrem."[24] From there Lambert revisits events both historical and mythic. He notes the invention of music and astronomy, the creation of written language, the codification of human and divine law, the construction of the temple at Jerusalem, Caesar's declaration of empire, the discovery of the True Cross, and the establishment of the kingdom of the Franks and the county of Flanders. Finally, at the very end of the list, he writes two lines: "Godfrey, son of Count Eustace of Boulogne, conquered Jerusalem in the year of our Lord 1099. Then Robert, fourteenth count of Flanders, established Godfrey as King of Jerusalem."[25] Thus, our pilgrimage begins at the city built by Cain, the original avatar of the City of Man, and it concludes with the arrival of the Franks at the classic earthly representation of the City of God, Jerusalem.

This diagram has, however, one troublesome incongruity, seemingly inconsequential but ultimately revealing of the bases of Lambert's thought and of his methods as a historian. If we add up the five totals he gives for each age of history, we arrive at the sum of 5,217. Lambert presents this figure directly just a few pages later, on folio 32v, in a brief world history attributed to Isidore of Seville, where he writes: "In the year 5217 of the world's foundation, Augustus reigned, Christ was born."[26] The anomaly grows out of this total. For at a later date, Lambert added some additional commentary, using a darker ink and writing in a somewhat finer, narrower script, visible in figure 3.1, between the diagram's title and the circle. It is a note intended to assure readers, first, that Lambert puts no credence in the notion of an apocalyptic year 6000, and second, that the year 6000 has already passed. He writes, alongside an antimillenarian thought from Isidore of Seville, "We say 'six ages' in place of 'six millennia,' whose end was reached in the year of the Lord 742."[27] Simply put, the numbers do not add up. If the year 742 A.D. were the year 6000 of creation, then the sum of the years from the first Five Ages of history should be 5,258. But, as noted, it is instead 5,217. However minor the inconsistency, Lambert himself confronts it directly. Returning to the short chronicle on folio 32v, immediately after announcing that there were 5,217 years until the Incarnation, Lambert wrote another very brief history, which concludes, "The sum of years from Adam to Christ is 5,257."[28]

The calculation of the world's age has thus led Lambert to two different totals, separated from each other by somewhere between forty and forty-two years. But this discrepancy does not result from contradictory evidence. While Lambert's sources (mainly the seventh-century encyclopedist Isidore of Seville and the fifth-century historian Orosius) do disagree about figures and chronology, they do not do so in a way that would lead to this specific mathematical impasse. The discrepancy also has nothing to do with concerns about millennial years. Both 1000 C.E. and the various readings of *anno mundi* 6000 had long since passed. But if the forty-year miscalculation has nothing to do with the millennium, it has everything to do with the Apocalypse.

To understand why, we must set aside conventional history and turn instead to prophecy, specifically to the *Life of Antichrist*, the treatise written around the year 950 by the cleric Adso of Montier-en-Der at the request of Queen Gerberga, wife of Louis IV of France and sister to Otto I of Germany. Lambert includes this text in the *Liber floridus*, though he attributes it erroneously to the fourth-century church prophet Methodius (or "pseudo-Methodius," as he is usually called in connection with the other prophetic text, "The Revelation," mentioned above). The background of Adso's treatise is well known. Gerberga was concerned about possible connections between the political turmoil in the late Carolingian court and about the rapidly approaching millennium, and she wished to learn from Adso as much as possible about the figure of Antichrist. In response, Adso wrote a short, imaginary biography of a figure yet to be born. It proved to be a remarkably popular book, surviving in some 170 manuscripts. Later scribes would alter its contents freely, but its core message remained the same: Antichrist would not appear as long as the Frankish monarchy survived.[29]

To be precise, Antichrist would not appear as long as the power of the Roman Empire endured in the West, whose authority, according to Adso, lingered in the government of the Franks. The model rests on the book of Daniel, where King Nebuchadnezzar dreamed of a great statue composed of four different types of metal: the head of gold, the chest and arms of silver, the stomach and thighs of bronze, and the legs of iron. The statue's feet were partly iron and partly clay. As Nebuchadnezzar watched, a stone not cut by human hands struck the statue's vulnerable and unsteady feet, bringing down the entire monstrous figure. Only Daniel could explain the dream, a representation of "what will happen in the Last Days."[30] The golden head was Nebuchadnezzar himself, the most splendid ruler the world had seen. The other metals were successor states, each inferior in beauty to the kingdom that had preceded it. But the last kingdom, like iron, would be strong and able to crush all in its path. Even this seemingly indestructible kingdom, however, would grow divided, as symbolized by its clay and iron feet, and God himself would strike it down and replace it with His own eternal empire.

What interpreters of Daniel, particularly St. Jerome, drew from Nebuchadnezzar's dream was a four-fold model of history as intriguing to Christian thinkers as the six-fold model described above.[31] Indeed, we have already seen Lambert combine these two programs in figure 3.2, where the last four ages of history bore the names of four separate dynasties. Mixing Jerome and Daniel, the golden head would be the Assyrians; the silver, the Medians; the bronze, the Persians; and the iron, Rome, whose weak-footed demise Jerome believed himself to be witnessing in the fourth century. Adso thought the same thing in the tenth century, and Lambert conjectured that his own twelfth-century world — with Salian imperial claimants at war against Roman popes — had stumbled still further from the old imperial grandeur.

These signs had taken on a still greater significance in light of the crusade. As the authority of the Roman Empire waned — or perhaps it had disappeared altogether by 1099 — a Frankish monarch, according to Adso "the greatest and the last of all the kings,"[32] would travel to the East and engage in combat around Jerusalem. If one follows the earlier prophecies of Pseudo-Methodius, which Lambert would eventually insert into the *Liber floridus*, the king of the Last Days would defeat Gog and Magog, for centuries locked away by Alexander the Great (the prison's location carefully marked on Lambert's world map),[33] and then reign in Jerusalem for seven years. Godfrey of Bouillon, who had defeated Turkish invaders and the Egyptian Babylon, would have seemed an unusually appropriate candidate for this prophecy. While not a Frankish king, his claims to Carolingian ancestry were well known, giving him a strong claim to Roman legitimacy. Godfrey was also able to claim that the Emperor Alexius had adopted him as son, thereby making him and his family potential claimants to the Eastern Empire as well. As a prince in Jerusalem with claims to both Greek and Roman rule, Godfrey looked very much like a viable ruler for the Last Days.[34]

But there are two obvious objections to viewing Godfrey this way. First, according to both tradition and accepted history, Godfrey never accepted the office of "King of Jerusalem" but preferred instead to be known, more modestly, as "Advocate of the Holy Sepulchre." But Lambert seems never to have heard this story. Godfrey was for him, simply, "King." The other objection is that, according to Adso, the emperor would arrive at Jerusalem and lay down his crown on the Mount of Olives. Godfrey, by contrast, had received royal authority only upon reaching Jerusalem. Adso's prophecy, however, is one of those texts in the *Liber floridus* that Lambert had revised. According to his version of Adso, after the ruler "has successfully governed his realm, he will finally come to Jerusalem and on the Mount Olives will receive a scepter and a crown and rule of the Christians."[35] The king will not give up his title in Jerusalem. Rather, he will accept a crown and then gird himself for battle.

Did Lambert believe this king of the Last Days to be a crusader king? Almost certainly he did. At the least, he saw the fulfillment of this prophecy and the story of the crusade as directly connected, since he literally placed them side by side in his book. The chronicle of Bartolph de Nangis follows immediately upon Adso's *Life of Antichrist*, the latter finishing on the recto side of folio 110 and the former beginning on the verso.

Unexpectedly, this model of historical-prophetic thought also provides the explanation for the chronological discrepancy noted earlier. Why did Lambert, upon adding his note from Isidore of Seville to his diagram, "The Ages of the World until King Godfrey," decide to make the first Five Ages of history 41 years longer? Why did he demonstrate in the diagram that the ages had lasted for 5,217 years and then argue in the margins that they had endured for 5,258? The answer is not that he changed the duration of any of the first Five Ages. Rather, he added 41 years to the Sixth Age. That is, at some point, he decided to begin the Sixth Age not with the birth of Christ but with the rise of Augustus, illustrated in yet another of his summaries of world history. There, between the summaries of the Fifth and the Sixth Ages of history, Lambert has placed an impressive illustration of the emperor Augustus seated on a throne in the posture of an Ottonian ruler and holding in his hand an orb with the three known continents mapped onto it, the image shown in figure 3.3.[36] Lambert surrounded the emperor with a passage from the gospel, referring to the census that led to Christ's birth in Bethlehem — from a Christian perspective the pivotal event of Augustus's reign. Below the throne Lambert has written, "On eight ides January he closed the doors of Janus."[37] In Rome, the doors of the Temple of Janus were closed only during rare times of peace.[38] Augustus thus effectively proclaimed world peace, opening the way for Christ's birth: "And so at that time, that is to say the year in which Caesar by the mandate of God established peace securely and truly, Christ was born, whose arrival that peace did serve."[39] Augustus reigned, Lambert would have learned from Isidore and others, for 56 years. But Christ

FIGURE 3.3. Emperor Augustus seated on a throne. Ghent, Universiteitsbibliotheek Gent, MS 92 fol. 138v. Photograph courtesy of Ghent University Archive.

did not choose to appear until the forty-second year of his rule. After 41 years, Christ sanctioned the Augustinian Peace. When Lambert realized the importance of this point, he altered his chronologies accordingly.

To link the Sixth Age of history to a political figure, rather than to Christ, was not an anodyne decision, and Lambert himself was probably never comfortable with having made it. The idea even seems to have set off a debate among the canons of Saint-Omer. In the church's copy of

Orosius's history, next to the passage about Augustus sealing the doors of Janus, a scribe, writing in a hand contemporary with Lambert's, wondered how else to interpret this information than "Caesar carried the image of Christ."[40] In a way that would have been entirely objectionable to conservative Augustinian historians and, presumably, to church reformers as well, Lambert linked man's salvation and man's political institutions. And perhaps for this reason more than any other the *Liber floridus* keeps circling back to the topic of chronology and to summaries of world history.

But Lambert was not alone in his preference for this model. Regardless of what Isidore might have believed about when the Sixth Age had begun (if he thought about it at all: some of the earliest manuscripts of his *Chronicon* do not even mention the Ages of History), a plurality of the surviving manuscripts put the dividing line at Augustus rather than with Christ.[41] In other words, readers and copyists by and large preferred to begin the Sixth Ages with a new empire, not with an incarnate savior. Biblical personalities and events do not by themselves, therefore, define a particular age. Rather, it is the conjunctions between Scripture and World Empire—a model that the Bible embraces through the vision of Nebuchadnezzar, where each part of the golden, silver, bronze, and iron statue embodies a new kingdom.

Out of this stew of ideas Lambert concocts his grandest and most original statement of world history, combining his thought on chronology, Scripture, and current events into a single arresting image (fig. 3.4). What this diagram seeks to present is a combination of the two dreams of Nebuchadnezzar. The first one, the dream of the statue, I have already discussed. The crowned and bearded aged figure is that statue. The youthful sleeper is Nebuchadnezzar. Growing out of the young king's groin—mimicking the iconography of the "Root of Jesse"—is a tree, the subject of the king's second dream. In that vision, a heavenly watchman—here a Christ-like man with unsheathed sword in the upper left-hand corner—ordered the tree, a symbol of pride, to be cut down, leaving only a stump surrounded by an iron ring. Thus, for a time, Nebuchadnezzar's rule would be brought to an end. In a decision wholly unjustified by Scripture, Lambert turned the statue into an axeman. It will be recalled that the statue symbolizes, through its various parts, all earthly kingdoms: Assyrian, Median, Persian, and Roman. The enforcer of justice in this picture—the one who acts

FIGURE 3.4. The dream of Nebuchadnezzar. Ghent, Universiteitsbibliotheek Gent, MS 92, fol. 232v. Photograph courtesy of Ghent University Archive.

TABLE 3.2   Six Ages, Elements, and Body Parts

First Age	golden head
Second Age	silver chest
Third Age	bronze stomach
Fourth Age	iron thighs
Fifth Age	lead legs
Sixth Age	mud feet

on behalf of Christ — is the embodiment of all secular might throughout world history including, bizarrely, Nebuchadnezzar's own rule.

Lambert also uses the statue to attempt the impossible: he tries to harmonize the model of the four kingdoms with that of the Six Ages of history, effectively to make four equal six. To do so, he actually revises Scripture and says that the statue is of composed of six elements (see table 3.2). The axeman's head is golden, his chest silver, his stomach bronze, his thighs iron, and then, puzzlingly, his legs are lead. His feet Lambert simply labels "mud." To the right of the statue, Lambert lists each age, the accompanying element, and the beginning and the end of that age — for example, "Age 1, golden, from Adam to Noah." To the left of the statue, Lambert again lists the elements and the ages, connecting them directly to the statue's body. In doing so, he gives the figure a name: *mundus,* or "the world." "*Mundus* in the first age has a golden head."[42]

This vision thus encompasses all history, but it also makes an argument about history, specifically about the Fourth Age. For the image more than anything else represents "what Daniel interpreted from the statue and the tree during the Babylonian Captivity at the end of the Fourth Age."[43] To emphasize the point, Lambert labeled the axe — the central element in the picture — with three words running just above the handle: "Fourth Age, iron." Bending chronology back on itself, the statue will, with its iron axe, strike down the tree and bring to an end to the golden era of Nebuchadnezzar (First Age). Lambert, however, was not overtly interested in Medians and Persians. Rather, as he wrote on the right-hand side of the page, just below the tree's lowest branches, "At one and the same time Babylon fell, and Rome rose, in the year before the coming of the Lord 752."[44] What we are seeing, then, is the moment when Rome (Sixth Age) replaced Babylon (First Age) on the historical stage, through a swing of the iron axe (Fourth Age). The chronologies and symbols necessarily intermingle.

TABLE 3.3   Three Ages of History

First Age: Creation to Babylon	3,342 years
Second Age: Babylon to Rome	1,164 years
Third Age: Rome to Christ	752 years

Prophetic time and historical time are not identical, but their patterns do overlap, the movements of each one dependent upon and taking cues from the other.

To make the point more elegantly, Lambert set aside the sixfold and fourfold models and replaced them, or perhaps complemented them, with a three-tiered system. He introduced this final historical scheme in the upper right-hand corner of the Nebuchadnezzar diagram (fig. 3.4): "From Adam to the founding of Old Babylon, which is in Persia, 3342 years. It survived 1164 years, and then Rome began. From there, it was 752 years to Christ. That is 5258 years"[45] (see table 3.3). These numbers are not entirely new, and we can be fairly precise about how Lambert arrived at them. Two of the numbers Lambert uses in this diagram, 1,164 and 752, come straight from Orosius. The Medians, Orosius writes, plundered Babylon after it had stood for 1,164 years.[46] Later, neatly dividing books six and seven, Orosius noted that in the year 752, after the founding of the city, the Emperor Augustus closed the doors of the temple of Janus, stating in the next chapter that Christ was born that same year.[47] To attain the other number, 3,342, Lambert simply added these other two figures together, 1,164 and 752, and then subtracted them from his preferred figure for the age of the world, 5,258 (see table 3.4).

By the time Lambert created the Nebuchadnezzar diagram, he had settled on a favorite model of historical calculation, a chronological-prophetic model that depended on the movements of empire as much as on the words of Scripture.

This revelation finally led Lambert, and leads us, back to the First Crusade. For a prophet such as Daniel was never so myopic as to reveal only one or even two specific incidents. The present and future do not simply reiterate the past: they are inseparable from it; they move with it. In the case of Daniel, as we learn from Scripture, the prophet saw in the dream of the statue not Nebuchadnezzar's own last days but everyone's Last Days. So the statue and Lambert's illustration do not just tell us the fate of a sleeping Babylonian king. They also depict the fall of Rome—the end of the second stage of history (Babylon) and the end of the third stage of history (Rome) in perfect allegorical harmony. Again, Lambert enables us to see this interpretation in one of the short texts inserted into the picture, this one just above the axe and just below one of the tree branches: "Babylon the Great has fallen, she with whom the kings of the earth have fornicated!"[48] It is a condensation of Revelation 18.2–3, a prophecy about the final collapse of Babylon before Christ's return to earth—events that would occur only with the end of Roman power and the advent of both the last world ruler and Antichrist.

Lambert's illustration thus represents the fall of Nebuchadnezzar at the end of the Third Age as well as the concordant fall of Antichrist at the end of the Sixth. Strengthening this interpretation, the young king of Babylon in this image bears a noticeable resemblance to the enthroned Antichrist Lambert had drawn earlier in his book (fig. 3.5).[49] They are both beardless, youthful men who wear similarly shaped crowns. And if the sleeping figure is both Nebuchadnezzar and Antichrist, Babylon and Rome, who is the standing figure, the statue, and the axeman? As a symbol for kingship, it is Rome, the power that shall replace Babylon. Perhaps it also represents Cyrus, the Persian king who effectively brought Babylonian rule to an end. It may be an aging world—*Mundus,* as Lambert names the figure—in the last throes of life. Or it might be, as the art historian Penelope Mayo has suggested, a crusader king.[50] It was the crusaders who had struck the most recent blow against the Saracens, the imagined agents of Antichrist. More specifically, in defeating the Fatimid armies at the battle of Ascalon, the Franks had defeated the literal incarnation of Babylon, since "Babylon" was the label they generally used for Egypt.

But how could Lambert possibly reconcile all these historical and prophetic ideas, especially since, by the time Lambert finished his book, Godfrey had been dead nearly twenty years and the Last Days had not mate-

TABLE 3.4   Lambert's Math

5,258 = total years of creation until the birth of Christ
1,164 = total years in the Second Age of history
752 = total years between the foundation of Rome and the birth of Christ
5,258 − (1,164 + 752) = 3,342
3,342 = total years between creation and the birth of Christ

FIGURE 3.5. Enthroned Antichrist. Ghent, Universiteitsbibliotheek Gent, MS 92, fol. 62v. Photograph courtesy of Ghent University Archive.

rialized? Perhaps the Seventh Age had not yet begun, but one of Godfrey's heirs — one of the men whose name Lambert had inscribed around his mystical Palm Tree — would finish what the Duke of Bouillon had begun. From an exegetical perspective, after all, one king of Jerusalem served the same allegoric or anagogic function as another. But it is also possible, as the diagram "On the Ages of the World" suggests, that the prophecies had been fulfilled, that Godfrey had been the king of the Last Days foretold by Adso and Methodius, and that Lambert now believed himself to be living in the Seventh Age.

If this were the case, Lambert would have some theological justification. Commentators since Jerome — rather than admit the possibility of a millennial kingdom of Christ on earth — had accepted the possibility that, after the Sixth Age and the fall of Antichrist, a short respite might occur. During this time of indeterminate length (it was, symbolically, forty-five days), any of the elect who had wavered during Antichrist's reign would be able to perform whatever penance God deemed necessary.[51] Perhaps the Franks were now living through such a time, in the aftermath of an improbable, apocalyptic series of victories around the cities of Jerusalem and Babylon. If so, secular history could continue for a few more years, and Lambert did allow for that possibility. In his schematic, annalistic chronicle of the Sixth Age in the *Liber floridus,* he has left blank spaces for several additional entries during the decades that would follow.[52] The last space left for future historians is marked "1291." It is an astonishingly prescient choice for a crusade historian to have made in 1115, since 1291 was the year of the fall of Acre and the traditional endpoint of the crusade era. Probably, though, Lambert had in mind the book of Daniel, who prophesied a 1,290-day period of abomination between the end of Jewish sacrifices and the victory of true religion.[53]

At the very least, Lambert's detailed and beautifully illustrated historic and prophetic speculations alert us to the signal importance the conquest of Jerusalem held for apocalyptic thinkers. It encouraged serious speculation about how current events fit into biblical prophecy and whether a new kingdom, established at the intersection between heaven and earth, which is to say Jerusalem, might yet be established. Whatever Augustine may or may not have prohibited, theologians like Lambert felt able to try to make sense of current and future events through the application of prophetic history. In particular — and in a way that seems to anticipate the elaborate system of correspondences developed by Joachim of Fiore — Lambert sought the meaning of current events through an analysis of parallels in biblical and ancient history. A new era had begun. Whether it was to be a Seventh Millennium of peace and Christian governance, or whether it was to be only a brief time of penance before the eventual return of Christ, perhaps in the year 1290, Lambert was in no position to say.[54]

The crusade was, therefore, important to apocalyptic thought and to apocalyptic thinkers. We might ask, correspondingly, if apocalyptic thought was important to the crusade? The question is difficult to answer. We will never know what mad dreams, hopes, and fears drove men to leave everything they knew and march east in 1096. Surely, though, the armies did include at least a few soldiers who imagined themselves fulfilling the divine plan, living an apocalyptic dream, and fighting against a fearsomely anti-Christian adversary over the heavenly city. Whether any of them on the march drew connections between their military activity and the haunting dreams of Nebuchadnezzar — perhaps inspired to do so by the priests, bishops, and monks scattered within their ranks — we can never know. We can be fairly sure, however, that one of them, Bohemond, who preached a sermon at Saint-Omer, did make this connection, at least in retrospect.

The evidence for this point survives in a miracle story of St. Léonard of Noblat, a saint known for his facility at securing the release of prisoners. Bohemond, who had been held captive by the Danishmend Turks from 1101 to 1103, credited his eventual release to St. Léonard, and when he began his preaching tour of Europe in 1106, he started with a visit to the saint's shrine. During his earlier imprisonment, as the story tells us, he and his friend Richard of the Principate reminisced together about battles around Jerusalem and Antioch. These happy thoughts gave way to fury as Bohemond railed against the Emperor Alexius, blaming Greek treachery for his current predicament. Recently Jean Flori and Luigi Russo have both called attention to how these passages might offer insight into the content of Bohemond's sermons in 1106, since his goal in preaching a new crusade was as much about overthrowing Alexius as it was about aiding Jerusalem.[55] Another aspect of Bohemond's discourse with Richard, however, is perhaps even more important: their consideration of the crusade's eschatological significance. The Franks in 1099 had, Bohemond and Richard agreed, fulfilled the dream of Nebuchadnezzar. At Nicaea and Antioch, the iron Persians were brought low; at Jerusalem and Ascalon, the stone Egyptians. Other tribes whom the Franks had faced — "Chaldeans" — were bronze and silver, and the Arabs were gold. All of these groups, "a gathering of all the wicked people, the Lord and the army of Christ fell upon like a storm and smashed like a clay pot, cast them down, and scattered them as dust upon the earth."[56]

It is not exactly Lambert's model of the Ages of history. Indeed, it does not really match any commentary on the book of Daniel. The very imprecision of the imagery makes it more likely that we are hearing here something approximating Bohemond's actual thoughts rather than the words of an educated cleric. And it is not surprising that he would say such things. Even more than Lambert, Bohemond dreamed of overturning empires and rewriting history. The place to turn for inspiration and edification on these subjects, as any moderately educated cleric could have told him, was the book of Daniel, the definitive statement on world history. For warlord, exegete, encyclopedist, prophet, and historian alike, the conquest of Jerusalem led to the same end — to dream anew the visions of Nebuchadnezzar and to see within them the fates of empires past and future, to believe that the actions of one man might bring to fruition the plans of God.

Notes

The author wishes to thank the editors of this volume and the organizers and participants at the Fordham Conference, as well as Dominique Barthélemy, Jean-Charles Bédague, Thomas Burman, Philippe Buc, Frédérique Lachaud, Thomas Madden, Meredith McGroarty, Christopher MacEvitt, Kevin Uhalde, Meghan Holmes Worth, Geoffrey Martin, and the librarians in the manuscript room at the University Library in Ghent; at the Salle des Manuscrits, Bibliothèque nationale de France, Paris; at the Institut de recherche et d'histoire des textes, Paris; and at the Herzog August Bibliothek, Wolfenbüttel.

1. The autograph copy of *Liber floridus* is Gent, Universiteitsbibliotheek, MS 92, available in a partial facsimile edition: Lambert, *Liber Floridus: Codex Autographus Bibliotheca Universitatis Gandavensis*, ed. Albert Derolez and Egied Strubbe (Ghent: In Aedibus Story-Scientia, 1968). All references to *Liber floridus* will cite both the manuscript folio number and the page number from the facsimile: "de celesti prato"; Lambert, *Liber Floridus*, fol. 3v, p. 8.

2. Albert Derolez provides his most comprehensive description of *Liber floridus* in *The Autograph Manuscript of the Liber Floridus: A Key to the Encyclo-*

pedia of *Lambert of Saint-Omer*, in *Corpus Christianorum Autographa Medii Aeui*, vol. 4 (Turnhout: Brepols, 1998). On the associative arrangement of the book's contents, see, among other locations, p. 161. Also, Albert Derolez, *Lambertus qui librum fecit, een codicologische Studie van de Liber Floridus-autograaf*, in *Verhandelingen van de Koninklijke Academie voor Wetenschappen Letteren en Schone Kunsten van Belgie*, vol. 89 (Brussels: Paleis der Academiën, 1978). Also, Léopold Delisle, "Notice sur les manuscrits du *Liber Floridus* de Lambert, chanoine de Saint-Omer," *Notices et extraits des manuscrits de la Bibliothèque nationale et autres bibliothèques* 38 (1906): 577–791.

3. In connection with this chapter's topic, see Penelope C. Mayo, "The Crusaders under the Palm: Allegorical Plants and Cosmic Kingship in the *Liber Floridus*," *Dumbarton Oaks Papers* 27 (1973): 31–67, and Daniel Verhhelst, "Les textes eschatologiques dans le *Liber floridus*," in *Use and Abuse of Eschatology in the Middle Ages*, ed. Werner Verbeke, Daniel Verhelst, and Andries Welkenhuysen (Leuven: Leuven University Press, 1988), 299–305.

4. Lambert, *Liber floridus*, fol. 76v, p. 156.

5. Published as *Chronica*, ed. G. H. Pertz, in *Monumenta Germaniae Historica, Scriptores* 5 (Hanover: Hahnsche Buchhandlung, 1844), 65–66.

6. Usually attributed to Bartolph de Nangis, *Gesta Francorum Iherusalem expugnantium*, in *Recueil des historiens des croisades: Historiens occidentaux*, 5 vols. (Paris: Académie des Inscriptions et Belles-Lettres, 1872–1906), 3:491–543 (hereafter *RHC Occ*). In *Liber floridus*, fols. 110v–128v; pp. 226–60. The autograph copy is missing a quire of Bartolph's chronicle.

7. Leiden, MS Voss. 31, fols., 84v and 85r. Less perfect copies are preserved in Bibliothèque nationale de France, MS Latin 8865, fol. 133r.

8. Lambert, *Liber floridus*, fol. 27v, p. 56.

9. This topic has been treated most recently and most judiciously by Nicholas Paul, "A Warlord's Wisdom: Literacy and Propaganda at the Time of the First Crusade," *Speculum* 85 (2010): 534–66. The idea of Bohemond as propagandist was most forcefully proposed by A. C. Krey, "A Neglected Passage in the *Gesta*," in *The Crusades and Other Historical Essays Presented to Dana C. Munro*, ed. L. J. Paetow (New York: F. S. Crofts, 1928), 57–78, and has been taken up more recently by Jean Flori, *Bohémond d'Antioche, Chevalier d'Aventure* (Paris: Payot & Rivages, 2007), 268–73. On Bohemond's itinerary, see Luigi Russo, "Il viaggio di Boemondo d'Altavilla in Francia (1106): un riesame," *Archivo Storico Italiano* 163 (2005), 3–42. On the second generation of crusade histories, see Jonathan Riley-Smith, *The First Crusade and the Idea of Crusading* (Philadelphia: University of Pennsylvania, 1986), 135–55.

10. The notion of an apocalyptic First Crusade has been presented most recently by Jean Flori, especially in *Pierre l'Ermite et la Première Croisade* (Paris:

Fayard, 1999); Matthew Gabriele, "Against the Enemies of Christ: The Role of Count Emicho in the Anti-Jewish Violence of the First Crusade," in *Christian Attitudes towards Jews in the Middle Ages: A Casebook,* ed. Michael Frassetto (New York: Routledge, 2005), 84–111; Peter Raedts, "Jerusalem: Purpose of History or Gateway to Heaven? Apocalypticism in the First Crusade," in *Church, Change, and Revolution,* ed. Johannes Van den Berg and Paul G. Hoftijzer (Leiden: E. J. Brill, 1991), 31–40; and Jay Rubenstein, "Godfrey of Bouillon versus Raymond of Saint-Gilles: How Carolingian Kingship Trumped Millenarianism at the End of the First Crusade," in *The Legend of Charlemagne in the Middle Ages: Power, Faith, and Crusade,* ed. Matthew Gabriele and Jace Stuckey (New York: Palgrave Macmillan, 2008), 59–75.

11. The most forceful case for millennial expectations around the year 1000 is Richard Landes, "The Fear of an Apocalyptic Year 1000: Augustinian Historiography, Medieval and Modern," *Speculum* 75 (2000): 97–145. On Joachim and the apocalyptic years 1260, see Marjorie Reeves, *The Influence of Prophecy in the Later Middle Ages: A Study in Joachimism* (Oxford: Oxford University Press, 1969; rpt., Notre Dame, IN: University of Notre Dame Press, 1993), esp. 45–70 and 175–90; also, on later belief in the apocalyptic year 1260, Delno C. West, "Between Flesh and Spirit: Joachite Pattern and Meaning in the *Cronica* of Fra Salimbene," *Journal of Medieval History* 3 (1977): 339–52.

12. Flori, *Pierre l'Ermite;* Flori, *La Guerre Sainte: La formation de l'idée de croisade dans l'Occident chrétien* (Paris: Aubier, 2001); and Flori, *L'Islam et la fin des temps: L'interprétation prophétique des invasions musulmanes dans la chrétienté médiévale* (Paris: Seuil, 2007).

13. Paul Alphandéry and Alphonse Dupront, *La chrétienté et l'idée de croisade,* 2 vols. (Paris: A. Michel, 1954–59). Also see the final comments of Guy Lobrichon, *1099: Jérusalem conquise* (Paris: Seuil, 1998), 136.

14. On the connections of reform and crusade, see Carl Erdman *The Origin of the Idea of Crusade,* trans. Marshall W. Baldwin and Walter Goffart (Princeton: Princeton University Press, 1977). On penance and pilgrimage as crusade motives, see Jonathan Riley-Smith, *The First Crusaders (1095–1131)* (Cambridge: Cambridge University Press, 1997), and Marcus Bull, *Knightly Piety and the Lay Response to the First Crusade: The Limousin and Gascony, c.970–c.1130* (Oxford: Clarendon Press, 1993).

15. Heinrich Hagenmeyer, *Peter der Ermite* (Leipzig: Otto Harrassowitz, 1879). Jean Flori, *Pierre l'Ermite,* argues both for Peter's importance as a crusade leader and perhaps as its inventor. See also E. O. Blake and Colin Morris, "A Hermit Goes to War: Peter and the Origins of the First Crusade," *Studies in Church History* 22 (1985): 79–107.

16. Augustine, *De civitate Dei (The City of God),* ed. B. Dombart and A. Kalb,

2 vols., *Corpus Christianorum Series Latina,* 176 vols. (Turnhout: Brepols, 1954–65), see vols. 47 and 48 (Turnhout: Brepols, 1955), 20.7: 709, where he acknowledges that he too used to subscribe to millenarian beliefs. See also G. Folliet, "La typologie du sabbat chez saint Augustin: son interprétation millénariste entre 389 et 400," *Revue des études augustiniennes* 2 (1956): 371–90, and more generally, R. A. Markus, *Saeculum: History and Society in the Theology of St. Augustine* (Cambridge: Cambridge University Press, 1970), 45–71.

17. Robert E. Lerner, "The Medieval Return to the Thousand-Year Sabbath," in *The Apocalypse in the Middle Ages,* ed. Richard K. Emmerson and Bernard McGinn (Ithaca: Cornell University Press, 1992), 50–71; pages 50–53 essentially suggest that Augustine's moratorium held, at least until Joachim of Fiore revolutionized apocalyptic speculation. See also in the same volume Paula Fredriksen, "Tyconius and Augustine on the Apocalypse," 36, who sees Augustine's prohibition as being successful among the intellectuals, though fear of apocalyptic years 6000 remained capable of stirring fears and hopes among the masses.

18. Not only did the prophecies of Methodius appear frequently in medieval manuscripts, but they would receive occasional updates to take into account current events; see Marc Laureys and Daniel Verhelst, "Pseudo-Methodius, *Revelationes:* Textgeschichte und kritische Edition. Ein Leuven-Groninger Forschungsprojekt," in *The Use and Abuse of Eschatology in the Middle Ages,* ed. W. D. Verhelst and A. Welkenhupen (Leuven: Leuven University Press, 1988), 112–36. The basic text is printed as Pseudo-Methodius, "Sermo de Regnum Cantium," in *Sibyllinische Texte und Forschungen,* ed. Ernst Sackur (Halle, 1898), 59–96. The most important contribution to this topic is Carl Erdman, "Endkaiserglaube und Kreuzzugsgedanke im 11. Jahrhundert," *Zeitschrift für Kirchengeschichte* 51 (1932): 384–414, which examines the production of prophetic texts in connection with the call to crusade.

19. Four of the five sums — for the First, Second, Fourth, and Fifth Ages — appear in an anonymous continuation of Fredegar's chronicle, *Patrologiae cursus completus: Series Latina,* comp. J. P. Migne, 217 vols. and 4 vols. Indexes (Paris, 1841–64), 71: cols. 675–98 (hereafter *PL*), specifically at col. 676. It is possible that Lambert was working from memory and that his faulty memory, once set to parchment, became authoritative.

20. Mayo, "Crusaders," 65–66, makes a similar observation.

21. The Latin reads, "Octavianus, Christus, apostoli, evangelistes, martyres, confessores, virgines. In hoc anno Domini MXCIX Godefridus dux cepit Hierusalem indictione VII," and "VI etas usque ad captam Hierusalem annos MXCIX" (Lambert, *Liber floridus,* fol. 20v, p. 42).

22. "Ordo regnorum principaliter regnantium" (Lambert, *Liber floridus,* fol. 19v, p. 40).

23. "Urbs ista, sepe preda facta regibus, / pessum dabatur obruenda funditus; / hac o beata captione civitas, / hinc promerens ut imperare debeas / ad teque regna christiana contrahas, / videbis orbis huc venire glorias / tibique matris exhibere gratias" (Guibert, *Dei gesta per francos,* ed. R. B. C. Huygens, in *Corpus Christianorum Continuatio Mediaevalis* 127A [Turnhout: Brepols, 1996], 7:14, 289–90 [hereafter *CCCM*]).

24. "Caim filius Adam primus civitatem primam quam Effrem vocavit condidit" (Lambert, *Liber floridus,* fol. 1v, p. 4). Cain calls the city "Enoch" or "Henoch" in Genesis 4:17. Lambert takes "Effrem" from Pseudo Methodius, recorded in *Liber floridus,* fol. 217r, p. 433. Augustine mentions Cain and Enoch in *City of God,* 15.1.

25. "Godefridus filius Eustachii comitis. Bolonie anno domini m xc iiii: Iherusalem cepit; Rotbertus quartus x comes Flandrie. Godefridum Hierosolimis tunc regem constituit" (Lambert, *Liber floridus,* fol. 1v, p. 4).

26. "Anno orbis conditi VCCXVII Octavianus regnavit, Christus natus est" (ibid., fol. 32v, p. 66).

27. The Latin reads, "Sex etates pro sex milibus dicuntur. finem facientes in anno domini dccxlii; Isidorus dicit."

28. "Summa annorum ab Adam usque ad Christum VCCLVII" (Lambert, *Liber floridus,* 32v, p. 66). He has revised this section to reach this sum. The final numerals in the total, "LVII," have been written over an erasure, and two of the other numbers have been tampered with as well, raising the possibility that originally there was no discrepancy. Or, if there was a discrepancy, Lambert, upon reflection, decided to correct it so that it was the right discrepancy.

29. The various renditions are in Adso Dervensis, *De ortu et tempore Antichristi,* ed. D. Verhelst, *CCCM* 45 (Turnhout: Brepols, 1976).

30. ". . . quae ventura sunt in novissimis temporibus" (Dan. 2:28). See also Flori, *L'Islam et la fin des temps,* 20–27.

31. Jerome, *Commentariorum in Danielem, Corpus Christianorum Series Latina* (Turnhout: Brepols, 1964), vol. 75a, 1.2.31–35, pp. 793–95.

32. ". . . ipse erit maximus et omnium regum ultimus" (Adso, *De Antichristo, CCCM* 45:26).

33. Lambert, *Liber floridus,* fols. 92v–93r, 190–91.

34. More fully made in Rubenstein, "Godfrey versus Raymond."

35. "Qui, postquam regnum feliciter gubernavit, ad ultimum Hierosolimam ueniet et *in monte Oliueti* sceptrum et coronam christianorumque obtinebit imperium" (Adso, *De Antichristo, CCCM* 45:149). Also, *Liber floridus,* fol. 109v, p. 222.

36. Lambert, *Liber floridus,* fol. 138v, p. 280.

37. ". . . viii idus ianuarii clausit portas Iani" (ibid.).

38. Orosius, *Historiae adversum paganos, PL* 31, col. 1058A, B. On the connection to Christ's birth, see also col. 669.

39. "Igitur eo tempore, id est eo anno quo firmissimam verissimamque pacem ordinatione Dei Caesar composuit, natus est Christus, cujus adventui pax ista famulata est" (Orosius, *Historiae adversum paganos,* col. 1058B).

40. "... in ipso ordine Cesar. Christi figuram portaret?" (Bibliothèque municipale Saint-Omer, MS 717, fol. 48v).

41. On occasion, the transition occurs earlier still, with Julius Caesar, since it is with Caesar that the Roman Empire proper begins. The most respected edition is Isidore of Seville, *Chronica,* ed. Theodore Mommsen, *Monumenta Germaniae Historica: Auctores antiquissimi,* vol. 11 of *Scriptores rerum Germanicarum* (Berlin, 1893), 391–506. This edition places the division at the birth of Christ, after the entry on Augustus; see ch. 237, p. 454. Of the twenty manuscripts Mommsen consulted, nine place the division at the reign of Augustus, only three with the birth of Christ. Paris, Bibliothèque nationale de France, MS lat. 1863, fol 30r, places the division between Caesar and Augustus. These irregularities make ironic the observation by Paul Merritt Bassett, "The Use of History in the *Chronicon* of Isidore of Seville," *History and Theory* 15 (1976): 278–92: "Even Augustus seems a more logical beginning point [for the Sixth Age], for he was the first Roman emperor"; see 286. John Victor Tolan notes the Augustinian division correctly, without mentioning the confusion; see *Saracens: Islam in the Medieval European Imagination* (New York: Columbia University Press, 2002), 6-7.

42. The two passages read, in Latin, "Etas. I. aurea. ab Adam usque ad Noe," and "Mundus in prima etate habens caput aureum."

43. "... interpretauit Daniel propheta dum esset in transmirgratione Babylonis, e statua et arbore in fine quarte etatis mundi" (*Liber floridus,* fol. 232v, p. 464). Mayo, "Crusaders," 60 and n113, overlooked this passage when she argued that the diagram does not conflate the two dreams.

44. "Uno eodemque tempore Babylon cecidit et Roma surrexit. anno ante adventum Christo DCCLII" (*Liber floridus,* fol. 232v, p. 464). The idea derives from Orosius: "And so in one and the same intersection of time, the one fell and the other rose ... Empire died in the East, and Empire was born in the West": "Siquidem sub una eademque convenientia temporum illa cecidit, ista surrexit: illa tunc primum alienigenarum perpessa dominatum, haec tum primum etiam suorum aspernata fastidium: illa tunc quasi moriens, dimisit haereditatem: haec vero pubescens, tunc se agnovit haeredem: tunc Orientis occidit, et ortum est Occidentis imperium" (*Libri,* 2:2, col. 747A).

45. "Ab Adam usque ad conditionem Babylonie veteris que est III. et ccc. xlii. Mansitque annis MCLXIIII. tunc. Rome incepta est. Inde ad Christum DCCLII. Hoc sunt VCCLVIII" (*Liber floridus,* fol. 232v, p. 464).

46. Orosius, *Libri*, 2:3, col. 747B.

47. Ibid., 6:22, col. 1057C, and 7:1, col. 1059B. The number 3,342 is Lambert's own, for Orosius states clearly that 3,184 years passed between the creation of the world and Babylon's foundation. To obtain this new number, 3,342, Lambert did not rely on history but on math. He started with 5,258, one of his preferred figures for the total number of years between Creation and Christ, and subtracted from it the other two quantities that he had learned from Orosius (the number of years that Babylon had existed and the number of years between the founding of Rome and the birth of Christ), leaving him now with the first two Ages, lasting 3,342 years. Orosius also observes that from the time of Ninus and Abraham to the birth of Christ was 2,015 years; see *Libri*, 1:1, col. 669B.

48. "Cecidit Babilon illa magna cum qua fornicati sunt reges terre" (*Liber floridus*, fol. 232v, p. 464).

49. Ibid., fol. 62v, p. 126.

50. Mayo, "Crusaders," 61.

51. The belief grew out of a discrepancy in the book of Daniel, which described a 1,290-day period of desecration and a judgment that would follow after 1,335 days, leaving an unexplained 45-day gap between the end of the time of tribulation and the Day of Judgment. Discussed by Robert E. Lerner, "Refreshment of the Saints: The Time after Antichrist as a Station for Earthly Progress in Medieval Thought," *Traditio* 32 (1976): 97–144.

52. Running in *Liber floridus* from 36v to 46r, pp. 74–93.

53. Dan. 12:11–12, the prophecy discussed above in n54.

54. Though to engage in a style of speculation that Lambert would have appreciated, if one adds the 42-year reign of Augustus to the year 1290, one arrives surprisingly close to the figure 1,335, the number associated by the Daniel with the time of Judgment, as discussed in the notes above.

55. Russo, "Viaggio di Boemondo," 6–16, and Flori, *Bohémond d'Antioche*, 260–64; see also Paul, "Warlord's Wisdom," 557–58.

56. *Vita et miracula S. Leonardi,* in *Acta Sanctorum,* ed. Jean Bollard, Jean Carnander, et al., 70 vols. (Paris: Société des Bollandistes, 1863–; rpt., Brussels: Cultures et Civilisations, 1965), Nov. 3, p. 164 (where the two men discuss the apocalypse) and p. 180 (where Bohemond delivers a sermon on the same themes): "Totumque hoc genus quasi vas figuli Dominus confregit Christique militia quasi turbo irruens in virtute Dei malignantium coetus dispersit, praecipitavit et tamquam pulverem terrae proiecit."

Part Two

Sites and Structures
Cities, Buildings, and Bodies

CHAPTER FOUR

Remembering the Crusades in the Fabric of Buildings

Preliminary Thoughts about Alternating Voussoirs

JERRILYNN DODDS

O N 31 MARCH 1146 King Louis VII of France traveled to the town of Vézelay. There, an unusually large crowd had assembled to witness ceremonies intended to visualize the launching of the Second Crusade. The king received a cross sent by Pope Eugenius III at a ceremony in which he and a group of nobles made their vow to join the crusade. He then joined the famed Cistercian preacher Bernard of Clairvaux on a dais at an outdoor public assembly, a production meant to enlist broad support for the crusade among the people. Little cloth crosses were to be distributed to promote the crusade in the crowd that gathered to hear Bernard. The great monastic leader and extraordinarily persuasive speaker had been chosen specifically by the pope, and his exhortation so moved those listening that there were not enough crosses, and he was forced tear off strips of his monastic habit to make more for the waiting crowd.[1]

This was an event for which the monks of Vézelay had waited for more than fifty years. William of Tyre tells us that in 1095 Pope Urban II had thought of holding the council that would launch the first crusade in either Vézelay or Le Puy but that finally he settled on Clermont.[2] There Urban had addressed a crowd of churchmen and laity, exhorting Frankish knights to make a militant pilgrimage to the Holy Land, to free the Eastern Christians and liberate the Holy Sepulchre. The churchman who played the protagonist's role at that original theatrical event was Le Puy's bishop, Adhémar of Monteil, who became the first to take the cross, as the pope's representative. But in 1146 it was a monk, Bernard, who would preach the call to the Second Crusade against the theatrical backdrop of Ste. Made-leine de Vézelay, a powerful and independent monastic church.

Vézelay would appear yet again as a site associated with the crusades in 1190, when Richard Lion-Heart, king of England, and Philip Augustus of France would begin the Third Crusade from the same site, against the backdrop of the same dramatic monastic church. These observations lead naturally to an older study of Vézelay's iconography — one received with alternate reverence and ambivalence in recent decades — and to the question of the interaction of monuments and the public remembrance of historical events.

The Church Fabric of Vézelay

In his powerful interpretation of the central tympanum of Vézelay of 1944, Adolph Katzenellenbogen suggested that its iconography reflected an "encyclopedic Mission of the Apostles" that "prefigures the new mission of the crusaders" (fig. 4–1).[3] Created after the First Crusade captured Jerusalem in 1099 and before the launch of the Second Crusade at its very threshold in 1146, he saw it as justifying and celebrating the crusades metaphorically, in language reflected in contemporary sources. William of Malmesbury reported Urban's command in language that echoes Christ's in the Mission of the Apostles, and Raymond of Aguilers, who fought in the First Crusade, reminded his readers that Jerusalem was captured on the fifteenth of July, "the day on which the apostles had dispersed throughout the world to fulfill their mission."[4] The crusaders were continuing the work of the apostles, following their mission to conquer the world for the Christian faith into faraway lands, to the exotic peoples represented in the carefully articulated archivolts of Vézelay's tympanum.

Scholars have recognized a significant number of other purposeful architectural allusions to the crusades in Romanesque architecture. The crusades had become more than merely a contemporary political event by 1099: they were now also integrated into the exegetical framework of salvation history. Linda Seidel's work, in particular, has recognized the presence of the crusades in every level of production of the churches of Aquitaine: craft, imagery, meaning, and the social and economic position of their patrons.[5] Ann Derbes has found specific reference to Adhemar of Le Puy and the First Crusade in frescos at the cathedral of Le Puy;

FIGURE 4.1. The Benedictine Abbey Church of Sainte-Marie-Madeleine de Vézelay, tympanum. Dedicated 1104. Photograph by Jerrilynn Dodds.

direct reference to the crusades has been uncovered at St. Gilles-du-Gard, Auxerre, in Templar churches throughout Europe, and at St. Denis.[6] The impact of the Holy Land in architecture has been demonstrated at Le Wast near Boulogne and can be traced in the churches of the Auvergne.[7] And Seidel has found in the construction of St. Lazare of Autun, Vézelay's ecclesiastical rival, the "physical experience" of a "miniature Holy Land" creating a metaphor between Autun's pilgrimage and the crusades.[8]

Subsequent studies have explored the intense and complex local meanings in Vézelay's tympanum, and some have argued for a Pentecostal iconography rather than a "Mission." More recently, the tympanum is seen as a conflation of a "Pentecost" and a "Mission to the Apostles," a combination present in the Cluniac lectionary and in lessons from Bede.[9] My goal in this chapter is not to take on the weighty subject of the tympanum of Vézelay but to offer an architectural argument that might serve to buttress Katzenellenbogen's thesis while pleading for an approach that seeks a palimpsest of meanings layering biblical, local, and global preoccupations that, like the crusades, infused the life of the monastery and monastic thought of the age.[10]

If the First Crusade was preached at Clermont, the Second was preached at Vézelay, not by a pope or bishop, but by Bernard of Clairvaux, arguably the most powerful monk in Christendom. In 1190, Richard Lion-Heart and Philip Augustus would begin the Third Crusade from Vézelay as well, choosing this site to combine their crusading forces for the march to Marseilles. The Third Crusade was a kings' crusade, and yet here too Vézelay was chosen as a site for the historic unification of often-hostile forces. It is possible then, that among its many meanings, the immediacy of this vision of Christ linking the crusaders' mission with that of the apostles could also manifest to a broad audience less concerned with monastic authority than those of the previous two crusades. It was perhaps the multivalent communication of its sculptural vision that made Vézelay a dramatic stage set for the launching of crusades.

Alternating Voussoirs

The parts of the Vézelay tympanum that distinguish its an iconography associated with Mission to the Apostles from that of a Pentecost alone lie primarily in the figures of exotic peoples of the world, whom (together with the sick and possessed) the apostles were tasked to baptize and cure through miracles.[11] At Vézelay these exotic peoples present some of the most inventive and intriguing images of the tympanum: the expressive imagined portraits of dog-headed Cynocephali, pig-nosed people, elephant-eared Pantoii, and the naked Maritimi, with their bows and arrows. Among these mythic peoples are also Jews and Arabs. Some join the procession on the lintel, but most occupy distinct trapezoidal compartments shaped like voussoirs, which create an arch over the dynamic image of Christ and the Apostles, lacking only a keystone, where Christ's head intrudes into its space. Their architectonic shape is more visible than the actual voussoirs of the tympanum arch, and the arresting images they convey — of exoticism, strangeness and deformity, possession and infirmity — can be seen both to define the Apostles' mission and to catapult it into the immediacy of the contemporary world.

These architectonic compartments that so pointedly contain the iconographic link between apostles, monks, and crusaders are echoed by the articulation of the corresponding voussoirs of the transverse arches of Vézelay's nave, so memorable for alternation between dark and light voussoirs (fig. 4.2).[12] This distinctive unusual disposition in the nave of a Romanesque church makes Vézelay immediately recognizable among its contemporaries, and I would suggest that the novel creation of voussoir-shaped compartments in the tympanum connect their sculptural expression of exotic and apostolic meaning to the bold polychrome voussoirs of the nave. Yet to understand why this structural morpheme might have been understood to carry through that meaning, we need to trace its history as well.

Banded arches of alternating dark and light voussoirs have been the subject of scholarly speculation for nearly a century. Henry-Russell Hitchcock, the architectural historian who combined sweeping breadth of subject with patrician authority, made banded arches the subject of a virtuoso article in 1911.[13] His ambitions to establish their origins in "hither Asia" were not fulfilled, but his meticulous dissecting of the history of the forms in building practice and ornamentation is still essential to understanding the problem posed by this practice. Hitchcock recognized that banded arches in exposed brickwork — those that alternated brick and stone — were distinct in practice and tradition from the alternating voussoirs created with marble revetment.

FIGURE 4.2. Vézelay, nave. The alternating voussoirs of the last three transverse arches (those furthest to the east) are reconstructions of Viollet-le-Duc. Photograph by Jerrilynn Dodds.

Banding with tiles in the brick tradition was a Roman technique derived from a need to stabilize and reinforce concrete, a technique virtually invisible for its early history because it was hidden in the interior of walls that were faced with brick, *opus reticulatum,* marble, or finished plaster. Banded arches like those at the remains of a Roman amphitheater of the second century in Bordeaux alternate dark tiles and lighter bricks in arches, but soon the availability of stone in Gaul saw the banding created with alternating brick and stone voussoirs. In vestiges of the city walls of Bordeaux, this work was no longer faced, so the alternation of materials became both constructive and ornamental.[14] The alternation of stone and brick became a common masonry technique under the late Roman Empire, one widely used in the kind of civic constructions that marked the territory of its northern colonies. At the baths of Trier, stone and brick straddle their twin functions of strengthening construction and enlivening the wall through the introduction of color and texture. Among the visual tropes born of this technique is the alternation of brick and stone in the extrados of its arched windows.

In northern Europe in the tenth and eleventh centuries, frame and fill construction sometimes retained the memory of these Gallo-Roman traditions. The Priory Church of St. Philibert de Grandlieu alternates compact stone courses with thin brick ones, and bristles with alternating dark and light voussoirs in its arcades. Banded arches are also present in the masonry that survives from Coutances's early eleventh-century church.[15] Ottonian architecture finds polychrome masonry and painted banded arches in a lively tradition that might relate to Byzantine sources or that might echo the marble voussoirs of Charlemagne's palatine chapel, restored in the beginning of the last century. These buildings compose a fascinating and essential subject for further study, a jungle of nineteenth- and twentieth-century restorations that still wait to be untangled.[16]

The second tradition for alternating the colors of arch stones grew from facing the walls of buildings with marble revetment. The earliest recorded examples of alternating marble voussoirs were also the product of Late Antique building: in the side aisles of the Hagia Sophia marble plaques of different colors form the impost and voussoirs of passage arches, and at St. Demetrios in Salonika before its fire in 1917, the entire nave arcade and parts of the gallery arcades were paneled with red and green marble voussoirs, which tied its interior together like a sumptuous checkered ribbon.[17] The use of the components of the arch itself as a structure for the design of marble revetment is characteristic of a Late Antique style that also employs trompe l'oeil representations of cornices, moldings, and curtained niches. It is part of the intimate play between architecture and ornament that draws the spectator into a pleasurable visual dual with the building itself.

The early Islamic use of alternating voussoirs was part and parcel of the Late Antique tradition. It slips into a general use of *opus sectile* decoration as a direct product of the need to create official buildings that spoke an authoritative common language of visual opulence in new, plural cities. They appear at Damascus in vestibules, a placement analogous to their location at the Hagia Sophia, but also in the earlier Dome of the Rock, where they weave the octagon arcade into a dramatic and memorable whole.

One monument, however, breaks the neatly bifurcated history of brick or marble banded arches and complicates our attempts to understand their appearance in Romanesque architecture. The first building campaign of the Great Mosque of Cordoba prominently featured the multiplication of banded arches composed of brick and stone in ten arcades of superposed arches in the prayer hall. These alternating voussoirs are confounding if one adheres to construction tradition to understand their pedigree and thus their meaning. They are, in terms of materials, traditionally linked to Merida's Roman aqueduct, which — though it does not possess banded arches — uses straight courses of stone and brick and superposed arches that suggest those of the Great Mosque.[18] But as we consider the significance of this sprawling oratory at the heart of Cordoba — the first monumental mosque constructed in the capital of a new kingdom, and what's more, a kingdom established by a royal exile of the almost entirely exterminated Umayyad family — the idea that its primary ornamental marker should be meaningful, rather than the result of a fortuitous visual whim, makes sense.

There is in fact an anomaly concerning the way the brick and stone banded arches of eighth century Cordoba function within the building that separates them from most banded arches within brick traditions. Those on the exterior portals of later additions to the mosque are ornamental and dislocated from the building's actual construction, which uses ashlar.[19] That is, they transform a wall of which they are not an integral constructional part, in the same way that marble revetment functions. Finally, unlike the vibrant and unpredictable use of banding in northern French masonry traditions, the alternating brick and stone voussoirs of Cordoba are substantial and even: they suggest in their scale and proportions the *opus sectile* voussoirs of the Dome of the Rock and Damascus more than the constructive banded arches of Roman and Byzantine tradition.

Damascus was a monument well known to Cordoba's new emir, Abd al Rahman I, a grandson of the Caliph Hisham born and educated in Syria. He narrowly escaped death at the hands of the Abbasids, who had overthrown and slaughtered his family. Fleeing across the face of the Mediterranean he would establish a kingdom at the edge of the Islamic world, in a place the Abbasids, intent on empowering the East of the Caliphate, chose not to defend. The Great Mosque of Damascus must have held enormous meaning for this exiled prince: it was the official mosque of the lost capital of the Umayyads, the monument that most profoundly marked their caliphate, now lost. Damascus could thus serve as a visual marker of Abd al Rahman's legitimacy as prince and of his particular right to continue the Umayyad line on this far-off western frontier.[20]

Banded arches were not a particularly significant motif in the decoration at Damascus; rather, they were one of many motifs that grew from the sumptuous decorative program of the mosque, which included revetment and mosaics. But for Abd al Rahman, who had access neither to the Byzantine mosaicists nor to the marble quarries of his forbearers, this was one motif that could be simulated with readily accessible materials. Moreover, it could be used to create a dramatic and opulent effect, like that of the marble revetment of select Umayyad public buildings. The alternating voussoirs of the Great Mosque of Cordoba were meant to become a beacon of Umayyad legitimacy on the Iberian Peninsula, in this first monumental mosque of the Umayyad capital. For more than three centuries, Abd al Rahman's descendents would expand and embellish the mosque, and over time the construction techniques would change. But the decoration of prayer hall arcades with alternating voussoirs would not change, presumably because their meanings as remote evocations of Damascus and Umayyad authority survived with each generation. In the final, eleventh-century additions to the mosque by Almanzour, the arches were constructed entirely of stone: the effect of revetment was achieved by painting alternating white and red voussoirs in a pattern that, like revetment, was not tied to the voussoirs below. It was the effect of alternation and polychromy that encased the message of Umayyad authority, a sense of continuity carefully preserved by each of Cordoba's rulers until their fall in the early eleventh century.

That the desire to evoke Umayyad Damascus survived the centuries in Cordoba is suggested by the opulent additions to the mosque of the last

FIGURE 4.3. Clermont-Ferrand, Notre Dame du Port, early twelfth century, east end. Photograph by Romary/Gnu.

half of the tenth century. A more wealthy and powerful al Hakam II, whose father, Abd al Rahman III, had declared the Spanish Umayyads to be caliphs, would add a sumptuous *mihrab* to the mosque, inviting artists from Constantinople to decorate it with mosaics and teach his eunuchs this exotic art. Ibn Idhari would later recount that al Hakam had "written to the king of the Rum (Byzantines) . . . and ordered him to send a capable worker, in imitation of that which al Walid ibn Abd al-Malik did at the time of the construction of the mosque of Damascus."[21] Al Hakam's act of patronage following his father's reclaiming the Umayyads' authority as caliph might be seen as completing the meaning of his ancestor Abd al Rahman I's mosque. It offers us an alternative for understanding the power of this motif in the overall design of this crucial official building; and these mosaics also simulate the effect of alternating voussoirs.

Like those in Cordoba, the alternating voussoirs of Vézelay straddle the two traditions of polychrome arches: constructional and revetment. Their effect is purposeful, and though they are constructional, the impression

FIGURE 4.4. Le Puy, Notre Dame, façade with polychromy of white sandstone and black volcanic breccia. First half of the twelfth century with later restorations. Photograph by Patrick Giraud.

created by this alternation of masonry voussoirs more resembles that of marble revetment. Vézelay's nave is distinctive when we see it against the backdrop of Burgundian Romanesque, but it is not unique: it also resembles Ottonian examples, which favored alternating voussoirs as a connection with Late Antique building, and probably with Aachen Vézelay's nave is not simply the natural outgrowth of its construction tradition. Contrasting masonry is used throughout Vézelay, but without regular patterning. Only in the voussoirs of the nave arches does it snap to attention, alternating regularly, and it does so in the original transverse arches (as well as in those more uniform painted voussoirs reconstructed by Viollet le Duc).[22] There is a purposefulness to the original use of the motif, which makes it worth exploring against the backdrop of the meaning that could be imputed to alternating voussoirs in the twelfth century. To do this, we need to consider Vézelay's connection to its visual fellows in twelfth-century Romanesque architecture: Clermont and Le Puy, the foundations to which William of Tyre would relate it in his memory of the First Crusade (figs. 4.3 and 4.4).

Memory, Bricks, and Stones

The Great Mosque of Cordoba, unlike most other buildings to use banded arches, would be wholly identified with this ornamental motif in a number of Christian communities in Spain. The mosque itself was constructed in an early medieval tradition of morphemes derived from Late Antique architecture that was a collective inheritance of the Mediterranean world. It used columns, Corinthian capitals (both *spolia* and new made), and horseshoe arches, like most Visigothic churches. Alternating voussoirs became a sign for the mosque, the form that distinguished it from buildings that shared so many of its architectural traditions, so that in the tenth-century Morgan Beatus, nothing more is required to vilify the impious Balthazar in a miniature illustrating the book of Daniel.[23] The form appears as well in tenth-century churches like Santiago de Penalba, in which a desire to evoke Cordoba reflects the ambivalence of Christians toward the peninsula's most glorious capital.[24]

We do not see alternating voussoirs again on the Iberian Peninsula until the twelfth century. Curiously, they appear at the monastery of San Pedro de Cardeña in Old Castile, as Cardeña becomes a Cluniac foundation. San Pedro had been given to the monastery of Cluny by King Alfonso VII on the occasion of the visit of Peter the Venerable to the Iberian Peninsula in 1142–43. Among the many motives for his trip, Peter the Venerable hoped to renew the once lucrative support the Castilians had afforded the abbey in the time of Alfonso's grandfather (Alfonso VI, 1040–r.1109). Alfonso, in turn, needed Peter's help in convincing the pope to codify his imperial pretensions through the appointment of a contested archbishop at Santiago de Compostela. But Peter also tells us in the *Liber contra sectam sine haeresim Saracenorum* that in Spain he hoped to contract for a translation of the Qu'ran with which he might refute Islam, a goal fulfilled by Robert of Ketton. Jose Luis Senra has chronicled the difficult and contested Cluniac takeover of Cardeña from its indigenous monks and the artistic transformation of the monastery: sculptors from Auxerre and Cluny decorated the capitals of a new cloister, which was built with robust columns and bound by a ribbon of banded arches. He has, moreover, chronicled the elaboration of legends of resistance and martyrdom of Cardeña's monks and their history with Islam, which would feed into the subsequent mythology of the monastery.[25]

As the Umayyad caliphate fell in the early eleventh century, the succeeding Taifa kingdoms would have increasingly intimate political and economic relationships with the northern kings. They were frequent allies and feudal clients of diverse Christian kings, and they were more difficult for Iberian Christians to exteriorize; to essentialize the way that crusader ideology would polarize the Muslims of the Holy Lands. The treasure that Alfonso VII's grandfather, Alfonso VI, had given the Cluniacs came from tribute paid him by his Taifa feudal clients. But the military and economic landscape had changed by the 1140's, and Muslim forces from outside the peninsula now threatened Alfonso VII's *Imperium.*

Alfonso VII became one of the first of the Castilian kings to officially style a military struggle with Muslims on the Iberian Peninsula as a crusade (though crusades had been fought on Spanish soil by the Aragonese, Franks, and others before). In April 1147, Pope Eugenius III granted a new crusading bull, *Divina dispensione,* which encouraged crusades against the pagan Wends in northern Europe and the "Saracens" in Spain, presumably in part because of a request by Alfonso. Alfonso's donation of the monastery of Cardeña to Cluny, then, puts its likely restoration sometime between 1145 and 1150, in a maelstrom of crusading rhetoric in both Castile and France. And the conflation of the two crusades — the Spanish crusade and the crusade to the Holy Lands — allowed for the conflation of the architectural languages of Cordoba to refer to both crusades.

The banded arches of Cardeña, like the banded arches of Vézelay, might appear as a talisman of the exotic mission of the crusader and relate it to the monastic mission. Pope Eugenius, like popes before him, conflated the "Saracens" of the divergent continents. But the fashioning of Muslims as "other" was an ideological leap more easily made by Frenchmen than by Castilians, and it is thus at a Cluniac monastery in Spain that the alternating voussoirs would come to be emblematic of the crusade, or the fight against an exotic Saracen foe. In its afterlife, Cardeña would come to be intensely associated with the fight against Islam as a polarized other. It is mythologized as the burial place of El Cid (in addition to that of his wife and horse), who is reconceived as a warrior dedicated to the eradication of Islam — so different from his career in life or from the poem that brought him fame. And polychrome masonry, echoing the alternating voussoirs of the cloister, accompanies this myth through the Baroque additions to the monastery, as emblematic of the exotic world that El Cid was believed to have conquered in the name of Christianity.

One wonders if Peter the Venerable, former prior of Vézelay and the man credited by Katzenellenbogen with Vézelay's iconographic plan, was responsible for the imagery of banded arches that so mark the Cluniac monastery of Cardeña and to what extent his hand binds the distinctive motive to both buildings. It is clear, however, that his trip cannot be seen the source of the motif — that Vézelay's nave was constructed between twenty and thirty years before the cloister at Cardeña. And though those who occupied Cardeña in the 1140's might well have been aware of the association of banded arches with Cordoba, the impulse to use them at Vézelay in relation to the tympanum and its imagery must have derived from a divergent source, or at least a different connection.

On 13 May 1143, returning from his trip to Spain, Peter the Venerable said mass at Le Puy, a logical stop on the shortest route back to Cluny. Although that stop cannot have influenced Le Puy's design, which was well on its way to completion by the time of Peter's visit, we can follow the great abbot and scholar, through his travels, into the larger world of Romanesque monuments that use banded arches.[26] The Cathedral of Le Puy, swathed in a striped cloak of white sandstone and black volcanic breccia, multiplies forms that can be linked to Islamic prototypes: polylobate arches, polychrome masonry, and doors framed with pseudo-Kufic inscriptions, which might have been begun around the time of Peter's visit.[27] And the tympanum of the little chapel of St. Michel d'Aiguilhe, with its reticulated ornamental masonry and fine sharp stone carving, recalls the Islamic luxury metalwork that Seidel evokes in her ground-breaking study of the façades of Aquitaine and their crusading patrons.[28]

The third great Romanesque church to use alternating voussoirs is the Basilica of Notre Dame du Port at Clermont, where the axial apsidal window clearly alternates dark and light voussoirs, a motif echoed in the other churches of the Auvergne.[29] Notre Dame du Port was built near the site where Pope Urban II preached the First Crusade; the same site at which Bishop Adhemar of Le Puy became his legate, the first to take up the cross and be the pope's representative on crusade.

These three monuments: Le Puy, Notre Dame du Port of Clermont, and La Madeleine at Vézelay, cannot be said to relate to each other as regards construction tradition, and yet all three display a regular alternation of voussoirs in some part of their arch design that is purposeful. Emile Mâle recognized the impact of Islamic forms at Le Puy, Clermont, and in the alternating voussoirs of Vézelay, which he attributed to monastic travels to Spain and in particular to the Great Mosque of Cordoba:

Let us assume that some of these monk-architects had pushed on as far as Cordoba, and the mystery is then explained . . . they could not resist the appeal of those curvilinear forms, of that alternation of colors. They took note of the shape of a bracket, of the design of a dome. Over their solid churches of stone and lava, they spread those airy graces of the East. Hence the profound seductiveness of the cathedral of Le Puy, which I had felt so often without being able to explain. One glimpses there the nostalgia of the artist who has once seen the kingdoms of light and cannot be consoled.[30]

He saw the connections in unabashedly Orientalist terms: repressed monk-architects, with whom Mâle movingly identifies, are seduced by pure form — by sensual form — that derives from the "East." While Mâle assumes that these masons were making essential formal decisions that would shape the appearance of centrally important buildings, he did grasp that the anomaly of these forms was undisguised. The appearance of the polychromy could not be rationalized as part of positivist thought, as the unconscious playfulness of a local tradition. In fact, it would be surprising to imagine that such bold visual gestures might be abdicated completely to the aesthetic decision of master masons.

The great monuments of twelfth century Romanesque that feature banded arches — Ste. Madeleine at Vézelay, Notre Dame du Puy, and Clermont — could have been built by patrons who were aware of the Great Mosque of Cordoba, but I believe they are linked to Islamic models through their desire to evoke the memory of the First Crusade. Clermont was built in the city of Urban II's call to the First Crusade; Le Puy was the seat of Adhemar, bishop of Le Puy and famous apostolic legate appointed by Pope Urban II; and Vézelay was a powerful monastic center that used the crusade, like its rival the Cathedral of Autun, as a means of embellishing monastic authority and enhancing its own pilgrimage. Its imagery would make the memory so palpable that it was the stage set for St. Bernard to preach the Second Crusade in 1146 and for the kings of England and France to begin the Third. Significantly, each of these architectural gestures was a local attempt to evoke the memory of the crusade, in each case for different reasons particular to its patrons, just as in each case the use of banded arches to recall the Holy Land was accomplished in a divergent technique. Thus, a Late Antique decorative technique used by the first Muslims to rule Jerusalem became the means by which crusaders marked the memory of their crusade. But it is not clear, as Mâle supposed, that the ultimate model for this motif was Cordoba.

Jerusalem

There we must go
Sell our fiefs
Gain the Temple of God,
Destroy the Muslims
    CRUSADER HYMN[31]

After unspeakable perils and adventures, appalling deprivation and suffering, Jerusalem fell to the crusaders on 15 July 1099. The crusaders had fulfilled the mission held out to them by Urban II, to embark "upon this holy pilgrimage"; to "set out on the road to the Holy Sepulcher, deliver that land from a wicked race and take it yourselves."[32] When the Holy Sepulchre was won, its value was located in its irrefutable centrality as the site of Christian revelation. But it was in ruinous repair, and Baldric of Dol would have us understand that this was known before the taking of the city. He recounts Urban as commenting upon its state of repair in his oration at Clermont: "Of the Lord's Sepulcher we have refrained from speaking, since some of you with your own eyes have seen to what abominations it has been given over."[33] It had been understood for centuries as a dome, a rotunda, from afar, and yet the rotunda that the crusaders found in 1099 was not a breathtaking sight.[34] The Constantinian rotunda had been demolished by the Fatimids in 1009 and rebuilt under constrained conditions, thanks to diplomatic intervention of the Byzantines by 1048. The crusaders would set about to construct a new Romanesque church, incorporating the older rotunda, in 1114.

Another domed structure on the other side of the city was renovated by the crusaders as well, though not rebuilt, perhaps because, in contrast to the Holy Sepulchre, it was gloriously ornamented and better cared for. "But why do we pass over the Temple of Solomon, nay of the Lord, in which the barbarous nations placed their idols contrary to Law, human and divine?" Urban is said to have asked in his oration of 1095.[35] Fulcher of Chartres, in his lurid account of the first days of the taking of Jerusalem,

FIGURE 4.5. Jerusalem, Dome of the Rock, interior. Seventh century. Photograph by Eric Matson/Library of Congress.

describes the crusaders ("the clerics and the laity") "going to the Sepulcher of the Lord and to his glorious Temple."[36] The "glorious Temple" was the Dome of the Rock, a building the crusaders believed, or chose to believe, commemorated a biblical sight as well. And within this space, the opulent and monumental rotunda of the Dome of the Rock was ringed by a circular arcade of alternating marble voussoirs (figs. 4–5).

The same concern with Late Antique marble ornament that connected Damascus with Cordoba in the eighth century was present in the most sumptuous of Islamic monuments in Jerusalem. The Dome of the Rock, the earliest of the grand Islamic monuments, was a building that used its Late Antique ornamental vocabulary as part of a statement meant to be read by the indigenous inhabitants of Jerusalem at the time of its construction in the seventh century. Perhaps for that reason, it moved quickly to the center of the Romanesque imagination in the twelfth century. Its opulent revetment, including quartered marble voussoirs of white and grey, became a distinctive marker of the building's interior. The alternating voussoirs, which embrace the rock at the building's heart like a garland, are a particularly bold rhetorical statement and a significant means by which the building is remembered. More elaborate, sumptuous, and exotic than the Church of the Holy Sepulchre, the Dome of the Rock was also an easier monument to allude to visually because of its polychrome masonry.

The Dome of the Rock and the al-Aqsa Mosque were not regarded as Christian holy sites during Jerusalem's Umayyad, Abbasid, and Fatimid periods, likely because their identification with Islamic functions was very much alive for the Byzantines who shepherded the Christian holy sites in Jerusalem under those rules.[37] Kuhnel sees a progression of identities assigned to the Dome of the Rock during the Middle Ages, and he traces their passage through time. Its identity for European Christians was transformed by the ninth century from that of an Islamic building understood to have been built on the site of the Temple of Solomon in the early Middle Ages to the actual Temple of Solomon: metaphorical meanings long associated with the buildings on the temple mount were thus concretized. In 870, a Frankish monk, Bernhard, identified the Dome of the Rock as the actual Temple of Solomon, saying that it was being used in his time as a "Saracen Synagogue."[38]

A number of these meanings from the ninth century have clear reverberations in Carolingian and Ottonian buildings, and though Alcuin's letter to Charlemagne calling Aachen "the Temple of the most Solomon" might certainly be a literary topos, its restored marble alternating voussoirs invite a closer inspection of the relationship.[39] By the crusader period, the Dome of the Rock became the Templum Domini and was converted into the "Church of the *Templum Domini*" immediately after the taking of Jerusalem.[40] Increasingly in the time of the First Crusade, the al-Aqsa Mosque was understood to be the Temple of Solomon or the Palace of Solomon, and it would serve as the center of government until 1119, when the Templars would come to occupy a section of it.[41] The Dome of the Rock became the Temple of the Lord. The crusaders alternatively saw it as the ancient temple of Solomon or as an ancient building constructed by a Christian emperor on the site of the temple where the Presentation at the Temple, the circumcision of Christ, and the expulsion of the money-lenders had taken place.[42] The renovated Templum Domini was consecrated in 1141, eight years before the Holy Sepulchre.

Within Jerusalem, the prominence of the Templum Domini sparked a rivalry between the buildings, and Nurith Kenaan-Kedar has traced the liturgy that reconciled and linked the Holy Sepulchre and the Templum Domini as the two sacred centers of the most sacred city. Processions for Palm Sunday, the Presentation at the Temple, the Purification of the Virgin, the consecration of the Church of the Holy Sepulchre, and the procession celebrating the crusader conquest of the city linked the Holy Sepulchre and the Dome of the Rock, as did the very coronation ceremony.[43] The processions constituted a ritual repossession of the monuments and the city, and they recalled as well the progress of the crusaders on that awful day in 1099. Finally the crusaders, Kenaan-Kedar tells us, "accustomed to regard Solomon's Temple as an ideal spiritual and literary prototype of a church, were confronted in Jerusalem with an earthly Templum Domini, built on the site of Solomon's temple, as well as with Solomon's palace (sometimes also called his temple)." She suggests that the two domes on the Temple Mount — the large dome of the Dome of the Rock and the smaller dome of the al-Aqsa Mosque — might thus have served as a model for the two domes of the restored Holy Sepulchre.[44]

The site of the Temple Mount, including both the Dome of the Rock and the al-Aqsa Mosque, was also the site of the most dramatic moments of the day of the crusaders' entry into Jerusalem. Fulcher of Chartres reminds us of the cruel and triumphant day, in an account that culminates in the Temple of Solomon: "On the top of Solomon's Temple many (Muslims) were shot to death with arrows and cast down headlong from the roof. Within this Temple about ten thousand were beheaded. If you had been there, your feet would have been stained up to the ankles with the blood of the slain. What more shall I tell? Not one of them was allowed to live. They did not spare the women and children."[45] In his chapter entitled "The Spoils Which the Christians Took," Fulcher recounts that Tancred "rushed to the Temple of the Lord, and seized much of the gold and silver and precious stones. But he returned it at the end."[46] The buildings on the Temple Mount contained, then, a memory of the triumph and the lucrative and glorious spoils of war as well. These meanings accompanied those of the "Templus eius gloriosum" that was celebrated.

In Western Europe, the Templum Domini and the Temple of Solomon were understood and revered as the physical buildings that evoked these real memories, as well as metaphorical ones. The Church of Le Wast in Boulonnias, with its zigzag voussoirs, must reflect an Abbasid portal of the al-Aqsa Mosque, which had become the Temple or Place of Solomon.[47] Ann Derbes has shown that frescoes from Le Puy make specific reference to Adhemar of Le Puy, the lamented bishop and papal legate who won fame and died on the First Crusade. Among the unusual images represented in the frescos is one of the constructions of the Temple of Solomon, the culmination of the crusaders' great victory and a metaphor for the triumph of the church.[48] At St. Gilles-du-Gard in Provence, meticulous sculpted models of the Dome of the Rock appear in two reliefs, showing its presence as a centrally planned dome building at the entry to Jerusalem, an image that could be read in biblical or contemporary terms.[49] The capacity of the Templum Domini as a building to evoke memory of the crusades was as potent as the Holy Sepulchre itself.

The Temple Mount was the site where crusaders covered in gore waded in the blood of the Muslims they had killed on the day they entered Jerusalem. The location of cathartic acts, the fervent spiritual culmination of the great miracle of the taking of Jerusalem, and the thrill of spoils of war could all be encased in a single visual memory, could all be sanctified and licensed. What the Templum Domini supplied for those who saw Jerusalem between 1099 and 1140 — for the first forty years of Latin presence there — was an opulent and exotic architectural vision to meet the fervent spiritual expectations and imaginations of those who had fought and yearned and imagined the spiritual power of Jerusalem.

Banded arches ought perhaps to be counted among the many visual expressions of the crusades that found their way back to Western Europe. The alternating voussoirs of the Dome of the Rock might well have become the visual shorthand for all of these meanings. As a motif it was eminently portable: it was, after all the same recognizable, easily replicable effect that had traveled from Damascus to Cordoba in the eighth century, crossing the frontier of construction and material to be brandished by Abd al Rahman I to evoke the legitimacy of Damascus and Jerusalem in his Iberian mosque. It also provided a monumental architectural gesture: bold, anomalous, and redolent with associations of Islam as an "other," banded arches could brand the crusader experience onto ecclesiastical and monastic experience in Western Europe.

Notes

For Alain le Craver

1. For the launching of the Second Crusade, see now Jonathan Phillips, *The Second Crusade: Expanding the Frontiers of Christendom* (New Haven: Yale University Press, 2007), 61–79.

2. William of Tyre, *Historia rerum in partibus transmarinis gestarum,* ed. R. B. C. Huygens, in *Corpus Christianorum Continuatio Mediaevalis 63,* 2 vols. (Turnhout: Brepols, 1986), 1:130.

3. Adolf Katzenellenbogen, "The Central Tympanum at Vézelay: Its Encyclopedic Meaning and Its Relation to the First Crusade," *Art Bulletin* 26 (1944): 141–51. The first to suggest the iconography might be the Mission to the Apostles was Abel Fabre, "Iconographie de la Pentecôte," *Gazette des Beaux Arts* 11 (1923): 33.

4. Katzenellenbogen, "The Central Tympanum at Vézelay," 49.

5. Linda Seidel, *Songs of Glory: The Romanesque Facades of Aquitaine* (Chicago: University of Chicago Press, 1981).

6. Anne Derbes, "The Crusading Cycle at the Cathedral of Le Puy," *Art Bulletin* 73, no. 4 (1991): 561–76; Carra Ferguson O'Meara, *The Iconography of the Façade of St. Gilles du Gard* (New York: Garland, 1977); Don Denny, "A Romanesque Fresco in Auxerre Cathedral," *Gesta* 25, no. 2 (1986): 197–202; and Elizabeth Brown and Michael Cothren, "The Twelfth-Century Crusading Window of the Abbey of St. Denis," *Journal of the Warburg and Courtauld Institutes* 159 (1986): 1–40.

7. Terry Allen, *A Classical Revival in Islamic Architecture* (Wiesbaden: L. Reichert, 1986), 74, and Camille Enlart, "L'église du Wast en Boulonnais et son portail arabe," *Gazette des Beaux Arts* 69 (1927): 1–11.

8. Linda Seidel, *Legends in Limestone, Lazarus, Giselbertus, and the Cathedral of Autun* (Chicago: University of Chicago Press, 1999).

9. Scholars arguing primarily for the Pentecost: Emile Mâle, *Religious Art in France, the Twelfth Century: A Study of the Origins of Medieval Iconography* (Princeton: Princeton University Press, 1978), 327–28; Peter Diemer, "Das Pfingstportal von Vézelay — Wege, Umwege un Abwege (einer Diskussion)," *Jahrbuch des Zentralinstitut fur Kunstgeschichte* 1 (1985): 77–89; Michael Taylor, "The Pentecost at Vézelay," *Gesta* 19 (1980): 9–15; see 9; and Peter Low, "'You who were once far off:' Enlivening Scripture in the Main Portal of Vézelay," *Art Bulletin* 85 (2003): 471–89. Some scholars see a conflation of Pentecostal and Mission symbolism, including Jean Adhémar, *La Madeleine de Vézelay* (Melun: Librairie d'Argences, 1948), 117; Kristin Sazama, "The Assertion of Monastic Spiri-

tual and Temporal Authority in the Romanesque Sculpture of Sainte-Madeleine at Vézelay" (Ph.D. diss., Northwestern University, June 1995), 58–68; and Emma Simi Varanelli, " 'Diversi, non adversi': L'interpretazione del timpano della Pentecoste di Vézelay, un unicum nel panorama dei modelli medievali della cominicazione visiva," *Arte Medievale*, n.s. 1, no. 2 (2002): 55–75.

10. Among those who focus the meaning of Vézelay's tympanum on local monastic identity and authority are the excellent study of Sazama, "The Assertion of Monastic Spiritual and Temporal Authority," and Low, "You who were once far off." Local concerns surrounding the aggressive economic policies of the monastery and its authority gave way to violent civic struggles that had famously culminated in the murder of Abbot Artaud in 1106. These are reflected in the tithers on the lintel, who act out an ideal of "political and economic subordination" to the monastery, in Barbara Abou-El-Haj's incisive words; see Abou-El-Haj, *The Medieval Cult of the Saints: Formations and Transformations* (Cambridge: Cambridge University Press, 1994), 24, and Abou-El-Haj, "The Audience for the Medieval Cult of the Saints," *Gesta* 30 (1991): 3–15. Judy Feldman Scott first identified the tithers and revived interest in Katzenellenbogen. The tithers join a wider procession of pilgrims and knights on Vézelay's lintel who might be those who come to Vézelay on pilgrimage or those who are part of the great militant pilgrimage to the Holy Land; see Scott's "The Narthex Portal at Vézelay: Art and Monastic Self-Image" (Ph.D. diss., University of Texas at Austin, 1986), and Katzenellenbogen, "The Central Tympanum at Vézelay," 150–51. The conflation of concerns surrounding local monastic identity and authority with the cosmic miracle of the taking of Jerusalem might reflect a reification of the discourse that grew out of the First Crusade, which sought, in Jonathan Riley-Smith's words, to "infuse secular life with monastic values" that "treat crusaders as temporary religious, professed into what looked to them like a contemporary monastery on the move" (*The First Crusade and the Idea of Crusading* [Philadelphia: University of Pennsylvania Press, 1986], 2.) In a world in which the monks of Vézelay struggled for spiritual and temporal powers, the tympanum can also be seen to link their apostolic identity both with local temporal and spiritual authority and with the most dramatic and cosmic miracle of the age. It visually generated a kind of *Historia,* which mustered apostolic history and the dramatic monastic metaphor at work in the crusades in their own struggles with the counts of Nevers, the bishop of Autun, and the commune of Vézelay.

11. See Sazama, "The Assertion of Monastic Spiritual and Temporal Authority," 60, for an excellent review of this issue.

12. The first three transverse arches of the nave are original, alternating white stone with darker stone quarried in Tharoiseau. The other six arches of the nave were originally constructed with this same effect, though those that survive are

reconstructions of Viollet-le-Duc. Kevin Murphy observes that iron oxide produced a darker color in the original stone, and that in the twelfth century arches the alternating voussoirs are not of uniform size. However, he demonstrates that in the reconstruction of Viollet-le-Duc, regularized voussoirs are painted to create a more regular effect of polychromy in the fourth through ninth arches, a technique immediately lamented by Merimée; see Murphy's *Memory and Modernity: Viollet-le-Duc at Vézelay* (University Park: Pennsylvania State University Press, 2000), 101–2.

13. Henry-Russell Hitchcock, "Banded Arches before the Year 1000," *Art Studies* 6 (1928): 175–91.

14. Ibid., 177–79.

15. Joel Herschman, "The Eleventh-Century Nave of the Cathedral of Coutances: A New Reconstruction," *Gesta* 22 (1983): 121–34.

16. Hans Belting, "Das Aachener Münster im 19. Jahrhundert: Zur ersten Krise des Denkmal-Konzepts," *Wallraf-Richartz-Jahrbuch* 45 (1984): 257–89; Jenny H. Shaffer, "Recreating the Past: Aachen and the Problem of the Architectural 'Copy'" (Ph.D. diss., Columbia University, 1992), esp. chs. 1 and 5; Matthias Untermann, " 'opere mirabili constructa' Die Aachener 'Residenz' Karls des Grossen," in *Kunst und Kultur der Karolingerzeit: Karl der Grosse und Papst Leo III in Paderborn,* ed. Christoph Stiegemann and Matthias Wemhoff (Mainz: P. von Zabern, 1999), 152–64; Michael Brandt and Arne Eggebrecht, eds., *Bernward von Hildesheim und das Zeitalter der Ottonen,* 2 vols. (Hildesheim: Bernward Verlag, 1993); and Werner Jacobsen, Uwe Lobbedey, and Dethard von Winterfeld, "Ottonische Baukunst," in *Otto der Grosse: Magdeburg und Europa,* ed. Matthias Puhle (Mainz: P. von Zabern, 2001), 1:251–82. At Charlemagne's Palace Chapel at Aachen, a much restored interior asserts a strong place for banded arches in its marble revetment. The interior of the centrally planned chapel, long believed to be the copy of a Constantinian or Justinianic building, is structured by eight sets of superposed arches, all divided by their revetment into black and white alternating voussoirs. In this way, the impact of the interior elevation of Aachen is comparable to that of the interior of the Dome of the Rock. Because the ornament grows from the architecture itself, it has a way of structuring our impression of each building's interior, of linking them despite their numerous typological divergences. See Gustav Kuhnel, "Aachen, Byzanz und die Fruhislamische Architektur Im Heiligen Land," in *Studien zur Byzantinischen Kunstgeschichte: Festschrift fur Jorst Hallensleben Zum 65. Geburtsstag,* ed. Birgitt Borkopp, Barbara Maria Schellewald, and Lioba Theis (Amsterdam: Adolf M. Hakkert, 1995), 39–57. Kuhnel asks if Charlemagne's chapel does not contain a "memory," an allusion to the Temple of Solomon, through the Dome of the Rock, a connection sought to enforce the literary links generated by the court between Charlemagne and Old

Testament kings. Though he posits that there are many models for Aachen, and he cites contemporary pilgrims who are not only aware of the Old Testament associations with the sites but also seem to believe that the stonework in particular marks the interior ("the Temple of Solomon with its distinctive stonework," 56). The complex layering of the iconography of Aachen allowed for the conflation of meanings, incorporating Charlemagne's Roman imperial ambitions and his metaphoric investment in Constantine, David, and Solomon. Any number of them could find an anchor in the Dome of the Rock as a model, and, if the restoration reflects the original disposition of the building, its alternating voussoirs came along with the broad building typologies, classical moldings, and capital types.

17. Hitchcock, "Banded Arches before the Year 1000," 180, imagined this decoration to be part of the fourth-century basilica, but it is largely dated to the second half of the fifth century today. See Richard Krautheimer and Slobodan Curcic, *Early Christian and Byzantine Architecture* (New Haven: Yale University Press, 1992), 128.

18. Manuel Gomez-Moreno, *Ars Hispaniae,* vol. 3, *El arte arabe espanol hasta los Almohades; Arte Mozarabe* (Madrid: Editorial Plus Ultra, 1951), 36.

19. Portals added in the ninth and tenth centuries use alternating voussoirs in blind arches and arcuated lintels. The building is ashlar-faced, with headers and stretchers in the Roman manner. The exterior's use of alternating voussoirs is uniquely ornamental.

20. Jerrilynn Dodds, *Architecture and Ideology in Early Medieval Spain* (University Park: Pennsylvania State University Press, 1990), 164n50, and Dodds, ed., *Al Andalus: The Art of Islamic Spain* (New York: Metropolitan Museum of Art, 1992), 15.

21. Muhammad Ibn Idhari al-Marrakushi, *Histoire de l'Afrique et de l'Espagne,* 2 vols. (Leiden: E. J. Brill, 1848–51), 2:392. See also Henri Stern, *Les mosaiques de la Grande Mosquée de Cordoue* (Berlin: De Gruyter, 1976), 6–7.

22. Murphy, *Memory and Modernity,* 101–2.

23. The association of the palace of Balthazar with the Umayyads through the use of alternating voussoirs was first established by Gonzalo Menendez Pidal, *Sobre miniatura espanola en la Alta Edad Media: Corrientes culturales que revela* (Madrid: Real Academia de la Historia, 1958), 30.

24. Dodds, *Architecture and Ideology,* 83–94, and Dodds, Maria Rosa Menocal, and Abigail Krasner, *Arts of Intimacy: Christians, Jews, and Muslims in the Making of Castilian Culture* (New Haven: Yale University Press, 2008), ch. 3.

25. José Luis Senra, "En torno a la restauracion de la memoria de la 'reconquista': Un escenario martirial en el contexto de la expulsion morisca," *Quintana* 3 (2004): 89–106.

26. The choir of Le Puy is thought to have begun sometime around 1095. The nave was probably completed in two campaigns, one in the early twelfth century, and a second, including the façade, by the mid twelfth century; see Walter Cahn, *The Romanesque Wooden Doors of Auvergne*, College Art Association Monographs, vol. 30 (New York: New York University Press, 1974).

27. Ibid., 11–34 and 59–83.

28. Seidel, *Songs of Glory*, 78–79.

29. Notably St. Austremoine at Issoire, Culhat, and St. Dier. Churches using volcanic stone also relate to Le Puy: St. Paulien and Le Monastier, for example. Smaller churches today can alternate painted dark and light voussoirs on their interior; much of the painting is later, but it needs to be examined with an eye toward an early example or initial impulse in the twelfth century. See in particular Saint-Martin at Cournon and Glaine-Montaigut.

30. Emile Mâle, *Art and Artists of the Middle Ages*, trans. Sylvia Stallings Lowe (Redding Ridge, CT: Black Swan Books, 1986), 37.

31. Guido Maria Dreves and Clemens Blume, *Analecta hymnica Medii Aevi*, 45b (Leipzig: O. R. Riesland, 1904), 78; quoted in Riley-Smith, *The First Crusade and the Idea of Crusading*, 45.

32. Robert the Monk, "Historia Hierosolymitana," *Recueil des historiens des croisades: Historiens occidentaux*, 5 vols. (Paris: Académie des Inscriptions et Belles-Lettres, 1872–1906), 3:728 (hereafter *RHC Occ.*); and Carol Sweetenham, trans. *Robert the Monk's History of the First Crusade: "Historia Iherosolimitana,"* Crusade Texts in Translation 11 (Aldershot, UK: Ashgate, 2006), 81.

33. Baldric of Bourgueil, "Historia Jerosolimitana," *RHC Occ.* 4:13; translation in Edward Peters, ed., *The First Crusade: The Chronicle of Fulcher of Chartres and Other Source Materials*, 2d ed. (Philadelphia: University of Pennsylvania Press, 1998), 7.

34. For the iconography of the Holy Sepulchre in Western Europe, the classic study remains Richard Krautheimer and Slobodan Curcic, "Introduction to an 'Iconography' of Medieval Architecture," *Journal of the Warburg and Courtauld Institutes* 5 (1942): 1–33.

35. Baldric of Bourgeuil, "Historia Jerosolimitana," *RHC Occ.* 4:13; trans. in Peters, *The First Crusade*, 7.

36. Fulcher of Chartres, *Historia Hierosolymitana*, ed. Heinrich Hagenmeyer (Heidelberg: Carl Winters Universitatsbuchhandlung, 1913), 304–5; trans. in Peters, *The First Crusade*, 79.

37. Kuhnel, "Aachen, Byzanz und die Fruhislamische Architektur," 51–55.

38. Ibid., 47.

39. Kuhnel, "Aachen, Byzanz und die Fruhislamische Architekture," 39–57.

Carol Heitz argues strongly for the relationship to Jerasulem through liturgical reference in *Recherches sur les rapports entre architecture et liturgie a l'époque carolingienne* (Paris: S.E.V.P.E.N., 1963).

40. Nurith Kenaan-Kedar, "Symbolic Meaning in Crusader Architecture; The Twelfth-Century Dome of the Holy Sepulcher Church in Jerusalem," *Cahiers archéologiques* 23 (1986): 109–17; see 113.

41. Ibid.

42. Heribert Busse, "Vom Felsendom zum Templum Domini," in *Das Heilige Land im Mittelalter. Begegnungsraum zwichen Orient und Okzident,* ed. Wolf-dietrich Fischer and Jürgen Schneider (Neustadt: Degender, 1982), 24–25, and Kuhnel, "Aachen, Byzanz und die Fruhislamische Architektur," 39–57. Kenaan-Kedar points out that some still considered that it might have been built by the Muslims, in "Symbolic Meaning in Crusader Architecture," 113.

43. Kenaan-Kedar, "Symbolic Meaning in Crusader Architecture," 114; Busse, "Vom Felsendom," 19–31; and Sylvia Schein, "The Temple between Mount Moriah and the Holy Sepulcher: The Changing Traditions of the Temple in the Later Middle Ages," *Traditio* 50 (1984): 175–95.

44. Kenaan-Kedar, "Symbolic Meaning in Crusader Architecture," 115.

45. Fulcher of Chartres, *Historia Hierosolymitana,* 301; trans. in Peters, *The First Crusade,* 77.

46. Fulcher of Chartres, *Historia Hierosolymitana,* 302–3; trans. in Peters, ed., *The First Crusade,* 78.

47. Allen, *A Classical Revival in Islamic Architecture,* 74, and Camille Enlart, "L'église du Waast en Boulonnais et son portail arabe," *Gazette des Beaux Arts* 69 (1927): 1–11.

48. Louis Reau, *L'iconographie de l'art chrétien,* 3 vols. (Paris: Presses Universitaires de France 1955–59), 2:291; cited in Derbes, "The Crusading Cycle," 574.

49. O'Meara, *The Iconography of the Façade of St. Gilles du Gard,* 97–130.

CHAPTER FIVE

Commemorating the Fall of Jerusalem

Remembering the First Crusade in Text, Liturgy, and Image

JAROSLAV FOLDA

$\mathcal{T}$HE EARLIEST ILLUSTRATED TEXTS of William of Tyre's *History of Outremer*, executed between 1244 and 1291, provide important evidence of the renewed interest in and awareness of the events surrounding the First Crusaders in the Holy Land.[1] This discussion will focus on the story of the First Crusade as presented in the first eight books — corresponding to the first eight miniatures — of various manuscripts of the *History*. The questions I propose to ask concern the broader crusading context in which continuations were given to these manuscripts and their cycles of illustrations were done. First of all, what was the situation when the first continuations to William's *History* were written, circa 1232, and the first illustrations were made, after 1244? With that in mind, why was it that the first illustrated *History of Outremer* manuscripts were produced from just after 1244 and the following years up to 1291? Then, in these early illustrated manuscripts, how was the story of the First Crusade presented in their imagery between 1244 and 1291? And finally, what happened to this imagery after 1291? To assess these issues, I begin by investigating how the fall of Jerusalem was commemorated in the twelfth and thirteenth centuries, starting with the triumph of the First Crusade.

After the conquest of Jerusalem by the First Crusade in 1099, the crusaders in the Latin Kingdom early on added a new festival day to the ecclesiastical calendar. On the ides of July, that is, 15 July, we find a commemoration in the earliest missals from the scriptorium of the Holy Sepulchre in Jerusalem (missals dating in the 1130s and 1140s), which reads as follows: "Festivitas Hierusalem quando capta fuit a Christianis."[2] Accordingly, in the 1130s, the conquest of the city was marked by a special liturgical celebration in Jerusalem. Joshua Prawer has described the progress of the solemn procession based on the *Barletta rituale:*

> Led by the patriarch very early in the morning, this [procession] passed from the Church of the Holy Sepulchre to the *Templum Domini,* the Mosque of Omar. Here a halt was made and prayers recited at the southern entrance, in that part of the Temple esplanade which faces the Mosque of al-Aqsa. From here, the procession wound its way across the esplanade to the burial place beyond the walls of those who fell in the conquest. Crossing the street of Josaphat it then proceeded to the northern part of the city walls. Here, not far from its north-eastern angle, a cross marked the spot where the knights of Godefroy [de Bouillon] first penetrated the city. At this place a sermon was pronounced by the patriarch to the assembled clergy and populace, and thanksgiving prayers commemorated the establishment of the Crusaders in the Holy Land.[3]

Thus the liturgical observance of the glorious conquest of the city in 1099 had relatively quickly taken its place with the other main festivals with major processions in Jerusalem, namely, those on Palm Sunday, at Easter, on Ascension Day, on Pentecost, and on the Assumption of the Holy Virgin. Therefore a triumphant victory in recent memory was elevated to the same status as the holiest events of the Gospels for the crusaders in the holy city of Jerusalem.

We can probably assume that the ecclesiastical commemoration of the capture of Jerusalem began immediately, possibly in 1101, following the untimely death of Godefroy de Bouillon on 18 July 1100. We do not know the exact date when the liturgical procession began to develop out of the spontaneous visitations of the Christian people of the city to the sites related to the conquest. As we have seen, they went to three places: first, the site where the crusaders first breached the walls and entered the city in July 1099; second, the place of the symbolic capture of the primary Muslim monument in the city, which the crusaders called the Templum Domini; and third, the cemetery of the fallen crusaders outside the city walls on the eastern side of the city. It is likely that just as the American Memorial Day commemoration emerged as a national day (Decoration Day) on 30 May 1868, a day to visit the cemeteries of fallen American soldiers in the Civil War, the crusader observance began with people visiting the graves of the First Crusaders. In any case, by 1131 there is ample evidence to suggest that a fully developed procession through the city existed and included all three sites. A few years later, in 1149, a new commemoration was added.

On 15 July 1149, the newly reconstructed and expanded crusader Church of the Holy Sepulchre was dedicated and a plaque was set up in the Chapel of Golgotha. The text read (in part):

> This place is holy, since Christ's blood had hallowed it before;
> Therefore no holiness we add by blessing it once more.
> The chapels that above the place and all round do lie
> Were consecrated on the dawn of 15th of July
> By Patriarch Fulcher and the rest of holy bishops they were blessed.[4]

The meaning of this commemoration was twofold. First, the dedication of the Church of the Holy Sepulchre was an event of the first importance to the crusaders and to the city of Jerusalem. Second, it was deemed appropriate to add to the commemoration of the capture of the city of Jerusalem in 1099 this august event, because the Church of the Holy Sepulchre was, after all, the focus of the crusaders coming to Jerusalem, and this church stood at the literal center of the Christian world.

The extant evidence for this additional commemoration being regarded as equal in importance and directly connected to the celebration of the capture of the city is found again in crusader liturgical manuscripts. In a Jerusalem sacramentary from the second quarter of the thirteenth century, we find the following entry for the ides of July: "Dedicatio ecclesie dominici sepulchri et liberatio ierusalem."[5] In addition, a royal psalter apparently commissioned circa 1225 for Isabel de Brienne, second wife of Frederick II, a manuscript known as the Riccardiana Psalter, spells out the pairing in more precise detail: "Dedicatio ecclesie S. Sepulchri, et festivitas ierusalem quando capta fuit a Christianis."[6] Therefore, the dedication of the Church of the Holy Sepulchre was meant to enrich the commemoration of the capture of the city in 1099 by focusing attention on the Holy Sepulchre, which was the ultimate goal of the First Crusade. So, from 1149 to 1187 this solemn liturgical observance was maintained, with the procession starting from the chapel of Golgotha in the Church of the Holy Sepulchre. But then came the cruel events of July and October 1187.

On 4 July the greatest crusader army assembled in the field during the twelfth century was defeated at the Horns of Hattin, and the holiest relic of the kingdom, the relic of the True Cross, was lost to Saladin. Three months later, on 2 October, Saladin received the surrender of Jerusalem from the crusaders, led by both Balian d'Ibelin and the patriarch. This terrible loss heaped on top of the catastrophic defeat at Hattin caused an immediate outcry for a new crusade to retake Jerusalem.

As the result of these events, new commemorations were developed for the fall of Jerusalem on 2 October 1187. On 20 October 1187 news of the battle of Hattin and the fall of Jerusalem first reached pope Urban III in Rome, and he died from the shock of the report. The new pope, Gregory VIII, wasted no time in issuing the call for a new crusade in his encyclical *Audita tremendi,* dated 3 November 1187. He refers to Jerusalem, the Holy Land, and the recent events, and says: "What a great cause for mourning this ought to be for us and the whole Christian people!"[7] Here, then, is the first commemoration of crusader Jerusalem effectively as a lament. Next, in conjunction with this letter the pope also prescribed special liturgical observances, obviously to support the new crusade he had called, but also to focus on the fall of Jerusalem as a context for the preaching of this crusade. He ordained a Lenten fast for Fridays in Advent for five years (1187–92), special prayers were ordered to be said for the liberation of the Holy Land and for the release of Christian prisoners in Muslim captivity, and a special mass was to be sung on those days.[8] At the core of this new mass, we find readings from Psalm 78, "Deus venerunt gentes."[9] This psalm, which begins, "O God, the nations have come into your inheritance; they have defiled your holy temple, they have laid Jerusalem in ruins," had long been seen as especially appropriate for portraying the miseries of Christian Jerusalem. Two of the four chroniclers who reconstructed the famous speech of Urban II at Clermont in 1095 had placed the words of this psalm in his mouth.[10]

In addition to these innovations, a new text, known as "L'Estat de la Cité de Iherusalem,"[11] appears in various Old French continuations to the translated *History* of William of Tyre, which are together known as the "Estoire d'Eracles." (The continuations vary in length and take the story of the crusaders up to the years 1231, 1248, 1261, and 1274.) In effect this text, "L'Estat de la Cité," therefore commemorates the city and the holy sites in and around Jerusalem for the reader, just as it was before the fall of

Jerusalem to Saladin and the Muslims in 1187. And it appears just as the liturgical procession to commemorate the taking of the city in Jerusalem ceases to take place, owing to the fall of Jerusalem to Saladin.

In 1198, when it became clear that the Third Crusade (1189–92) and the German Crusade (1197–98) were not able to retake Jerusalem, a new crusade was called by pope Innocent III — the ill-fated Fourth Crusade, which attacked, captured, and sacked Constantinople in 1204 but did not continue on to the Holy Land and did not attempt to recapture Jerusalem. In the aftermath of that catastrophic expedition, Innocent III persisted nonetheless with his vision of a great crusade to recover the Holy Land. In April 1213 he tried again, calling the Fifth Crusade.

It was Innocent III who added the next major observances to the practice of commemorating the fall of Jerusalem. His directives were contained in the papal encyclical *Quia major,* which was promulgated in April 1213 in conjunction with his bull calling for the Fourth Lateran Council to assemble in 1215. In Innocent's words: "We decree and command that once a month there must be a general procession of men separately and, where it can be done, of women separately, praying with minds and bodies humbly disposed and with devout and fervent prayer, that merciful God will relieve us of this shameful disgrace by liberating from the hands of the pagans that land in which he accomplished the universal sacrament of our redemption."[12] During this procession, the crusade was to be preached. Fasting and almsgiving should be joined to prayer. Directions for observance are also offered:

> And every day during the celebration of mass, when the moment has come after the Kiss of Peace when the saving sacrifice is to be offered for the sins of the world . . . everyone, men and women alike, must humbly prostrate themselves on the ground and the Psalm [78] . . . should be sung loudly by the clergy. When this has been ended reverently with this verse, *"Let God arise, and let his enemies be scattered: and let them that hate him flee from before his face"* [Ps. 67, *Exsurgat Deus*], the priest who is celebrating must chant this prayer over the altar: "O God, who disposes all things with marvelous providence, we humbly beseech thee to snatch from the hands of the enemies of the cross the land which thine only-begotten son consecrated with his own

blood and to restore it to Christian worship by mercifully directing in the way of eternal salvation the vows of the faithful here present, made for its liberation, through the same Christ, Our Lord, Amen."[13]

Despite these commemorations—the fervent prayers and the liturgical observances—Jerusalem was not, alas, recovered by the Fifth Crusade (1217–21). However, when Frederick II negotiated Christian access to Jerusalem and the other holy sites by treaty with Sultan al-Kamil in 1229, the full commemorations of the fall of Jerusalem no doubt continued or resumed, both the celebration of the 1099 victory and the lament over the loss of Jerusalem and the relic of the True Cross in 1187. Only the crusade expeditions themselves paused during the ten-year truce, until 1239. We know the commemoration of the 1099 victory and the 1149 dedication continued because of the entry in the Riccardiana Psalter executed in the Latin Kingdom about 1225, already mentioned above.[14] But of course the liturgical procession to the Templum Domini and the Templum Salomonis did not continue because the crusaders did not have access to the Haram al Sharif or any of the major Muslim holy sites after 1229.

We can be confident that the commemoration of the fall of Jerusalem in 1187 also continued because, first, Frederick II had negotiated access to the holy city while excommunicated, and therefore he could not legally be recognized as a valid crusader; second, there is no evidence that pope Gregory IX (1227–41) revoked any of the liturgical directives issued by his predecessors; third, only the primary Christian sites of Jerusalem were accessible to pilgrims and crusaders under the treaty, but all Muslim sites, even those with significant Christian associations, such as the Dome of the Rock, revered as the Templum Domini, and the al-Aqsa Mosque, formerly the residence headquarters of the Templars, were off limits to all Christians; and fourth, the Latin Kingdom had now subsided into a more or less permanent condition of weakness for which aid was desperately needed.

When the ten-year truce ran out in 1239, a new crusade was organized, but neither Thibaut IV of Champagne nor Richard of Cornwall was able to retake Jerusalem between 1239 and 1241. Then, three years later, disaster struck again. On 23 August 1244, Khwarismian Turks swept down from northern Syria and captured Jerusalem. Jerusalem fell again and would never be retaken by the crusaders, either by treaty or by military action.

Responding to this new catastrophe in December 1244, King Louis IX vowed to lead a new crusade to recapture Jerusalem, which had been overrun by the Khwarismian Turks. Four years later, in 1248, Louis set out on an expedition that suffered a grievous defeat at al-Mansourah in the Nile delta, the result of which was that Louis himself was captured and had to be ransomed in 1250. It was clear that yet a new crusade would have to be organized to attempt to liberate Jerusalem. In 1252, while Louis IX was still in the Holy Land, directing efforts at refortifying major crusader cities, a papal letter ordained that during the daily mass, when prayers for the crusade were said, the bells of all churches should be tolled for Jerusalem so that persons at work or at home could privately say a *pater noster* or other prayer for the crusade.[15] What must Louis IX have thought and felt when he heard those bells? This daily commemoration thereby joined monthly processions begun by Pope Gregory VIII in the aftermath of the catastrophic loss at Hattin and the subsequent loss of Jerusalem and the set prayer of the priest at mass installed by Innocent III in 1213.

Thus, all through the thirteenth century — indeed, after 1187 — we can observe that the crusade and the fall of Jerusalem were constantly being commemorated liturgically and brought to the attention of Christians in Western Europe and in the Latin East in various ways, for various reasons. Indeed, as the predicament of Jerusalem and the Latin Kingdom grew worse, the number of commemorations grew.

Why were these commemorations observed? I propose the following important reasons, among others: for the purpose of doing penance for past failures; as a way of stimulating prayers for the success of the crusade movement aimed at regaining the holy city; in order to recruit people to take the cross; and as a method of making it possible for everyone to participate in the crusade, whether they played an active role in the expedition or not.

With this in mind, we see that the fall of Jerusalem was especially commemorated whenever a new crusade was being preached, in the period from 1187 to 1291. Therefore, the fall of Jerusalem was commemorated frequently and in various special ways for a variety of reasons throughout this period. Indeed, we might ask, was the fall of Jerusalem in 1099, the glorious victory won by the First Crusade, still being commemorated liturgically after 1244? No doubt it was, in special circumstances, but the liturgical calendar of the Perugia Missal makes it clear that by the 1250s, when this crusader manuscript was done in Acre, the 15 July commemoration had dropped out of regular observance in the Latin Kingdom.[16] While the bells tolled at mass after prayers for the crusade were said, the commemoration of the fall of Jerusalem had become a continuous lament.

So it was with regard to liturgical and ritual commemorations, but after 1244, with the final fall of Jerusalem, and in the period 1245 up to 1291, the glorious victories of the First Crusade came to be remembered in the newly illustrated Old French manuscripts of William of Tyre's *History of Outremer*. Consider what the standard cycle of illustrations for the first eight books of the *History of Outremer* was between circa 1260 and 1291. For our purposes here I am selecting for discussion only miniatures from manuscripts painted in the crusader states.[17]

Even though book 1 begins with ten chapters telling the history of Jerusalem from the time of Heraclius (610–40) and the cruel bondage that Christians had endured during most of that nearly five-hundred-year period, the artistic imagery begins at chapter 11 with the story of pilgrims coming to the Holy Sepulchre in the late eleventh century. In particular, it tells of the coming of Peter the Hermit, a man described by William of Tyre, quoting Statius, as "small of stature and insignificant in person; but 'in that small body, a greater valor reigned.' "[18] Peter prayed at the sepulcher and met with the patriarch of Jerusalem, Simeon, who told him of the afflictions of the Christian people in the Holy Land (fig. 5.1).[19] Peter promised to take a letter from the patriarch to the pope and to the kings and princes of the West, "to bear witness to your exceeding great affliction with all diligence, and to invite earnestly one and all without delay to provide a remedy."[20]

A variant of this story is the uniform choice in all these early manuscripts done by crusader artists, *not* the speech of Urban II at Clermont, which appears at chapters 14 and 15! How remarkable that this holy man and pilgrim, Peter the Hermit — not the pope — is remembered as the first advocate for bringing aid to the Holy Land, in effect as the originator of the First Crusade. It is an interesting choice at a time when the loss of Jerusalem was being lamented, and later lamented even more poignantly in the wake of the death of Pope Gregory X in 1276 and the dissolution of his grandiose plans for a new crusade. Viewed in terms of this miniature,

FIGURE 5.1. Peter the Hermit at the Holy Sepulchre. Paris, Bibliothèque
nationale de France, MS fr. 9084, fol. 1r, bk. 1. Photograph courtesy of the
Bibliothèque nationale de France.

the crusaders in the Holy Land were remembering Peter the Hermit and
wishing for a new holy man to come to their aid.

In book 2 William of Tyre writes about the First Crusaders en route to
Constantinople. Godefroy de Bouillon is discussed in chapter 2 and beyond, substantial attention is given to prince Bohemond of Taranto in
chapter 13 and beyond, but Adhemar, Bishop of Le Puy and papal legate
on the crusade, only appears later, beginning at chapter 17. The imagery
of book 2 uniformly illustrates the First Crusaders setting out on their
march to the Holy Land. But choices could be made as to who they were.
In the Paris Bibliothèque national de France MS fr. 9084, these men are
remembered as resplendent knights in full armor;[21] in MS PLU.LXI.10,
Biblioteca Laurenziana, Florence, however, it is the beloved bishop of Le
Puy who is singled out.[22]

Once the crusaders left Constantinople in 1097 they were faced with
their first major challenge, capturing the ancient city of Nicaea. Nicaea

was the ancient home to the First Ecumenical Council in 325, and in 1196 it was a major walled city controlled by the Seljuk Turks. In the late thirteenth century, Nicaea was once again a city under Byzantine control, only regained from the Franks when the Latin Empire was ended in 1261. Book 3 describes the siege and conquest of Nicaea in chapters 1–13, including the capture of the Turkish leader's wife, who attempted to flee by crossing the lake adjacent to the city. These crusader illustrators focused on the siege of Nicaea in their individual styles, with or without the story of the capture of Qilij Arslan's wife, in celebrating the first major victory by the First Crusade.[23] This would have been an especially poignant memory in the late thirteenth century, when the Latin Empire of Constantinople (including Nicaea) had recently fallen (in 1261) to the Byzantines and the crusaders in the Latin Kingdom had just lost Antioch (in 1268) to the Mamluks.

The First Crusade achieved other victories crossing Anatolia after the taking of Nicaea in June 1097, but no conquest was more important than that of the ancient city of Antioch on the Orontes. Indeed, William of Tyre devotes most of his next three books to the complicated and wonderful story of the crusader siege: entry by subterfuge, conquest of the city, and then fight for survival against a superior Turkish attacking army at Antioch. The result was that Bohemond was established as the new crusader prince, despite Byzantine claims on the city. Crusader artists celebrated this great victory at highly charged moments in the Latin East: just after the fall of Antioch in 1268 to the Mamluks in most manuscripts, or in one important case, a few years before the Mamluks attacked Antioch, in a codex written and illustrated in Antioch itself, namely, MS Pal. Lat. 1963, Biblioteca Apostolica Vaticana, Vatican City.

Book 4 discusses the initial siege by the crusaders. The illustrators represent the attack with emphasis on chapter 15, which tells of the siege engines the crusaders used to weaken the walls and protect their men from sudden assaults out of the city gates.[24]

Book 5 recounts the peril of the crusaders who, after a seven-month siege, were faced with the threat of a major Turkish relieving army that was on the way to raise the siege of Antioch. Motivated by this danger, Bohemond made contact with a Christian inside Antioch, a man named Firuz Benizerra, or Firuz "the Breastplate-maker." Bohemond arranged for Firuz to allow the crusaders to enter the Tower of the Two Sisters (today,

FIGURE 5.2. Soldiers of the First Crusade attacking Antioch. Paris, Bibliothèque nationale de France, MS fr. 9084, fol. 53r, bk. 5. Photograph courtesy of the Bibliothèque nationale de France, Paris.

St. George), which he controlled. On the night of 2–3 June 1098 Firuz let down a ladder from his tower so that Bohemond and his men could enter. The crusaders then opened the gates and swarmed into the city. The artist of the Lyon manuscript represents the betrayal of the city by Firuz, who appears on his tower with the key to the city. Below, the crusaders enter the city through the opened city gate.[25] The artist of MS fr. 9084 conceives of this event less in a literal narrative fashion than as a grand depiction of the conflict of West and East, with the crusader knights and infantry attacking and entering the city defended by Turkish soldiers throwing rocks and shooting arrows. No more glorious memory of the victorious First Crusaders was ever conceived by medieval artists, East or West (fig. 5.2).[26]

The imagery for the start of book 6 reliably follows up on these representations of the triumph of the First Crusade at Antioch. But in the miniature in the Vatican MS Pal. Lat. 1963 the artist has depicted Antioch with extraordinary definition: we see the walls of the city flowing along the mountainous terrain rendered from observed reality (fig. 5.3).[27] Not

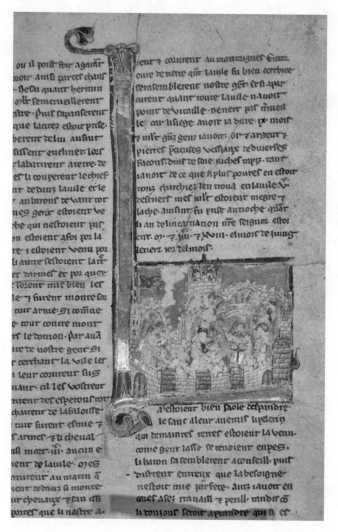

FIGURE 5.3. Soldiers of the First Crusade killing Antiochenes. Rome, Vatican City, Biblioteca Apostolica Vaticana, MS Pal. Lat. 1963, fol. 49r, bk. 6. Photograph courtesy of the Biblioteca Apostolica Vaticana, Vatican City.

only do we see Mount Silpius, with the citadel on the slightly lower peak to the north, but we also see the cleft in the mountains nearby, demonstrating that this artist had intimate knowledge of the city. The rendering is so exact that I have argued that the artist must have been working in Antioch when he painted the miniatures in this manuscript. And he was working there at a crucial moment in the history of the city, when Antioch had become the prime target of the feared Mamluk sultan Baybars in the later 1260s. This artist is remembering the miraculous success of the First Crusade in 1097 at a time when the Principality of Antioch was hoping that a similar miracle would save their city in the face of the Mamluk threat.

At book 7, the crusader cycle of miniatures regularly includes an image of the diplomatic embassy the First Crusaders sent to the Emperor of Constantinople. The purpose of this embassy was to inform the emperor of the conquest of Antioch and to request that he come to aid the First Crusade as it started south on the quest to conquer Jerusalem, as he was bound to do by treaty. The story of this ill-fated embassy occurs in book 7 at chapter 1, fol. 59r, but the artistic choice for this cycle could have been made in favor of a number of other events in this book. One wonders if the appearance of this standard image of a crusader envoy before the emperor under the domes of the city of Constantinople could refer to the lingering hope by the crusaders for a new Byzantine alliance in the 1260s, to aid Antioch in its coming hour of need.

Finally, in book 8, the First Crusade reaches the holy city of Jerusalem. The miniature that culminates the story of the First Crusade at the start of book 8 is simple and direct. It is either the imagery of chapter 3, which is represented in response to the words of William of Tyre: "Jerusalem lies upon two hills. . . . The peak on the west is called Sion. . . . The other hill to the east is called Mt. Moriah."[28] Or, not surprisingly, this miniature could also be a narrative of the siege and triumphant conquest of Jerusalem by the First Crusade, which is told in chapters 6 through 20.[29] In either case it is an image meant to bring to mind the capture of Jerusalem on 15 July 1099. As William of Tyre says in chapter 24, the last chapter of this book, a decree was issued on this day "in order that the memory of this great event might be better preserved." "It was ordained that this day be held sacred and set apart from all others as the time when, for the glory and praise of the Christian name, there should be recounted all that had been foretold by the prophets concerning this event."[30] So the images we see in these manuscripts, in fact in almost all manuscripts of this text, include an image of the holy city, Jerusalem the Golden.

This is not the place for me to discuss the images chosen for the cycle of miniatures in those manuscripts produced in Western Europe during the same period, circa 1250 to 1291. Suffice it to say, the Western cycle of miniatures is independent of those done in the crusader East; they show different choices at the start of certain books, choices made from a Western point of view far from the Holy Land. One could say they are more diverse and discursive, somewhat less focused on Nicaea and Antioch. But their commemoration of Jerusalem at book 8 is comparable to what we see in the crusader books.

At this point two observations can be made. First, it is extraordinary that the first illustrations of William of Tyre's *History of Outremer* manuscripts took place shortly after Jerusalem fell in 1244 to the Khwarismian Turks. Second, art historians have long noted that the beginnings of secular book illumination began in Paris about this time, in mid-century, and so it did. But for the *History of Outremer* these new illustrated books served a particular function. I propose that the production of these new illustrated manuscripts of William of Tyre's *History of Outremer* as one of these new secular books was directly stimulated in response to this event, with the commemoration of the taking of Jerusalem in 1099 by the First Crusade in mind. Even though Western Christendom was universally lamenting the recent loss of Jerusalem, the dream of retaking the holy city was still very much alive.

Following the development of what we might call standard cycles of illustrations for the manuscripts made in the West and in the Holy Land between 1250 and 1291, changes start to develop in later manuscripts, following the loss of Acre and the fall of the crusader states in Syria Palestine, in 1291. All of these manuscripts were made in Western Europe. What was the context for their production? First of all, in the wake of the fall of Acre, Pope Nicholas IV issued the encyclical *Dirum amaritudinem calicem* for the recovery of the Holy Land, in August 1291.[31] Then, in response to the papal encyclical, many new plans were put forth to mount a new crusade, in effect a new version of the First Crusade, which would retake Jerusalem for Christianity. Numerous "recovery treatises" were issued, starting with the *Liber recuperationis terrae sanctae,* by Fidenzio of Padua, and continuing with the famous treatises of Pierre Dubois and Marino Sanudo, among others, stretching from 1291 to the 1320s and beyond.[32] Meanwhile, after the fall of Acre in 1291, illustrated manuscripts of William of Tyre's *History of Outremer* were produced at an impressively intense level. Whereas there are nineteen illustrated codices of this text extant from the years 1245–91, a period of nearly fifty years, in the relatively short nine-year period from 1291 to 1300 we find a surge of twelve new illustrated manuscripts executed: ten in France and two in Italy.[33] How is the commemoration of the First Crusade and the taking of Jerusalem dealt with in these newly commissioned books?

Let me suggest some of the major points by selecting two examples from these manuscripts done in France between 1291 and 1300. In the first place, new imagery is introduced, which reflects renewed interest in and attention to the First Crusade. Sometime before 1300, shortly after the fall of Acre to the Mamluks in 1291, which effectively ended the crusader states on mainland Syria/Palestine, an artist somewhere in northern France, in the region of Picardy, illustrated a manuscript of William of Tyre's very popular *History of Outremer*.[34] The core text of this manuscript was written in Old French, translated from the original Latin, and a continuation, also in Old French, had been added, taking the story of the crusaders in the Holy Land up to 1232. The miniatures he painted include striking reminders of the First Crusade, including the only representation of Pope Urban's speech at Clermont in 1095 to appear in any extant miniature done for manuscripts with this text. Here you see the unique image: Urban speaking about Christ, Christian pilgrims, and infidels in the holy city (fig. 5.4).[35]

Then, shortly after MS 137 was completed, in about 1300, another manuscript of the *History of Outremer* was written and illustrated in or near Paris.[36] In this codex the artist of the basic *History of Outremer* text, carrying the story of the crusaders in the Holy Land up to the early 1180s, included a full set of images of the First Crusade at Antioch and Jerusalem. The images for books 6 and 8, the sieges of Antioch and Jerusalem, respectively, show a somewhat more expanded narrative than the ones seen before 1291. Clearly, focus on the events of the First Crusade in these manuscripts reflected the intense contemporary interest in mounting a new crusade to regain the Holy Land after 1291.

What happens after 1300 in these illustrated *History of Outremer* codices? What follows in the eighteen Old French manuscripts of William of Tyre's *History of Outremer* illustrated between 1300 and 1500 is that this focus continues, but with changes in iconography mutatis mutandis. Consider this final example: In Flanders about 1450 a beautifully illustrated version of this text was done (Amiens, Bibliothèque municipale, MS 483)

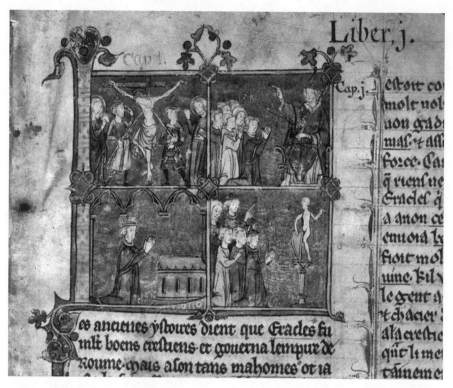

FIGURE 5.4. Speech of Urban II at Clermont calling for the First Crusade. Baltimore, Walters Art Museum, MS 137, fol. 1r, bk. 1. Photograph courtesy of the Walters Art Museum, Baltimore.

for Jean V de Créquy. Once again we see at book 5 and at book 8 the crusaders in camp preparing to besiege Antioch and Jerusalem, respectively (fig. 5.5).[37] These are the traditional choices for the illustrations of these books going all the way back to the second half of the thirteenth century. But here of course there is a novel iconographic twist in the story. The depiction of the First Crusaders at Antioch and Jerusalem is modernized with contemporary plate armor and weaponry—including cannons, heralding the age of gunpowder in warfare. The commemoration of the First Crusade is renewed here in all the immediacy of the imagery of the Hundred Years' War. The dream of a new "First Crusade" clearly vividly continued in the age of the conquest of Constantinople (1453) and the fall of Rhodes (1522) at the hands of the Ottoman Turks.

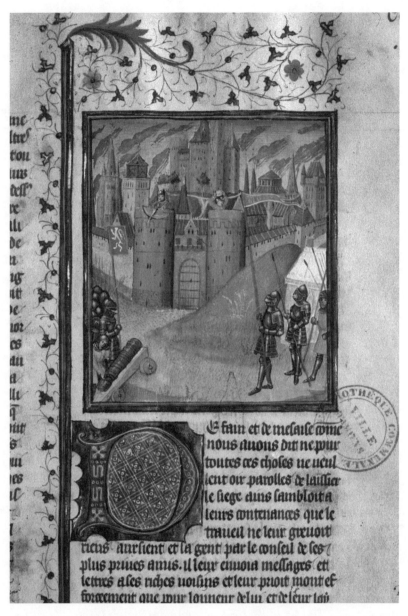

Le train et de melaile come
nous auons dit ne pur
toutes ces choses ne ueul
lent oir parolles de laillier
le liege auis lambloit a
leurs contenances que le
traueil ne leur greuoit
rieus aurlient et la gent par le conleil de les
plus pruues amis. Il leur cuuoia mellages et
lettres a les riches uoilins et leur prioit mout ef
forcement que pour louneur de lui et de leur loi

FIGURE 5.5. Soldiers of the First Crusade camped in front of Antioch. Amiens, Bibliothèque municipale, MS 483, fol. 32r, bk. 5. Photograph courtesy of the Bibliothèque municipale, Amiens.

In conclusion, consider the following three points: First, the commemoration of the First Crusade in medieval Europe had a vigorous and long history in ritual and image, starting shortly after the events of 1099 in the Holy Land, and then extending up to the end of the Middle Ages in Western Europe. Second, the illustrations of the story of the First Crusade begin, significantly, only a few years after the final fall of Jerusalem to the Khwarismian Turks in 1244. The fall of Jerusalem appears to be an important stimulus to the initiation of secular book illumination in vernacular texts in the crusader states, in terms of this example of the *History of Outremer*. Third, following the fall of Acre in 1291, original and creative examples abound for the commemoration of the story of the First Crusade in illustrated manuscripts of William of Tyre's *History of Outremer* up to the end of the fifteenth century. As Western Europeans contemplated the fall of Jerusalem and the loss of the crusader states, they continued to look to the glorious victory of the First Crusade to inspire them to recapture the Holy Land once again.

Notes

1. Of these illustrated codices, eight were done in France, one in England, and eight in the Holy Land. Most of those from the Latin East were executed in Acre from the 1250s to 1291, but at least one was done in Antioch before 1268. The usual format was one miniature at the start of each book of the *History*, with variable numbers of images given to the text of the continuation. For the source of my information, see below, n17.

2. Rome, Biblioteca Angelica, MS D.7.3, fol. 4v (Jerusalem, early 1130s), Paris, Bibliothèque nationale de France (hereafter BnF), MS lat. 12056, fol. 5v (Jerusalem, early 1140s). See Hugo Buchthal, *Miniature Painting in the Latin Kingdom of Jerusalem* (Oxford: Clarendon Press, 1957), 116.

3. Joshua Prawer, *The Latin Kingdom of Jerusalem* (London: Weidenfeld & Nicolson, 1972), 176–77 and n30.

4. Theodorich, in *Jerusalem Pilgrimage, 1099–1185,* ed. John Wilkinson, Joyce Hill, and W. F. Ryan (London: Hakluyt Society, 1988), 286–87. See also Jaroslav Folda, *The Art of the Crusaders in the Holy Land, 1098–1187* (Cambridge: Cambridge University Press, 1995), 228–29.

5. London, British Library, Egerton MS 2902, fol. 4 (Jerusalem or Acre, 1229–41). See Buchthal, *Miniature Painting,* 116.

6. Florence, Biblioteca Riccardiana, MS 323, fol. 4 (Jerusalem or Acre, ca. 1225). See Buchthal, *Miniature Painting*, 116.

7. Gregory VIII, "Audita tremendi," in *The Crusades: Idea and Reality, 1095–1274*, ed. and trans. Jonathan Riley-Smith and Louise Riley-Smith (London: E. Arnold, 1981), 65.

8. Christoph T. Maier, "Crisis, Liturgy, and the Crusade," *Journal of Ecclesiastical History* 48 (1997): 632.

9. Amnon Lindner, " 'Deus venerunt gentes': Psalm 78 (79) in the Liturgical Commemoration of the Destruction of Latin Jerusalem," *Medieval Studies in Honour of Avrom Saltman*, ed. Bat-Sheva Albert, Yvonne Friedman, and Simon Schwartzfuchs (Ramat-Gan: Bar Ilan University Press, 1995), 146.

10. These chroniclers are Baldric of Dol and William of Tyre.

11. Jaroslav Folda, *Crusader Art in the Holy Land, from the Third Crusade to the Fall of Acre, 1187–1291* (Cambridge: Cambridge University Press, 2005), 42–45.

12. Innocent III, "Quia maior," in Riley-Smith and Riley-Smith, *The Crusades: Idea and Reality*, 123.

13. Ibid., 123–24.

14. See above, n6.

15. Maier, "Crisis, Liturgy, and the Crusade," 638.

16. Buchthal, *Miniature Painting*, 116.

17. For a list of these manuscripts, see Jaroslav Folda, "Manuscripts of the *History of Outremer* by William of Tyre: A Handlist," *Scriptorium* 27 (1973): nos. 4 and 6, p. 92, nos. 69, 70, 71, 72, 73, 78, p. 95. See also the discussion of these manuscripts in Folda, *Crusader Art in the Holy Land,* as cited on 713–14. The selection of scenes found in manuscripts done in Western Europe was different to some extent and merits separate consideration in some other discussion.

18. William of Tyre, *A History of Deeds Done beyond the Sea,* ed. and trans. Emily A. Babcock and August C. Krey, 2 vols. (1941; rpt. New York: Columbia University Press, 1976), 1:82.

19. See, e.g., Paris BnF, MS fr. 9084, fol. 1r, in Buchthal, *Miniature Painting*, pl. 135f. For a color picture of Peter the Hermit praying at the Holy Sepulchre and leading a group of crusaders in Lyon Bibliothèque municipale (hereafter Bm) MS 828, fol. 1, see Monique Rey-Delqué, ed., *Les Croisades: L'Orient et l'Occident d'Urbain II à Saint Louis, 1096–1270* (Milan: Electra, 1997), 5.

20. William of Tyre, as in n18, vol. 1:83.

21. See, Paris BnF MS fr. 9084, fol. 20v, in Buchthal, *Miniature Painting*, pl. 136a.

22. See Florence, Biblioteca Laurenziana MS PLU.LXI.10, fol. 24r, in Jaroslav Folda, *Crusader Manuscript Illumination at Saint-Jean d'Acre, 1275–1291* (Princeton: Princeton University Press, 1976), fig. 141. For a color picture of Bishop Adhemar leading the First Crusaders in Lyon Bm MS 828, fol. 15v, see Rey-Delqué, *Les Croisades,* 127.

23. See, e.g., Paris BnF MS fr. 2628, in Buchthal, *Miniature Painting,* pl. 130b. For a color picture of the siege of Nicaea and the capture of the wife of Qilij Arslan in Lyon Bm MS 828, see Rey-Delqué, *Les Croisades,* 220.

24. See, e.g., Lyon Bm MS 828, in Buchthal, *Miniature Painting,* pl. 131a. For a color picture of this miniature on fol. 33r, see Silvia Rozenberg, ed., *Knights of the Holy Land: The Crusader Kingdom of Jerusalem* (Jerusalem: Israel Museum, 1999), 158.

25. See, e.g., Lyon Bm MS 828, in Buchthal, *Miniature Painting,* pl. 131b. For a color picture of this miniature, see Rey-Delqué, *Les Croisades,* 176.

26. See, Paris BnF MS fr. 9084, fol. 53r, in Buchthal, *Miniature Painting,* pl. 135f.

27. For a color picture of this miniature in Vatican City BAV MS Reg. Lat. 1963, fol. 49r, see Jaroslav Folda, *Crusader Art: The Art of the Crusaders in the Holy Land, 1099–1291* (Aldershot, UK: Lund Humphries, 2008), fig. 88.

28. See, e.g., Florence, Biblioteca Laurenziana MS PLU.LXI.10, fol. 80v, in Folda, *Crusader Manuscript Illumination,* fig. 147.

29. See, e.g., Paris BnF MS fr. 2628, fol. 62v, in Buchthal, *Miniature Painting,* pl. 131e.

30. William of Tyre, *A History of Deeds Done beyond the Sea,* ed. and trans. Babcock and Krey, 1:378.

31. Sylvia Schein, *Fidelis Crucis: The Papacy, the West, and the Recovery of the Holy Land, 1274–1314* (Oxford: Clarendon Press, 1991), 74–75.

32. Norman Housley, *The Later Crusades, 1274–1580: From Lyons to Alcazar* (Oxford: Oxford University Press, 1992), 22–38. For a list of treatises on the recovery of the Holy Land, see Schein, *Fidelis Crucis,* 269–70.

33. These statistics are derived largely from my doctoral dissertation: Jaroslav Folda, "The Illustrations in Manuscripts of the *History of Outremer* by William of Tyre" (Ph.D. diss., Johns Hopkins University, 1968), vol. 2. For a summation of the dating of these manuscripts, see Folda, "Manuscripts of the *History of Outremer,*" 1:90–95.

34. Baltimore, Walters Art Museum (hereafter WAM) MS 137, a codex formerly in the Ashburnham collection. See Lilian M. C. Randall et al., *Medieval and Renaissance Manuscripts in the Walters Art Gallery,* 3 vols. (Baltimore: Johns Hopkins University Press, 1989), 1:123–27, cat. no. 50.

35. WAM MS 137, fol. 1r, in Folda, *Crusader Manuscript Illumination,* fig. 273.

36. WAM MS 142, one of the two base codices for the early Paulin Paris edition of the Old French text of the *History of Outremer.* See, Randall et al., *Medieval and Renaissance Manuscripts,* 1:133–38, cat. no. 53.

37. See Folda, "Illustrations in Manuscripts of the *History of Outremer,*" 1:498–502.

CHAPTER SIX

Erasing the Body

History and Memory in Medieval Siege Poetry

SUZANNE CONKLIN AKBARI

𝔉OR MEDIEVAL READERS, THE experience of crusade could be recollected through two distinct discursive forms: the historical narration of chronicle accounts and the poetic narration found in the literary forms of epic and romance. This distinction is, needless to say, a false binary: as scholars such as Nancy Partner and Gabrielle Spiegel have shown, there is often a strongly literary quality to even the most sober historiography, and as Robert Stein and Robert Hanning have shown, a rich vein of historiography runs though the most elaborately poetic texts of the High Middle Ages.[1] This chapter explores the nexus of historiography and poetics through a particular focus on two Middle English poems, both titled *The Siege of Jerusalem* even though they recount two very different historical moments: one describes the fall of Jerusalem to the crusaders in the late eleventh century, following the historical account of William of Tyre, while the other narrates the fall of Jerusalem to the invading Roman army in the service of Titus and Vespasian in the first century. The essay places these two accounts of the siege of Jerusalem in the context of the literary tradition centered on the violent fall of imperial cities, especially the abundant literature devoted to Troy. The context offered here is a broad one, ranging from antiquity through the early modern period and even — in the case of Ismail Kadare's novel *The Siege* — as far as the present day. This breadth is necessary in order to bring out the ways in which the siege and fall of a city are used as a kind of narrative shorthand to encapsulate complex moments of historical change. One might describe the function of poetics in this mode of writing as a "crystallization" of a temporal shift, making visible what is normally unable to be seen. Accordingly, I focus particularly upon this process of crystallization through poetics, as symbolic forms — first, the city itself; second, the male body; third, the tomb that encases the body — are used to mark significant moments in history, points of rupture that mark a discontinuity between one period of time and another.

In earlier work on *The Siege of Jerusalem*, I argued that it is fruitful to juxtapose the fourteenth-century alliterative poem of that name, which focuses on the fall of Jewish-ruled Jerusalem to the invading Roman armies of Titus and Vespasian in the first century, with the fifteenth-century Middle English work of the same name, which is based on the Latin chronicle of William of Tyre (through an Old French intermediary) and recounts the fall of Muslim-ruled Jerusalem in the late eleventh century to the Christian armies of the First Crusade.[2] While these two works narrate very different historical moments, they share a common focus on the central role of the city in the unfolding of sacred history. In each text, the fall of the city marks a significant moment in the articulation of the divine plan: the fall of Jerusalem in the first century paves the way for the foundation of a Christian Rome and, ultimately, the establishment of papal rule, while the fall of Jerusalem in the eleventh century brings about not only Christian rule of the Holy Land but also — at least in the views of the first generations of crusade chroniclers — the imminent End Times.[3] One way of analyzing these works, pursued in my own earlier work as well as (in far richer detail) in Suzanne Yeager's *Jerusalem in Medieval Narrative*, is by viewing them within the multiple and polyvalent traditions of writing about Jerusalem: the holy city was at once the center of prediasporic Jewish community, the site of Christ's ministry and crucifixion, the symbolic center of the world as seen on medieval maps, and the spiritual homeland of every devout Christian soul.[4] Another way of analyzing these works, which I pursue here, is to displace Jerusalem as a singular, unique phenomenon and instead to examine depictions of the besieged city more broadly to see the common ground of these narratives. In this way, it is possible to develop a fuller understanding of how narrations of siege enabled premodern writers to make sense of historical change.

It is important to emphasize that this is not simply a question of literary genre, studied so well by Malcolm Hebron; instead, what is at stake is the particular notion of time that is articulated in narrations of siege.[5] In siege literature, time is depicted as being not only cyclical, governed by the repetitive movement of *translatio imperii,* but also linear, moving in a relentless forward march. This linear motion, moreover, is not continuous but teleological, driven toward a climactic goal. In siege literature, these two modes of temporality are placed in opposition so that the linear forward thrust of time, which steadily builds up pressure only to erupt in the destruction of the city, is perpetually at odds with the cyclical movement of time, in which periods succeed one another in turn, and each climactic moment proves to be simply yet another point in a regular sequence. This tension is expressed concretely in three symbolic forms: the shape of the city itself, bounded by its encircling walls; the body of the warrior, whose wounds reflect the vulnerability of the city he defends; and the tomb of the fallen warrior, which memorializes the site of human death, civic ruin, and imperial change. Bodies, alive or dead, mark points in time: in the form of the tomb, the site of the body remains as a focal point to give structure to historical time after the turning point of the fall of the city; in the form of the dismembered corpse, the body is eradicated in order to emblematize a site of erasure in historical memory.

The next section of this chapter, "The Poetics of Siege," offers a brief survey of the ways in which *translatio imperii,* or the succession of empires, is expressed in siege literature from antiquity through the twelfth century, including the *Aeneid* and the *Roman de Troie.* "Des-Troying Jerusalem" examines *The Siege of Jerusalem* texts in the light of the Troy literature of the previous section, observing how closely the besieged city of Jerusalem conforms to the Troy model and considering how the treatment of warrior bodies in another twelfth-century siege poem, the *Roman de Thebes,* relates to the depiction of Jewish bodies in the alliterative *Siege of Jerusalem.* Finally, "Suspended Bodies" turns to siege literature that builds upon historical models developed within the tradition of crusade literature centered on Jerusalem. These texts include the fourteenth-century *Sege of Melayne,* which recounts the assault of Charlemagne's Christian army on Muslim-held Milan, as well as an early modern adaptation of *The Sege of Melayne,* entitled *Capystranus.* In this sixteenth-century work, the conflict of Christian and Muslim is displaced from Milan to Eastern Europe, while the Arab Muslim adversary is replaced by the Ottoman Turk. The chapter closes with the modern revisioning of these premodern texts found in *The Siege,* a novel by the Albanian writer Ismail Kadare. Like the medieval works, Kadare's *Siege* focuses on the borders of Europe and the Islamic world, but this time the text witnesses the phenomenon of siege not only from within the walls but also from without and narrates the experience of siege from the perspective of Christian and Muslim, Eastern European and Ottoman Turk. In Kadare's novel, as in the premodern works discussed here, the walls of the city are refracted through the symbol of the male body, which at once establishes a spatial border and marks the site of historical rupture.

The Poetics of Siege

Siege poetry inhabits a peculiar place in literary history. From the fall of Troy to the fall of Jerusalem, the climax of siege literature — that is, the fall of the city — marks a transitional moment in which two things happen: a nation dies and is reborn, and imperial might passes from the hands of the past into the hands of the future. Siege poetry plays a special role among these fundamentally historical narratives, imposing form upon the memory of past glory and upon the imagined promise of future power. As a genre, siege poetry participates in what we might call an "imaginative historiography," in which poetic form is coupled with symbolic forms — especially the body — in order to produce a coherent image of the past.

For many medieval readers, the main example of the city under siege was Troy — not the Troy story recounted by Homer (which was known only indirectly) but the one nested inside book 2 of Virgil's *Aeneid,* studied by generation after generation in the schools of medieval Europe.[6] Safely harbored in Carthage, Aeneas tells Dido about his past, explaining how he escaped from the ravaged city. The whole of the *Aeneid* is situated, temporally, in the liminal space that separates the fall of one great empire — Troy — from the rise of another — Rome. Troy falls before the *Aeneid* begins; Rome rises after the *Aeneid* ends. Aeneas's journey south to Carthage and north to Latium knits together these two civic points of imperial might, creating a narrative of supersession: Troy dies and is replaced by Rome, fathered by "pater Aeneas." Other historical accounts of Rome produced in antiquity, however, describe the movement of empire in less teleological terms. Most important among these is the universal history composed in the last years of the Roman Empire by Paulus Orosius at the request of his mentor, St. Augustine. Orosius, like Virgil, gives an account of the place of Rome in imperial history. Unlike Virgil, however, who creates a narrative of supersession in which Rome replaces Troy, Orosius sketches out a four-part model of what he named, influentially, *translatio imperii:* the translation, or movement, of empire.

In Orosius's view of history, *imperium* passes from one great city to the next, following the four points of the cardinal directions: imperial power arose first with Babylon in the east; moved upward into the north, with the defeat of Darius by the Macedonian Alexander; then downward into the south, with the rise of Carthage; and finally to the west, with the rise of Rome. This four-part succession gives way to — is itself entirely superseded by — the birth of Christ, whose new Christian empire is the fulfillment and the replacement of Augustus Caesar's Rome.[7] In spite of the disjunction between the two-part narrative of Virgilian *imperium* and the four-part narrative of Orosian *translatio imperii*, later historians had no trouble integrating the two, as Lee Patterson has shown.[8] The fall of Troy was simply inserted, along with the fall of Thebes and the biblical histories of kings and patriarchs, into new universal histories. *Imperium* could be passed on through conquest, as in Orosius's formulation, or through gene-alogical descent, as in the *Aeneid;* whether mediated through the spilling of blood or through blood inheritance, however, *imperium* was fundamentally portable.[9] Imperial might was thought to travel from place to place, anchored for a time in a great city, inevitably destined to fall and be replaced by another ruling city. This view of history was manifested not only in universal histories, which set out the whole span of the past within the scope of a single work, and in the "integrated chronologies" that appear in medieval manuscript miscellanies, but also broadly in medieval history-writing. The reader of the popular history of Alexander the Great, for example, would know that this was part of a larger narrative of *translatio imperii*, in which the Persian Darius relinquished his rule to the Macedonian conqueror. Readers of literary texts — the romances of Alexander, of Thebes, of Troy — read with a similar awareness, knowing that this poem was just part of a bigger story, the story of "imperial translation."

In a sense, then, medieval historiography already imposes a form on the past: that of sequence or succession, of *translatio imperii*. The event of the siege marks the transition from one stage of imperial might to the next. But what about the *poetry* of siege? Poetics imposes a different form on our knowledge of the past, as Gabrielle Spiegel has shown in her important work on medieval French chronicles. As Spiegel points out, early manuscripts of one important universal history, the *Histoire ancienne jusqu'à César,* written mainly in prose, include verse sections to express transhistorical, eternally valid moral precepts; later manuscripts generally suppress the verse, but one late redaction of the *Histoire ancienne* actually inserts the whole of the *Roman de Troie* into the text.[10] Clearly, verse and prose were thought to have very different functions in the writing of history. Sometimes, verse was thought to be inferior, even deceptive; at other times, it was seen as desirable and even necessary. Poetry "re-members" the past — that is, it both recalls it through memory and gives it intelligible form. We might wish to describe the narration of history in verse as "imaginative historiography," recognizing that while historical events form the backbone of such texts, poetic form makes the "matter" of the work accessible to imagination and able to be preserved in memory.[11]

To illustrate this process, it is useful to turn to the scene of the fall of Troy recounted in the *Aeneid.* Here, the liminal status of *imperium* — suspended between the past rule of Troy and the future rule of Rome — is epitomized in the male body: namely, the corpse of Priam lying before the altar. It might seem peculiar to embody the fallen city in masculine rather than feminine terms; after all, a range of texts, modern and premodern, identify territory as metaphorically feminine. The act of conquest is figured as an act of sexual possession, as we see (for example) in the prologue to *The Book of John Mandeville,* where the reconquest of Jerusalem by Christian crusaders is described as the rescue of a helpless woman.[12] The same option of identifying the city in feminine terms appears in the *Aeneid,* when Aeneas recalls how Ilium, before the Greeks came, was "for many years a queen."[13] Once the siege begins, however, not the female body but the male is the object upon which the fall of imperial power is staged. To put it another way, while the female body can be used to represent territory, the male body represents the immaterial power that sustains rule over that territory.

Book 2 of the *Aeneid* expresses the fall of the city in microcosm, through the fall of the individual male body. Moreover, the liminal status of *imperium,* temporarily suspended between Troy and Rome, is also expressed both in the topography of the city and in the description of the male corpse. As the imperial city walls are transformed into the "ashes of Ilium" (*Iliaca cineres,* 2.431), the Greek invaders penetrate as far as the "threshold" (*limen,* 2.441) of the palace. Aeneas tells how he found his way through a secret passage that winds its way into the most interior, protected space within the Trojan city: "There was an entrance," he states — literally, a second *limen,* or "threshold" (2.453) — "with secret doors, a passage running from hall to hall of Priam's palace, a postern gate apart" (2.453–55).[14] In the past, Hector's wife used to bring their little child to visit his grandfather. Now this secret passage is overrun by the Greeks, says Aeneas, who pour in like rushing water: "Not with such fury, when a foaming river, bursting its barriers, has overflowed and with its torrent overwhelmed the resisting banks, does it rush furiously upon the fields in a mass" (2.496–98). The metaphor of the rushing river comes alive in the floods of blood spilled "amid the altars," where Aeneas sees Priam "polluting with his blood [*sanguine foedantem*] the fire he himself had hallowed" (2.501–2). Here again, the Greeks are said to be perched "on the threshold" (*in limine,* 2.500), marking the liminal space and the liminal time of this remembered crucible of imperial flux.

The death of Priam, a few lines later, makes it clear that this moment is a temporal threshold. Priam is dragged before the altar and slaughtered: he "lies a huge trunk upon the shore [*litore*], a head severed from the shoulders, a nameless corpse" (iacet ingens litore truncus, / avolsumque umeris caput et sine nomine corpus, 2.557–58).[15] The sacred inner room of the palace at Ilium is a deeply interior, hidden space; simultaneously, however, this most interior space is also a "*limen,*" or "threshold," located at the center in spatial terms but on the margin in temporal terms. The body of Priam lies, metaphorically, upon the shore, the littoral space that marks the dividing line between one era of imperial might and its successor.

There are at least three formal frameworks within which the phenomenon of siege can be expressed: one of these, as we have seen, is the historiographical, in which siege is repeated again and again at each stage of the process of *translatio imperii.* A second framework for siege literature can be found in the philosophy of Boethius, which was widely diffused in medieval culture: in the Boethian tradition, the rise and fall of individual men, as of empires, can be seen as a manifestation of the capricious turns of Fortune's wheel or — more profoundly — as a manifestation of the fundamental instability of the created world. A third framework within which siege can be expressed is poetic or, more precisely, tragic: as Aristotle puts it in the *Poetics,* the components of the tragic plot include not just the change in action (*peripateia*) and the change in knowledge (*anag-noresis*) but also the "scene of suffering" (*pathos*).[16] This is the moment of slaughter, of wounding, the moment when tragedy is expressed upon the body: the paradigmatic case, for Aristotle, is the self-mutilation of Oedipus. In medieval siege poetry, the fall of the city is the moment of change, and that moment is simultaneously expressed within these three frameworks: historiographical, Boethian, and tragic.[17] The tragic "scene of suffering" is the moment when change is made visible, and that moment is played out through the medium of the male body.

If we turn now to a widely disseminated Old French version of the Troy story, the *Roman de Troie* of Benoît de Saint-Maure (1160–70), we find that the *Aeneid*'s Trojan "scene of suffering" — that is, the slaughter of Priam — is refracted into a series of such scenes, in which mutilated male bodies serve as temporal markers of the progression toward the final resolution of the siege. The repetition of these "scenes of suffering" mimics the repetition of imperial rise and fall that is fundamental to the process of *translatio imperii,* with the sequence of fallen male bodies serving as metonyms for the sequence of fallen empires. In other words, the whole history of *translatio imperii* is recapitulated in the seemingly endless wait for the fall of Troy. The sequence of bodies described in the *Roman de Troie* begins with the body of Hector, which, after being mutilated by the Greeks, is returned to Priam and enclosed in a "precious tabernacle" (*tabernacle precios,* 16651):[18] here, the wounded body of the king's first-born achieves the status of martyr, his body preserved like a relic. This process is reenacted with the body of Troilus, which (like Hector's) has been dragged around the field after death (21447), and the body of Paris, which is encased in a "costly sarcophagus" (*chier sarquel,* 23038).[19] The sequence of mutilated male bodies concludes with that of Priam; unlike the bodies of his sons, however, Priam's body finds no resting place and is instead left on the ground, before the altar of Ilium.

The sequence of dismembered and then memorialized male bodies in the *Roman de Troie* is not limited to the sons of Priam. The Greek Achilles is also part of the tragic sequence: his body, however, is so badly mutilated that restoring it to a semblance of wholeness proves far more difficult than for the broken bodies of Hector, Troilus, and Paris. The fragments of Achilles' body are instead burned, and the ashes placed in a remarkable "costly vessel" (*cher vaissel,* 22470) made of a single ruby. This exquisite reliquary is, in turn, held in the hands of a golden image in the likeness of Achilles' beloved Polyxena. This figure is then placed at the summit of a wonderful monument, surmounting "a little sphere made of a single topaz, clear and beautiful." In spite of the difficulty in reconstituting the broken members of the wounded body of Achilles, this warrior's tomb is the most perfectly beautiful, perfectly shaped, exquisitely begemmed, of them all. As the poet puts it, "it was seen as a marvel" (*A merveille fu esgardee*, 22426).

The tomb of Paris, which comes in the sequence immediately after the sumptuous monument of Achilles, raises the stakes even higher. Instead of being made of gold, this "costly sarcophagus" (*chier sarquel*, 23038) is made of "a single jasper touched with green: / Never in all the history of the world / Was there a richer vessel" (*un vert jaspe goté: / Ainc en cest siecle trespassé / Ne fu veüz plus cher vaissel*, 23039–41). But the magnificence of this tomb is not what sets it apart: the tomb of Paris, in the *Roman de Troie*, actually becomes a resting place or sanctuary for the precious emblems of empire, as Priam removes his imperial insignia and places them upon the body in the tomb. He removes his ring and places it on his son's right hand; he places the crown on the head of the corpse. The poet writes, "Ne vuelt que Grieu seient seisiz" (23061), not simply that he did not want the Greeks to take the emblems, but literally that they "not be seized of them," not take legal possession of them.

Priam's resistance of the inexorable current of *translatio imperii* is, of course, futile. The poet states that the marble walls of Troy are "as smooth as ice, resplendent in the sun: they are green and blue, yellow and vermillion. They are high and straight, adorned with embattlements; no lance or spear can strike them" (23096–100).[20] These mirroring walls, refracting the light of the sun into a spectrum of colors, are only a deceptive image of imperial might: the *Roman de Troie* goes on to recount an interminable series of bloody battles followed by short pauses when the onslaught of siege gives way, however briefly, to a fragile moment of stasis. Ultimately, however, the shining walls of Ilium are penetrated in a bloodbath that finds the Trojan horses "up to their chests in red blood" (*Tresqu'as ventres sunt li destrier / En sanc vermeil*, 24372–73). After another period of truce, the onslaught begins again, in which "the base of the walls and the gates, head on and below and above, are besieged and nearly taken" (24465–67).[21]

After this, the poet states ominously, "the Trojans will never come out again" (*ja Troien n'en istront mes*, 24468).

Finally, on a "dark night" (oscurs, 26050), the palace is assailed (26055); women and children are slaughtered (26058). The oscillation between active siege and fragile truce comes to its climax, the pavement completely wet with blood (26068) and the altar desecrated by the blood of Priam (26148). Interestingly, in the *Roman de Troie*, the death of Priam is almost anticlimactic: instead of a teleological movement toward a final resolution in the sack of Troy as recounted in book 2 of the *Aeneid*, we find a state of suspension, in which a sequence of male bodies demarcates brief moments of equilibrium in the perpetuation of siege. Each time, the broken male body, marked by many wounds or even dismembered, is carefully reconstituted, restored to a state of symbolic wholeness. Even where the body is so leaky and fragmented that it cannot be embalmed, as in the case of Achilles, the powdery ashes are placed in an urn made of a single gem, placed in a monument that epitomizes the highest achievements of human art. This movement toward the restoration of wholeness, in the poetry of siege, comes to an end only with the death of the last of the warriors, as Priam himself is sacrificed. At this moment, the power of empire is released, to travel forth to the next city on its transnational itinerary.

Des-Troying Jerusalem

The poetics of siege sketched out above is based on the paradigmatic case of Troy, known during the Middle Ages not only through the ubiquitous school text of the *Aeneid* but also through a host of alternative versions, in Latin and in romance vernaculars. Combined with the Orosian model of *translatio imperii*, in which a series of imperial centers — Babylon, Macedonia, Carthage, and ultimately, Rome — succeed one another in a sequence of bloody battles, the case of Troy provided a crucial paradigm for the description of how one order of rule might succeed another. Medieval readers eagerly integrated the history of Troy with the Orosian account of imperial succession, adding Trojan genealogies and even entire narratives of the fall of Troy into late medieval adaptations of Orosius: in one extreme case, a fourteenth-century adaptation of the thirteenth-century *His-*

toire ancienne jusqu'à César actually inserts the whole of the *Roman de Troie* into the sequence of *translatio imperii*. The siege and fall of Jerusalem was similarly integrated into Orosian historiography, with a whole series of medieval chronicles integrating the history of Jewish diaspora (in the version of Josephus, as transmitted by pseudo-Hegesippus) within the sequence of imperial history. The fall of Troy and subsequent dispersal of its inhabitants, who — according to medieval chroniclers and writers of romance — went on to found the ruling houses of Europe, corresponds to the parallel account of the fall of Jerusalem and subsequent diaspora. In this implicit comparison of Troy and Jerusalem, both cities have a supersessionist relationship to Rome: Troy gives rise to Rome in the national narrative first inscribed in the *Aeneid*, just as Jerusalem gives rise to Christian Rome in the ecclesiastical narrative recounted in the many redactions and adaptations of Josephus's history of the Jewish Wars (*Bellum Iudaicum*). The alignment of the fall of Troy with the fall of Jerusalem, and their common participation in the larger trajectory of Orosian *translatio imperii*, is perhaps most fully expressed in the *Flores historiarum* of Matthew Paris, in which the chronologies of Jewish and Trojan history are alternately recounted until both give way to the linear sequence of successive imperial powers as they devolve from Babylon, to Persia, to Greece, to Rome.[22]

Writers seeking to provide an account of the crusader conquest of Jerusalem inevitably built upon the foundation of these patterns of historical narration, a tendency that was furthered by the ways in which Christian rule was understood to participate in the sequence of *translatio imperii*. Implicitly in Orosius's history, but quite explicitly in the *City of God*, composed by his mentor Augustine, the empire of Christ succeeds and supersedes the empires of this world, replacing the temporal rule of man with the eternal rule of God. Accounts of the siege of Jerusalem in 1099 and subsequent establishment of the Christian kingdom could readily draw upon Orosian models of imperial succession to make history intelligible, to give a regular pattern to the passage of time. In addition, the supersession of temporal rule by divine rule, implicit in Orosius and explicit in Augustine, added a slightly different sense of time to historical accounts of the crusader conquest of Jerusalem: while *translatio imperii* implies a series of successive periods of rule, each one anchored by a single imperial city, the supersessionary model implies a climactic — even apocalyptic — concept of time, in which one mode of being is simultaneously fulfilled and replaced by another. This double chronology, which yokes together repetitive sequence with climactic fulfillment, is highlighted in siege literature centered on Jerusalem.

Like siege literature centered on the city of Troy, the siege literature of Jerusalem highlights the Aristotelian "scene of suffering," expressed powerfully in the spectacle of the wounded male body. The nature of the city of Jerusalem as depicted in this literature, however, varies widely: it is sometimes envisioned as the specific, historical city, sometimes as the metaphorical Jerusalem — that is, any Christian community besieged by unbelievers or even the individual soul besieged by sin.[23] While in the narratives of siege described previously, the paradigmatic body is the male warrior — whether the aged Priam, clothed in armor and holding his sword, or his son Hector, first in a series of Trojan princes to suffer and die for his city — the paradigmatic body in Jerusalem siege narratives is that of the suffering Christ. In view of these parallels, it is surprising that siege literature centered on Jerusalem has often been seen as distinct from historiographical siege literature, such as the poems of Troy or Thebes.[24] This is a mistake, I would argue, because medieval universal histories and integrated chronologies are utterly explicit in their inclusion of Jerusalem within the sequence of besieged cities. Even Orosius includes an account of the siege of Jerusalem in 70 C.E. in his universal history; he does not, however, include Jerusalem in the sequence of imperial cities that have participated in the transmission of *translatio imperii*. For Orosius, Jerusalem is nothing more than a used-up vessel: he likens it to a womb that has served its purpose by giving birth to the Christian Church and is now empty and worthless.[25]

By the twelfth century, however, the siege of Jerusalem by Titus and Vespasian had become useful as a typological prefiguration of a crucial moment in history: that is, the conquest of Jerusalem by European Christians during the First Crusade. For Lambert of Saint-Omer, whose *Liber floridus* is an early twelfth-century compilation of texts all centering on this climactic moment in salvation history, the siege of Jerusalem by the Christians is both a repetition and a fulfillment of the siege of Jerusalem by the first-century Romans. His integrated chronologies make room for these repeated conquests of Jerusalem within the sequence of *translatio imperii*.[26] Some medieval vernacular texts with the title *The Siege of Jerusalem* describe the capture of the city by the Romans in the first century; others with the same title refer to the conquest of Jerusalem by the Christians in the First Crusade. This double-edged historiographical impulse is evident in the fourteenth-century anonymous Middle English alliterative *Siege of Jerusalem*, which explicitly recounts the conquest of the city by Titus and Vespasian in the first century but implicitly recounts the crusader attack on Jerusalem by consistently depicting the Romans in terms of medieval Christian warriors. Conventionally, in siege literature, those who are within the besieged city are those who suffer, and the reader is invited to experience compassion for them. In *The Siege of Jerusalem*, however, this convention is complicated by the text's ambivalence with regard to the position of the Jews. Trapped within the city, lacking food and water, they are pitiable; as the enemies of Christ and the Church, however, they are contemptible. The extremity of their suffering produces horrible effects, including the cannibalism of a child's body by its mother. This scene is at once repulsive and empathetic, as the mother, insane with hunger, offers up the body of her son for her fellows to eat in a grotesque parody of the Virgin Mary offering up her Son in the Eucharist.

In *The Siege of Jerusalem*, the scene of suffering is ubiquitous: all those contained within the city suffer in mind as well as in body, tormented by the knowledge of the behaviors they have been driven to as much as by their hungry and thirsty bodies. The most spectacular suffering, however, is that of the Jewish high priest Caiphas, who is publicly crucified along with his twelve "clerkes" in a grotesque parody of Christ and his apostles. The poet recounts their horrible fate:

> Domesmen upon deyes demeden swythe
> That ech freke were quyk-flyn, the felles of clene:
> First to be on a bent with blonkes to-drawe,
> And suth honget on an hep upon heye galwes,
> The feet to the firmament, alle folke to byholden,
> With hony upon ech half the hydeles anoynted;
> Corres and cattes with claures ful scharpe
> Four kagged and knyt to Cayphases theyes;
> Twey apys at his armes to angren hym more,

That renten the rawe flesche upon rede peces.
So was he pyned fram prime with persched sides
Tille the sonne doun sette in the someretyme.

. . . .

The kyng lete drawen hem adoune whan they dede were,
Bade: "A bole-fure betyn to brennen the corses,
Kesten Cayphas theryn and his clerkes alle,
And brennen evereche bon into browne askes."

(697–708, 717–20)[27]

The body of Caiphas serves as a microcosm of Jerusalem. His body is torn apart and burned to ashes, scattered to the winds; the city walls soon suffer the same fate, beaten down into "poudere" (1284). In the end,

Nas no ston in the stede stondande aloft,
Morter ne mude-wall bot alle to mulle fallen:
Nother tymbre ne tre, Temple ne other,
Bot doun betyn and brent into blake erthe.

(1289–92).

Every wall, including those of Solomon's temple, are broken down and beaten into powder. These fragmented walls, demolished into "black earth," correspond to the broken bones of Caiphas, reduced into "brown ashes."

Like the cannibalistic mother who is a parody of the Virgin Mary, Caiphas and his followers are a feeble imitation of Christ and his apostles; they differ, however, in that no memorial or commemorative place remains to recall that they ever lived. The annihilation of the walls of the city, repeated in microcosm in the annihilation of the bodies of the Jewish men, is a visible manifestation of the erasure of the community of the Jewish nation. Superseded by the Church, the community of the Jews could be seen only as the detritus of the past. These powdery ashes, all that is left of the warriors of Jerusalem, are very different from the bodies of the warriors described in the *Aeneid* or the *Roman de Troie*. While Achilles' body is also reduced to ashes, because it was too badly wounded to be embalmed and preserved, it is placed in a monument so artful, so rich, and so pure — its receptacle made of a single ruby — that the effect is that of a reliquary. Although a reliquary contains only a few physical remnants of the saint's body, these few bones or teeth are linked across time through the glorified flesh that will ultimately be reunited with the soul: the saint is thus manifested, wholly and completely, through the fragments preserved in the reliquary. Achilles' body is preserved in a similar way, though his "precious vessel" owes its transcendent perfection to art rather than to any link with the divine.

To find a more precise analogue to the treatment of Jewish bodies in the *Siege of Jerusalem,* we must turn to another Old French siege poem closely related to the *Roman de Troie:* that is, the roughly contemporary *Roman de Thebes* (ca. 1150). Narratives of the fall of Thebes resemble narratives centered on Troy, with the important proviso that the imperial lineage of Thebes is a genealogical dead end, very different from the prolific heritage of Troy. The twin sons of Oedipus and his mother, Jocasta, are doomed to be born of a single womb and to end up in a single tomb. Like the *Roman de Troie,* the *Roman de Thebes* is preoccupied with the need to restore the fragmented body of the warrior into a state of wholeness; this effort is complicated, however, by the peculiar genealogy of Thebes.[28] The sons of Oedipus, Polyneices and Etiocles, are locked in warfare, each trying to claim his inheritance of the city of Thebes. They are drawn together by love and repelled by hate. This is particularly evident in the scene of their joint death: the "red blood" that flows from the wounded body of Etiocles causes his twin, Polyneices, to be moved by "pity." When Polyneices embraces his twin, Etiocles is correspondingly moved by the reciprocal emotion of "passionate hatred" (*mout iriez,* 9788), and shoves a knife between the joints of his brother's armor. The two bleed to death in each other's arms, glued together by love and hate. The death of the twins marks the moment in which Oedipus's self-mutilation is completed: the poet ends his account of their death by stating, "Now both of the brothers are dead: both because of the sin of their father, which he never ceased to mourn bitterly, and because of his eyes, which he wounded and wrenched out because of anguish, for he had taken his mother as wife" (*Roman de Thebes,* 9811–16).[29] The tragic moment begins when Oedipus gains terrible knowledge and inflicts a double wound on his own body; it is completed when the twins destroy one another and the doomed lineage comes to an end.

The ambivalent status of the twins — neither fully united nor fully separated — complicates the usual effort to restore the wounded body of the warrior to a state of wholeness. Following the battle, Theseus, the ruler of Athens, seeks out the bodies of Polyneices and Etiocles on the field and tries to bury them. The bodies continue to battle even after death, so Theseus has them cremated; two flames leap up from the pyre as the brothers continue to wage war upon each other. Finally, Theseus comes up with a plan to immure the brothers into a single space, a precious "vessel" like that containing the ashes of Achilles in the *Roman de Troie.* The fighting begins again, however, and the vessel ruptures as the powdery ashes "burst forth." In some respects, the attempt to immure the remains of Polyneices and Etiocles is a special case; in other ways, however, it repeats the standard forms of siege poetry, in which containment and wholeness is the necessary punctuation to the bloody release of the siege.

In narratives of Thebes ranging from the first-century *Thebaid* of Statius onward, the siege and destruction of the city is symbolically expressed through the bodies of male warriors, just as in the narratives of Troy. In the *Roman de Thebes,* however, the male body is not a focus for memorialization as it is in the *Roman de Troie,* marked as whole and perfect even after death: instead, it is characterized by decay and dissolution. This twelfth-century precedent is a crucial background for the depiction of the male body in the late medieval *Siege of Jerusalem,* where the male body is similarly a metonym for the city that does not survive in the form of a memorial tomb but rather is broken down into dust and scattered to the winds. In the *Roman de Thebes,* the ashes of the Oedipal twins, perpetually at war and bursting out of the golden vessel provided by Theseus, represent an only slightly more permanent monument than the scattered ashes of Caiphas. The legacy of Thebes is abjected from the national historiographies of Europe, just as the legacy of post-Incarnational Judaism is abjected from Christian history. The body of the warrior, symbolic representation of the city, and by extension, of the period of rule that ends with the city's ultimate fall, represents that legacy. For Troy, the enduring wondrous monument to the fallen hero underscores the permanence of the Trojan legacy; conversely, for Thebes as for Jerusalem, the scattered ashes of the Theban warrior or the Jewish priest reflect the rejection of the cultures they emblematize.

The siege literature of Jerusalem, as noted above, is complicated by the many referents that Jerusalem could potentially have in the medieval imagination: the historical city, whether of the first century or the eleventh; the community of the faithful, united in the Church; the individual soul, yearning for salvation; or the Heavenly Jerusalem, to be experienced at the end of time. In historiographical terms, Jerusalem has a comparably complex polyvalence. Accounts of Jerusalem in the first century, as in the alliterative fourteenth-century poem I have discussed, also refer implicitly to the events of the eleventh-century siege by the crusader armies; similarly, accounts of the crusader siege carry within them the memory of the early history of siege upon the holy city. This historiographical polyvalence is evident, as Michael Johnston has shown, in the compilation of the alliterative *Siege of Jerusalem* in the London Thornton manuscript, where it is surrounded by a sequence of crusade materials. Johnston demonstrates that this deliberate contextualization "gives voice to a militant Christian historiography," first recounting "the supersession of the Jewish community, then turning to the threat of Islam."[30] The placement of the siege and fall of Jerusalem just after an account of Christ's Passion and just before crusade narratives on the destruction of Islam, he argues persuasively, turns the poem into "a piece of triumphalist and imperialist Christian historiography."[31] By establishing a historiographical context for reading the poem, the compiler of the London Thornton manuscript capitalizes on what we might call the "double chronology" of siege literature, in which each iteration of the fall of the city is simultaneously an evocation of other moments of imperial conquest.

The ambivalence found in the alliterative *Siege of Jerusalem,* in which the Jews are at once pitiable and contemptible, leads to an inversion of the economy of siege in subsequent accounts of Jerusalem. As we have seen, conventionally in siege poetry, those within the walls are those who suffer; those outside the gates are the aggressors. While those outside the walls may suffer and even die, they are not the victims who are sacrificed in the climactic moments of siege. This balance — victims inside, aggressors outside — is inverted when siege poetry focused on Jerusalem becomes part of crusade literature, so that the suffering of those *outside* the walls becomes the reader's empathetic focus. This can be seen clearly in a fifteenth-century Middle English work having the same name as the alliterative fourteenth-century poem discussed above, *The Siege of Jerusalem.* This prose text is a Middle English translation of the Old French *Eracles,* an adaptation of the Crusade chronicle of William of Tyre.[32] Although the late medieval prose version, published by William Caxton, shares a title with the fourteenth-century poem, the Caxton *Siege of Jerusalem* inverts the binary opposition of tormentor and sufferer, placing the scene of suffering not within the walls but outside. The Christians who besiege the city from outside the walls suffer the pangs of thirst after the Muslims within the gates "stopped the mowthes of thyse fontaynes and of the Cysternes . . . ffor they thought that the pylgryms for lacke of waters sholde not mayntayn theyr siege to fore the toun" (254.17.20).[33] The Christians also experience severe hunger due to the scarcity of food, as "a cowe was worth four marc weight of syluer, which a man might haue at begynnyng for echt or ten shyllyngis. A lamb or a kyd was at sex shyllyngis, whiche to fore was worth but thre or four pens" (144.29–32). Through this series of inversions, the Caxton *Siege of Jerusalem* switches around the conventional dynamic of besieger and besieged, in which the besieger is the aggressor and those who are besieged suffer want, deprivation, and — ultimately — death. Here, the pangs of hunger and thirst are experienced by the Christians encamped outside the walls, not the Muslims within Jerusalem. In other words, in the Caxton *Siege,* the dynamics of siege are turned inside-out, so that the scene of suffering is displaced from the central spectacle and instead placed at the periphery.

This displacement of the scene of suffering from center to periphery affects the way in which the suffering male body is identified with the besieged city and, consequently, the representation of historical time in siege literature. Instead of the body of the warrior being made eternal, as in the *Roman de Troie,* through the creation of a monument that marks the fall of the city and the subsequent transit of temporal power from one imperial center to another, the body of the warrior remains permanently in a liminal state, marking the ambivalent relationship of the present moment to that remembered past. In the alliterative *Siege of Jerusalem,* as in the *Roman de Thebes,* the scattered dust of the male bodies represents a culture that is necessarily abjected from the history of imperial succession, whether the post-Incarnational Jewish community or the incestuous lineage of Oedipus and Jocasta. Both lineages continue to remain in historical memory, integrated within the chronicle tradition and in poetic retellings of history; simultaneously, however, they are cut off from lineal participation in the present through the account of dissolution and scattering expressed symbolically through the male body. In the Caxton *Siege,* the precedent established in earlier siege poetry centered on Jerusalem is inverted, so that the scene of suffering is situated not with the reviled antagonists within the walled city (as was the case in the alliterative *Siege of Jerusalem*) but with the protagonists who tenaciously besiege the walls in spite of their own pain and hunger. This inverted model of siege would prove central to late medieval and early modern depictions of war waged on behalf of Christ against the unbelieving enemy.

Suspended Bodies: Marking the Border of Europe

Late medieval siege literature builds upon precedents developed within the tradition of crusade literature centered on Jerusalem, as can be seen in the fourteenth-century *Sege of Melayne,* which recounts the assault of Charlemagne's Christian army on Muslim-held Milan, as well as in the sixteenth-century *Capystranus,* an early modern adaptation of the *Sege of Melayne* that displaces the conflict of Christian and Muslim from Milan to Eastern Europe and replaces the Arab Muslim adversary with the Ottoman Turk. The *Sege of Melayne* is part of the Charlemagne cycle of romances, featuring the familiar figures of Roland, Oliver, and Bishop Turpin. Turpin is at once a warrior and a priest, having much in common with the hybrid figures described in the chronicles of the crusades: he expresses his priestly function in conventional terms, offering the sacrifice of the Mass on the battlefield (881–910), but he also throws himself into battle, leading an army of priests in place of the usual company of soldiers. Perhaps Turpin's most striking quality, however, is the way in which he undergoes bodily suffering on behalf of his community, in a dramatic spectacle that at once evokes both the prolonged suffering of Christ in the Passion and the fragmented bodies of the warriors we have seen in other siege poems.

Unlike all the examples discussed thus far, Turpin's body is not a dead body: instead, it is a body suspended between two states of being, perpetually hidden from view. After Turpin is sorely wounded, Charlemagne asks to examine his wounds and to provide a doctor. Turpin refuses, insisting on keeping his body sealed off — deprived of food, of water, and unable to be viewed — until the siege comes to its climax. Refusing to allow Charlemagne to see his wounds, Turpin insists upon imitating the suffering Christ:

Criste for me sufferde mare.
He askede no salve to His sare,
Ne no more sall I this tyde.
I sall never ette ne drynke
Ne with myn eghe slepe a wynke,
Whate bale [pain] als ever I byde,
To yone cité yolden bee
Or ells therfore in batelle dye —
The sothe is noghte to hyde.
     (*Sege of Melayne* 1345–53)[34]

Like the body of Caiphas, the body of Turpin is a microcosm of his community. It represents not only the individual suffering body of Christ but also the collective body of Christ — that is, the Church. This is made apparent in a passage where the bloodied bodies of the warrior host are reflected in the terrain of the battlefield itself:

But one the morne the Cristen stode,
A thowsande, over theire fete in theire blode,
Of their awenn wondes wane.
Othere refreschynge noghte many hade
Bot blody water of a slade
That thurghe the oste ran.

                    (1201–6)

The bloody stream running through the host is a eucharistic image that at once evokes the body of Christ in the Passion, the eucharistic host, the bodies of the suffering warriors, and the battlefield itself.[35] All these are unified into a single body, a singular warrior of Christ who besieges the heathen city in the course of a Holy War.

The wounds of Turpin become the focus of attention in the *Sege of Melayne,* as Charlemagne repeatedly begs him to remove the clothing that hides them. After the first injury, Charlemagne asks to see the wound (1184–86); Turpin refuses. After the next wound, Charlemagne asks again (1339–42); Turpin remains silent. Finally, the only surviving manuscript of the poem breaks off just a few lines after Charlemagne, brought to tears by the sight of the suffering Turpin, laments this "floure of presthode" who "will no man his wondes late see" (1584, 1589). Turpin's withholding of the sight of his wounds serves two functions. First, the refusal to uncover is also a refusal of "medicine" (salve, 1188, 1347) that might heal the wounds, and hence part of the overall vow of fasting that Turpin has undertaken, in imitation of Christ's suffering. Second, the refusal to uncover keeps Charles and his knights in a state of tension: I will not eat or sleep, Turpin declares, until the "city be yielded" (1352). The wounds are hidden, and will stay hidden, until the climax of the siege.

On one level, the body of Turpin is a metonym of the city, his clothing covering his wounds in the same way that the walls cover the city. On another level, however, the body of Turpin is a microcosm of siege itself: not just the geography of siege, but the temporality of siege. In this respect, Turpin's body recalls the earliest example of the alignment of body and city we have observed here, the liminal body of Priam in the *Aeneid,* which marks a threshold in time. The enormous pressure upon the city walls is simultaneously exerted upon the body of Turpin, and that pressure will be released — either in life or in death — only when the walls finally give way. His speech is the speech neither of the dead nor of the living: it is the speech of one who is suspended between two states of being. Paradoxically, the hidden nature of his wounds is precisely what makes visible his liminal status. In his mirroring of Christ's passion, Turpin is himself a threshold between the human and the divine.

Although only a single manuscript of the *Sege of Melayne* survives today, the poem must have enjoyed some degree of popularity because it gave rise to an early modern poem with a very similar structure, plot line, and Turpin-like hero. *Capystranus,* named after its own warrior-priest, the Franciscan St. John Capistrano, recounts the siege of Hungary by the Ottoman Turks in 1456.[36] The poem survives in fragments of three early printed editions by Wynkyn de Worde, dating from about 1515 and 1530. Where the *Sege of Melayne* inveighed against the "Saracen" threat, *Capystranus* instead condemns "the Turkes" and, in particular, the individual "false Turke" (68) who rules the Ottomans, "Machamyte, that Turke untrue" (58; that is, Sultan Mehmed II).[37] Mehmed had captured Constantinople in 1453 and moved northward toward Belgrade in the summer of 1456; St. John Capistrano, together with Hungarian reinforcements, entered Belgrade and successfully held off the Ottoman army. This poem draws upon the *Sege of Melayne* for many elements, including the warlike behavior of the heroic priest and his tendency to rail against the Virgin Mary when she fails to help the Christian troops (489–500). The striking difference in *Capystranus* concerns the inversion of suffering that we saw in the *Sege of Melayne,* and which also appears in the Caxton *Siege of Jerusalem:* in those works, those outside the walls are the sufferers, and those within the walls remain unknown and unremarked. Conversely, in *Capystranus,* the Christians are within the besieged city, appealing for help from above when it appears that earthly help is not enough. When the walls begin to fall and the slaughter of women and children begins, the only place to turn for help is above. Fleeing to the top of the tower, Capystranus reenacts the desperate flight from siege we saw in Priam's Ilium, recounted in book 2 of the *Aeneid.* But where Priam flees inward, to a private space at the heart of the palace, Capystranus flees upward, to the summit of the tower, to ask for help. Although salvation comes by means of divine intervention, it is striking that the enemy is no longer described in religious terms, as the "Saracen," but in national terms, as "the Turke."[38] *Capystranus* thus marks an end point in siege poetry in the crusading tradition, as collective identity begins to be identified in terms of national identity instead of religious orientation.

A similar historical episode of attack on Europe by the Ottomans forms the plot of *The Siege,* a novel by Albanian writer Ismail Kadare, written in 1969 and published in 2008 in an English translation by David Bellos. Even though a novel, strictly speaking, lies outside a study of the poetics of siege, it is striking to note some of the ways in which the temporality of premodern siege literature continues to be manifested in this twentieth-century work. Drawing upon a wide range of historical sources, Kadare situates his siege in an unnamed Albanian town, in the period just before the fall of Constantinople in 1453. In this respect, it complements *Capystranus,* which is set immediately after the fall of Constantinople. Written in the extremely closed society of Maoist Albania, Kadare's novel can be read as a political allegory, a veiled expression of the fear that non-Soviet-aligned Communist nations experienced after the invasion of Czechoslovakia in 1968. For our purposes, however, Kadare's *Siege* is useful in the way that it highlights the ambivalence of the scene of suffering. As we have seen, from the *Aeneid* onward, siege literature normally represents the scene of suffering within the walls of the city. Only with the integration of Jerusalem into the genre of siege literature do we find suffering displaced from within the walls onto the encampments without; crusade literature, both poetic and historiographical, perpetuates this displacement, emphasizing the plight of the Christian invaders of the Holy Land at the expense of the displaced local inhabitants. Texts such as *Capystranus*, reflecting the early modern Ottoman threat posed not just to Christendom but also to Europe, return to the conventional model of siege, where suffering takes place inside the walls.

Kadare's novel plays effortlessly with these conventions, foregrounding the suffering outside the walls by devoting the main narration to the Ottoman court chronicler sent to report on the success of the mission, but integrating the suffering within the walls by including short passages — almost letters in a bottle — from the Christians locked up inside. Resisting any easy judgment concerning right and wrong, good and bad, Kadare instead draws the reader's attention to the inexorable forward thrust of time. When the siege begins, the Ottomans march toward the city along the old Roman road ("Via Egnatia," 4),[39] while the defending Christians bring into the city the same icon of the Virgin that had, one hundred years earlier, given a neighboring city "the strength to repulse the Normans" (4). Implicitly, this conquering imperial force is simply one in a series that have come in the past, and the novel's conclusion makes it clear that both the onward pressure of history and the immediate pressure of siege will continue into the future. The Quartermaster tells Çelebi, the Ottoman court chronicler, "Every spring . . . when the green shoots reappear, we will return to these parts" (287). The ultimate success of the siege is inevitable: whether in this iteration or in the next, or in the next one after that, the city will fall, with this particular siege being "a dress rehearsal for [the] onslaught on the Western Rome" (290). At the same time, however, the victims of siege enjoy a different kind of victory: as the Quartermaster of the Ottoman troops puts it, "we are making them immortal . . . by our own hand" (287).

When, in an apparent miracle, the rains come and the Ottoman army retreats, the siege is both over and not yet over: the immediate iteration of siege has ended, but the endless tide of siege presses on. The time of conquest lies ahead, in the future; nonetheless, in Kadare's novel as in the earlier siege literature, the male body continues to stand as a symbol of the movement of power from one imperial center to another. Because the time of that movement of power — that is, *translatio imperii* — still lies in the future, the body itself also continues to remain merely potential and not actual. The novel closes with an account of the death of the Pasha by his own hand after the failure of the siege (313), followed by an apparently causeless miscarriage that results in the death of the Pasha's unborn male child. The aborted body is never made visible, instead appearing only as a repetitive "bleeding" (319, 321) experienced by the Pasha's concubine. This body is not reduced to ashes or scattered in fragments, like the male bodies of the *Siege of Jerusalem* or the *Roman de Thebes*. Instead, it lies prior to the time of full embodiment, as its potential for coming into being lies in as yet unrealized future. The Ottomans *will* come, the city *will* fall, and a new empire *will* rise. It's just a matter of time.

We might say that the body of the warrior is itself the "matter of time." We saw how, in the *Aeneid*, the body of Priam is described as "a huge trunk upon the shore," a liminal object in a liminal space, concealed behind a secret "threshold" (*limen*, 2453) that offers no protection from the invading host. Priam's body marks the in-between space, the metaphorical shoreline that temporally separates empire from empire in the movement of *translatio imperii*. In the *Roman de Troie*, the fragmented bodies of warriors are sumptuously entombed in an attempt to refashion the broken body into wholeness, to take it outside of time through the eternal power of art. This transcendence of local time is emphasized in the comment on Achilles' tomb that "no knight had ever been interred more richly" and echoed in the description of Paris's marvelous tomb: those who see it say that "no king's son had ever had a more beautiful one." Even without the exquisite art of the craftsman, the powdered ashes of the warrior's body can still be part of an effort to conquer time, if not through memorialization, then through dematerialization. Following the model of the dissipated Oedipal lineage in the *Roman de Thebes*, The *Siege of Jerusalem* provides the symbolic spectacle of the body of Caiphas. Transformed into scattered ashes, his body represents in microcosm the dissolution of the community of the Jews and heralds a new era in Christian salvation history. The wounded body of Turpin, poised between wholeness and dismemberment, moves to a different temporal plane as the scene of suffering becomes eternal. Through identification with the suffering Christ, Turpin is suspended outside time, embodying both the unified community of the Christian host and the temporal weight of the siege itself. The body is at once whole and fragmented, opened up in wounds but participating in the wholeness of the divine. In each of these works, the matter of the warrior's body is a crystallization of the human attempt to control time. It is a formal, poetic effort to restrain the forward pressure of translation and to hold back the inevitable climax of siege.

Notes

1. Nancy F. Partner, ed., *Writing Medieval History* (New York: Bloomsbury, 2005); Gabrielle M. Spiegel, *The Past as Text: The Theory and Practice of Medieval Historiography* (Baltimore: Johns Hopkins University Press, 1999), and Spiegel, *Romancing the Past: The Rise of Vernacular Prose Historiography in Thirteenth-Century France* (Berkeley: University of California Press, 1993); Robert M. Stein, *Reality Fictions: Romance, History, and Governmental Authority, 1025–1180* (Notre Dame, IN: University of Notre Dame Press, 2006); and Robert W. Hanning, *The Vision of History in Early Britain* (New York: Columbia University Press, 1966).

2. On the two *Siege of Jerusalem* works, see Suzanne Conklin Akbari, "Placing the Jews in Late Medieval English Literature," in *Orientalism and the Jews,* ed. Ivan Davidson Kalmar and Derek J. Penslar (Hanover, NH: University Press of New England, 2005), 32–50; see also Suzanne Conklin Akbari, *Idols in the East: European Representations of Islam and the Orient, 1100–1450* (Ithaca: Cornell University Press, 2009), 124–35.

3. On the imminent apocalypse and its precipitation by the crusader conquest of Jerusalem as expressed in the historical writing of Lambert of Saint-Omer in his *Liber floridus,* see Akbari, *Idols in the East, 75–89.*

4. Suzanne M. Yeager, *Jerusalem in Medieval Narrative* (Cambridge: Cambridge University Press, 2008).

5. Malcolm Hebron, *The Medieval Siege: Theme and Image in Middle English Romance* (Oxford: Oxford University Press, 1997). On the siege genre, see also Suzanne Conklin Akbari, "Incorporation in the *Siege of Melayne,*" *Pulp Fictions of Medieval England: Essays in Popular Romance,* ed. Nicola McDonald (Manchester: Manchester University Press, 2004), 22–44.

6. On Virgil as a school text, see Christopher Baswell, *Virgil in Medieval England: Figuring the Aeneid from the Twelfth Century to Chaucer* (Cambridge: Cambridge University Press, 1995), 41–83. The *Aeneid* supplemented the chief Latin Troy narrative of the Middle Ages, the *De excidio Troiae* of Dares of Phrygia. See Louis Faivre d'Arcier, *Histoire et geographie d'un mythe: Le circulation des manuscrits du "De excidio Troiae" de Dares le Phrygien (viiie–xve siècles),* Memoires et documents de l'Ecole des chartes 82 (Paris: Ecole des chartes, 2006).

7. On the quadripartite succession of empire in Orosius, see Suzanne Conklin Akbari, "Bodies and Boundaries in the *Roman de toute chevalerie*," in *Postcolonial Approaches to the European Middle Ages: Translating Cultures*, ed. Ananya Jahanara Kabir and Deanne Williams (Cambridge: Cambridge University Press, 2005), 105–26, esp. 106–11, and Fabrizio Fabbrini, *Paolo Orosio, uno storico* (Rome: Edizioni di storia e letteratura, 1979), 364–65.

8. On the disjunction of Orosian/Augustinian and Virgilian historiographical modes, see Theodor E. Mommsen, "Orosius and Augustine," in *Medieval and Renaissance Studies*, ed. Eugene F. Rice Jr. (Ithaca: Cornell University Press, 1959), 325–48. In *Chaucer and the Subject of History* (Madison: University of Wisconsin Press, 1991), Lee Patterson perpetuates Mommsen's distinction but points out how twelfth-century chroniclers such as Otto of Freising influentially worked to "subvert" the division of Orosian/Augustinian and Virgilian historiographical modes: "Asserting the primacy of an institutional unity denominated 'Christendom,' whose existence was marked by its political formation into the significantly named Holy Roman Empire, Otto declared that historical actuality should be endowed with provisional legitimacy" (90). See also Lee Patterson, *Negotiating the Past* (Madison: University of Wisconsin Press, 1991), 157ff., and Hanning, *Vision of History*, 1–43.

9. On the symbolic function of blood in conceptions of lineal descent as related to *translatio imperii*, see Zrinka Stahuljak, *Bloodless Genealogies of the French Middle Ages: "Translatio," Kinship, and Metaphor* (Gainesville: University Press of Florida, 2005), ch. 5: "Translations of Genealogy."

10. "The verse moralizations [of the *Histoire Ancienne*] are scattered throughout the text in fairly regular intervals, but are notably absent from the sections that deal with Theban and Trojan history and that recount the death of Aeneas and Alexander—that is, from precisely those parts of the work most indebted to romance verse narrative" (Spiegel, *Romancing the Past*, 108).

11. On "imaginative historiography" and "imaginative geography," see Akbari, *Idols in the East*, 287–88.

12. On the gendered language of this passage, see Iain Macleod Higgins, *Writing East: The "Travels" of Sir John Mandeville* (Philadelphia: University of Pennsylvania Press, 1997), 35–36.

13. "The ancient city falls, for many years a queen" (urbs antiqua ruit, multos dominata per annos [*Aeneid* 2.363]). Virgil, *Aeneid*, trans. H. Rushton Fairclough and G. P. Goold, Loeb Classical Library 63–64, 2 vols. (Cambridge, MA: Harvard University Press, 1916; rpt. 1999).

14. "Limen erat caecaeque fores et pervius usus / tectorum inter se Priami postesque relicti / a tergo . . ." (*Aeneid* 2.453–55).

15. Note that Aeneas witnesses the carnage but gets away, reassured by his mother, Venus, that she will not rest until she has "set thee safely on thy father's threshold" (*patrio te limine sistam, Aeneid* 2.620).

16. On the three components of the plot in tragedy, see Aristotle, *Poetics* 11.1–5, in *Aristotle: Poetics; Longinus: On the Sublime; Demetrius: On Style,* Loeb Classical Library 199, ed. and trans. Stephen Halliwell (Cambridge, MA: Harvard University Press, 1995).

17. On the intersection of Boethian, Aristotelian, and historiographical models of change in Chaucer's "Knight's Tale" and *Troilus and Criseyde* and in Christine de Pizan's *Livre de la Mutacion de Fortune,* see Suzanne Conklin Akbari, "Small Change: Metaphor and Metamorphosis in Late Medieval Literature" (unpublished manuscript).

18. *Le Roman de Troie publié d'après tous les manuscrits connus,* ed. Léopold Constans, *Société des anciens textes françaises,* 6 vols. (Paris: Firmin Didot, 1904–12); cited parenthetically in the text by line number; translations are my own.

19. The monumental scope of this sarcophagus evokes not only the golden sarcophagus said to contain the body of Alexander in the roughly contemporary Anglo-Norman *Roman de toute chevalerie* (ca. 1170) but also the tomb of the Persian king Darius described in the *Alexandreis* of Walter of Châtillon (ca. 1178; 7.42–77). In Walter's *Alexandreis,* Darius's fabulous monument is said to include a perfectly accurate rendition of the world map upon a globe surmounting the tomb. Darius's cartographic monument may have a common source with the *Roman de Troie*'s description of Paris's sarcophagus, which is followed in the text by an otherwise inexplicable geography of the world.

20. ". . . plus plein de glace, / Vert sunt e pers, jaune e vermeil; / Molt reluisent contre soleil, / Haut sunt e dreit e bataillié: / N'i atendreit lance n'espié" (23096–100).

21. "Li pan des murs e li portal / Entor e amont e aval / Furent asis e bien de pres" (24465–67).

22. For a more detailed account of the alignment of the fall of Troy and the fall of Jerusalem and the place of both episodes within Orosian historiography, see Suzanne Conklin Akbari, "Between Diaspora and Conquest: Norman Assimilation in Petrus Alfonsi's *Disciplina Clericalis* and Marie de France's *Fables,*" in *Cultural Diversity in the British Middle Ages: Archipelago, Island, England,* ed. Jeffrey Jerome Cohen (New York: Palgrave Macmillan, 2008), 17–37, esp. 20–21.

23. On the metaphorical Jerusalem of the Christian community (or the individual soul), see Yeager, *Jerusalem,* esp. 108–34.

24. A notable exception is Hebron, *The Medieval Siege.*

25. On Orosius's view of Jerusalem, see Akbari, *Idols in the East,* 119–21.

26. On Lambert's integrated chronologies, see ibid., 79–80.

27. *The Siege of Jerusalem,* ed. Ralph Hanna and David Lawton, *Early English Text Society,* o.s. 320 (Oxford: Oxford University Press, 2003); cited parenthetically in the text by line number.

28. Parenthetical citations are from the *Roman de Thèbes,* ed. Guy Raynaud de Lage, 2 vols. (Paris: Champion, 1966–1971); cited in the text by line number; translations are my own.

29. Ore sont mort andui li frère
    et pour le pechié de leur pere
    que il onques nul jor n'amerent,
    et pour ses eulz qu'il defolerent,
    qu'il s'avoit tret pour la dolor
    que sa mere ot prise a oisour.
    (9811–16)

30. Michael Johnston, "Robert Thornton and *The Siege of Jerusalem,*" *Yearbook of Langland Studies* 23 (2009): 130.

31. Johnston, "Robert Thornton," 128.

32. On the relationship of the Middle English *Siege* printed by Caxton to its French and Latin precursors, see Akbari, *Idols in the East,* 126–28.

33. *Godeffroy of Boloyne; or, The Siege and Conqueste of Jerusalem,* ed. Mary Noyes Colvin, *Early English Text Society,* e.s. 64. (1893; rpt., Oxford: Oxford University Press, 1926); cited parenthetically in the text by page and line number.

34. *The Siege of Milan,* ed. Alan Lupack, in *Three Middle English Charlemagne Romances* (Kalamazoo, MI: Medieval Institute, 1990); cited parenthetically in the text by line number.

35. For a more detailed account of the Eucharistic language of the *Sege of Melayne,* see Akbari, "Incorporation in the *Siege of Melayne.*"

36. For the historical events see Norman Housley, "Giovanni da Capestrano and the Crusade of 1456," in *Crusading in the Fifteenth Century, Message and Impact,* ed. Norman Housley (Basingstoke, UK: Palgrave Macmillan, 2004), 94–115 and 215–24.

37. *Capystranus,* ed. Stephen H. A. Shepherd, in *Middle English Romances* (New York: W. W. Norton, 1995; rpt. 2003); cited parenthetically in the text by line number.

38. On the terminology of "Saracen" as a simultaneously religious and national/ethnic category, see Akbari, *Idols in the East,* 155–59, and Katherine Scarfe Beckett, *Anglo-Saxon Perceptions of the Islamic World* (Cambridge: Cambridge University Press, 2003), 116–39. On the shift from religious to national alterity in late medieval and early modern Orientalism, see Akbari, *Idols in the East,* 284–85.

39. Ismail Kadare, *The Siege,* trans. David Bellos (Toronto: Doubleday Canada / Bond Street Books, 2008); cited parenthetically in the text by page number.

CHAPTER SEVEN

The Servile Mother

Jerusalem as Woman in the Era of the Crusades

DAVID MORRIS

𝔄 MONG THE SEVERAL VERSIONS of Pope Urban's speech at Clermont, that of Robert of Rheims, written around 1107, presents a distinct curiosity.[1] In Robert's version of events, the pope fervently recounted the alleged atrocities of the Saracens, even mentioning the "abominable rape of women."[2] Shortly thereafter, Urban described the plight of Jerusalem, a city held captive by Christ's enemies and enslaved by "those who do not know God" (*ab ignorantibus Deum ritui gentium ancillatur*).[3] While these elements are not found in some of the earliest accounts of the crusade, such as the anonymous *Gesta Francorum,* Robert's account of the pope's sermon were clearly meant to confer upon Jerusalem the powerful image of an abused and oppressed woman. Specifically, Robert's use of the word *ancillatur* by necessity made the holy city an *ancilla,* a defiled slave woman of the Saracens. Urban apparently further painted this anthropomorphic vision of Jerusalem for his spellbound audience, claiming that "she seeks therefore and desires to be liberated, and she does not cease to implore you to come to her aid. From you especially she asks for help, because, as we have already said, God has conferred upon you above all nations great glory in arms."[4] By invoking these powerful images of subjugation, defilement, and abuse, Robert shows the pope making a conceptual link between the purported rape of women and the violation of a fully feminized Jerusalem.

To understand the origins and the resonance of this image, one must first trace its "pedigree" through the textual culture that would have been known to medieval people, considering the centrality of the Bible in the mental landscape of the Middle Ages. In many cultures, places of origin such as a city or a country generate powerful feelings of attachment that result in the use of the language of parenthood to describe these foci of collective loyalty. By necessity, this linguistic development results in a highly gendered conception of place. Scripture generally prefers feminine terms and applies them to countries, as well as to cities, such as Jerusalem. The Bible's gendered conception of the city is striking because the feminization of towns involves not only the language of parental affection but also that of marriage and sexuality.

This development emerged in the ancient Middle East, where there existed a long-standing tradition of identifying cities as female deities, who were the consorts of the masculine gods whose temples they contained.[5] This metaphor could easily be applied to the spiritual monotheism of the ancient Hebrews, their capital, Jerusalem, and the Temple. Yet the Jewish understanding of this relationship between male deity and female city differed from earlier precedent. Although endowed with a feminine persona, at no point did Jerusalem itself become a goddess.[6] The Hebrews could also see this marriage metaphor in negative terms: if Jerusalem was the wife of Yahweh, she could also be described as a shameless adulteress if the Hebrews proved unfaithful to the covenant.[7] The various Old Testament prophets tried to capture the essence of this mentality by using feminine metaphors to describe the city, thereby conveying the full complexity of the these social and spiritual relationships.[8]

As Jerusalem assumed a greater role in the historical development of the Jews, many of the Old Testament prophets equated that city with the Hebrew people and their covenant with God.[9] This relationship can be seen clearly with Ezekiel's description of God "courting" the city of Jerusalem. God saw Jerusalem growing into full womanhood, with her breasts fully formed and her long hair fully grown:[10] "And I passed by you and saw you and behold, your time was the time of lovers, and I spread my garment over you and covered your ignominy. And I swore to you, and I entered into a covenant with you, says the Lord God, and you became mine."[11] Ezekiel goes on to describe God adorning Jerusalem with extravagant clothes and jewelry,[12] while in a similar vein, Isaiah urges the holy city to don her garments.[13]

However, the language of sexual defilement often came into play whenever the prophets denounced infidelity to the covenant, to the "marriage" as it were, with God. Isaiah exclaims, "How has the faithful city, that was full of justice, become a harlot?"[14] In the Book of Lamentations, Jerusalem groans and turns her face away, since all who once honored her have seen her nakedness.[15] In Chapter 16 of Ezekiel, the author shows God condemning a resplendent Jerusalem: "But trusting in your beauty, you played the whore because of your renown, and you have prostituted yourself to every passerby to be his."[16] Through Ezekiel, God actually calls Jerusalem an adulteress,[17] angrily assuming the role of cheated husband: "Wherein shall I cleanse your heart, says the Lord God, seeing you do all these the works of a shameless prostitute?"[18]

While these passages describe Jerusalem as a proactive entity seeking out her "lovers," other visions of a fully sexualized Jerusalem could also be passive. In Ezekiel, Jerusalem has breasts that have been fondled, as "she played the harlot in Egypt."[19] Likewise, the Babylonians came "into her bed of love," and they "defiled her with their fornications and she was polluted by them and her soul was glutted with them."[20] In Lamentations, Jerusalem's enemies have stretched out their hands "to all her desirable things, for she has seen the Gentiles enter into her sanctuary."[21] Considering that Jerusalem is addressed as a widow at the very beginning of Lamentations, the subsequent account of the city's violation at the hands of her enemies has a sexual undercurrent, conjuring the image of her defilement.[22] Thus, in the midst of these various passages that show Jerusalem as a sexually exploited woman, there is an emerging conception of the feminized city as a victim.

None of these observations is meant to detract from the maternal aspects of Jerusalem found in the Old Testament. For instance, Ezekiel denounces Jerusalem as a treacherous mother, who hands over her children to destruction.[23] From a more positive standpoint, the maternal vision of the holy city is perhaps most clear in Isaiah, when he tells the Hebrews to rejoice in Jerusalem's favor: "That you may suck, and be filled with the breasts of her consolations, that you may milk out, and flow with delights, from the abundance of her glory."[24] Of course, the language of parenthood could go both ways, with the city conceived in filial terms in relation to God: Babylon is described as a daughter in Isaiah,[25] while Jerusalem is addressed as such in Lamentations.[26]

These motifs persisted into the New Testament. In his letter to the Galatians, St. Paul makes the distinction between the earthly Jerusalem and the heavenly Jerusalem, a distinction that would profoundly shape later Christian exegetical discourse. According to Paul, the earthly Jeru-salem represents the Old Law that Christ has superseded. This city is described as a bondwoman (or in the Vulgate, *ancilla*) who shares in the servitude of her children.[27] He then describes the heavenly Jerusalem, "that Jerusalem, which is above, is free, which is our mother."[28] Thus Paul presents his readers with two evocative visions of Jerusalem, either as subservient *ancilla* or as "our mother." In the Book of Revelation, the heavenly Jerusalem is indeed an actual city, with lofty walls, a specified number of gates, and very exact dimensions.[29] Yet Jerusalem is also dis-tinctly anthropomorphic. She comes out of God resplendent in beauty, "prepared as a bride adorned for her husband."[30] In another passage, an angel describes her as the wife of the Lamb.[31]

Building upon scriptural precedents, Latin patristic authors often used feminized images of the holy city to advance their exegetical works, and in so doing, they reinforced the cultural and literary resonance of this mental image. For instance, Jerome explored Paul's dichotomy between Jeru-salem as *ancilla* and as mother in his commentary on Galatians 4:25. While Paul identified the earthly Jerusalem with Hagar and with the Old Law, Jerome identified the heavenly Jerusalem with the Church, calling her "the mother of the saints."[32] He elaborated upon Paul's link between Jerusalem and the Genesis story of Hagar and Sarah. Sarah prefigured the heavenly Jerusalem because she was barren until she gave birth to Isaac, the first of Abraham's legitimate progeny; the Church, identified with the Jerusalem "that is free and the mother of the saints,"[33] was also infertile until the birth of Christ, who represents the first of a new line of spiritual progeny.[34] The need to distinguish between the Jews,[35] as the illegitimate children of Abraham born of the slave Hagar, and the Christians, as the legitimate children of Abraham born of his wife Sarah, only enhanced these various feminine conceptions of Jerusalem, as a city both terrestrial and celestial.[36]

These themes form the central vision of Augustine's *City of God,* in which Augustine used the image of the bondwoman to explain how the material city fulfills its servile role as a reflection of Jerusalem, "the free mother." He enhanced Paul's vision of the spiritual Jerusalem, painting an even more vividly anthropomorphic picture of the city: "Moreover, we are to understand Jerusalem not as the one who is in servitude with her chil-dren, but the one who is our free mother, who according to the Apostle is everlasting in heaven. There, after the labors belonging to life's anxieties and worries, we will be comforted like her small children, borne upon her shoulders and on her lap."[37]

Augustine has employed the evocative imagery of motherhood to describe the relationship between the city of God and its "citizens." In Isaiah's maternal vision of the city, Jerusalem has breasts at which her children are weaned, while Augustine has embellished this conception, giving her shoulders and a lap on which her children are to be consoled.

In all these ways, Christian exegesis reinforced the use of the feminine Jerusalem as a spiritual symbol, an idea often mirrored in liturgy, art,[38] and hymnology.[39] This is not to say, however, that the historical understanding of Jerusalem was lost upon Christian exegetes. While Paul might have made the distinction between the city as *ancilla* and as *mater,* Augustine held that both visions are thoroughly intertwined since the terrestrial city symbolizes or prefigures the celestial one.[40] Indeed, he argued that no prophecy pertains only to the earthly Jerusalem, but either to the heavenly city or to both cities.[41] Thus Solomon's construction of the Temple, a historical event in the earthly city, also prefigured the heavenly city.[42] David reigned in the earthly Jerusalem as a son of the heavenly Jerusalem.[43] Indeed, Augustine calls the earthly Jerusalem a "shadow of the one to come" (*umbra futuri*).[44]

Early medieval exegetes maintained these allegorical and historical readings of the feminine city. According to the Carolingian-era theologian Paschasius Radbertus, the heavenly Jerusalem refers to the Church of Christ in allegorical terms,[45] but the Book of Lamentations also refers to the actual distress suffered by the historical city at the hands of the Babylonians and even more fully at the hands of the Romans under Vespasian and Titus, who destroyed the Temple in 70 C.E.[46] In a similar vein, Hrabanus Maurus equates the defilement of Jerusalem in Ezekiel with all the times the Temple and the Holy of Holies were defiled by the infidel: by the Babylonians, Antiochus, Pompey, and ultimately by Vespasian and Titus.[47]

It was the use of this ancient imagery to describe the immediacy of Jerusalem's subjugation and its application to her contemporary travails at the hands of the Muslims that represented a genuine innovation on a rhetorical and an exegetical level. What changed circa 1100 that allowed centuries of interpretation to become suddenly applicable to the contemporary city, both as mother and as bondwoman? Several explanations could be advanced for why this interpretive shift happened when it did. Indeed, the eleventh century witnessed the opening of routes across Central Europe and the Mediterranean, possibly resulting in a much greater volume of pilgrimage. The era also witnessed an increasing theological and devotional focus on Christ's humanity — hence a greater desire to experience the site of Christ's passion, death, and resurrection.[48] Yet this interpretive shift can also be understood in light of the Gregorian Reform and the Investiture Contest, specifically, in terms of what connotations the word *ancilla*, often in conjunction with the maternal or bridal imagery traditionally associated with the Church, acquired in the discourse inspired by these upheavals in the years and decades before the First Crusade.

Pope Gregory VII (r. 1073–85) often used the image of the *ancilla* to describe the plight of Holy Mother Church, oppressed by temporal interests, contrasting it to the reforming ideal of the *libertas ecclesiae*. In a letter from 1073, addressed to Bishop Roderic of Chalon-sur-Saône, Gregory denounces the princes "of our time who have ravaged the Church of God by selling it with wicked avarice, and who have trodden their mother underfoot" in a manner befitting a slave woman.[49] Writing to Archbishop Sicard of Aquileia, Gregory claims that "the rulers and princes of this world" oppress the Church like a lowly *ancilla* (*quasi vilem ancillam opprimunt*),[50] while he warns Bishop Altmann of Passau to administer his diocese well, "so that the bride of Christ is not regarded instead as a bondwoman."[51] This image of an *ancilla* being trampled upon was also used by Paul of Bernreid in his *vita* of Gregory to describe King Henry IV's oppression of the whole Church.[52] Likewise, Anselm of Lucca attacked the antipope Guibert of Ravenna by describing the current state of the Roman Church with the heated language of adultery: Jerusalem, that is, Holy Church, had been made into an adulteress because of Guibert and his master, King Henry.[53] Anselm then draws on imagery from Isaiah, "The mistress of the nations has become like a widow because the king of Babylon possesses her."[54] After citing the passages where Christ names Peter head of the Church, Anselm declares that "whoever is corrupted by the usurpation of another authority is no longer the bride of Christ, but an adulteress; she is not free, but a slave woman" (*non iam sponsa Christi sed adultera, non libera sed ancilla convincitur*).[55]

From this perspective, no great leap of the imagination is required to take the vision of the Roman Church, the servile mother oppressed by temporal princes, and apply it to Jerusalem, servile mother of the Church oppressed by infidel princes. Indeed, it is difficult to see how the crusading image of Jerusalem as a distressed mother, a battered and oppressed slave woman, could not have been influenced by reform discourse and polemic. Whether it was actually Pope Urban himself or the first generation of chroniclers who made such a connection is almost beside the point: this contemporized vision of a servile mother, applied first to the Western Church and then to the holy city, likely emerged in the reforming circles of the late-eleventh and early-twelfth centuries. This conceptual link of course further demonstrates the well-known and intimate connection between the Gregorian Reform and the crusades.

However, it also speaks to a trend more commonly associated with medieval apocalyptic, the so-called actualization of scripture — that is, identifying images from the Bible with specific people, places, and situations in the contemporary world. Thus the often spiritual, allegorical exegesis that had held sway since late antiquity, a paradigm established by Tychonius and St. Augustine, was partially offset by more literal, contemporized readings. Granted, it would take decades before the heated rhetoric of those dual upheavals of the late-eleventh century, the Investiture Contest and the First Crusade, profoundly shaped the work of serious biblical exegetes, such as Joachim of Fiore (d. 1202), Alexander the Minorite (d. 1271), and finally Nicholas of Lyra (1270–1349) in the fourteenth century. Yet the scale of the transformation is quite striking when we compare earlier exegesis, such as the *Glossa Ordinaria,* with Nicholas of Lyra, the most widely used biblical commentator in the later Middle Ages, who reads the events of the First Crusade directly into his exposition on the Apocalypse.[56] Bernard McGinn has suggested that this profound shift in the way Latin Christians read scripture had its origins in the polemical exchanges of the Investiture Contest, as the reformers and their opponents used images, chiefly from the Book of Revelation, to denounce any number of vices or villains perceived to be undermining their conception of the Roman Church.[57] For example, Rupert of Deutz identified both King Henry and the antipope Guibert with the beast of Revelation 13:1,[58] while a proimperial tract from the 1090s denounces the reformers as "those who have received the mark of the beast and adore his image," identifying them with the whore of Babylon.[59]

The words of scripture were born anew in the events of the time, and in this volatile milieu, the imagery long associated primarily with Jerusalem in either a spiritual or a historical sense could conceivably be made tangible in the form of the contemporary city. Thus the invocation of the feminine Jerusalem, which became a consistent feature of crusade discourse, must itself be seen in this larger context. These rhetorical flourishes collectively demonstrate a change in how medieval people related their understanding of their world to their understanding of the Bible. The cry of this servile woman purportedly heard at Clermont shows how the vision of Jerusalem — like other biblical figures and images over the course of the Middle Ages — came to life in a most striking way.

Yet did Pope Urban actually make this allusion in 1095? It is impossible to know for certain. The reference is not found in any of the other five early accounts of the sermon. Guibert of Nogent, who was not an eyewitness, makes passing reference to the church of Jerusalem as "the mother of the churches" in his version of the speech, but this reference is likewise not found in any of the other, earliest versions.[60] Regardless of who first used the image of Jerusalem as woman, either as bondwoman or as mother, it became a common device in the accounts written within a generation of the First Crusade. Like Guibert's account, most of these feminine conceptions invoke the language of motherhood. Near the beginning of his *Gesta Tancredi* (probably written before 1118),[61] Ralph of Caen refers to the crusade as "that glorious labor that restored to our mother Jerusalem her inheritance."[62] Baldric of Dol describes Jerusalem as a woman in both roles, as mother and as captive: when the crusaders besieged Jerusalem, they came not as stepsons attacking their stepmother, but as sons who had come to rescue their mother.[63] They besieged her "not to capture one who was free, but to free one who was captive."[64] The anonymous coauthor of the crusading poem *Historia Vie Hierosolymitane*[65] calls Jerusalem "the first head of the churches, the mother and nurse of the holy disciples, and witness of life-giving miracles, hallowed by the blood of the first martyrs."[66]

In his history, Fulcher of Chartres describes the resolution of a jurisdictional conflict over the city of Tyre in vividly anthropomorphic terms:[67] "Justly Jerusalem like a mother rejoices over her daughter Tyre at whose right hand she sits crowned as befits her rank."[68] Indeed, Fulcher explains his choice of words within the context of ecclesiastical organization: "Where there was a metropolis, which is interpreted 'mother city,' there were metropolitans who presided over three or four cities within the province of the mother or greater city."[69] Viewed in this light, the holy city is a mother in a twofold sense, both as the mother of the Christians who had come to liberate her and as the mother of the various smaller cities within her ecclesiastical province, her "daughters." This dual understanding is apparent with Ralph of Caen's address to the city, "Behold your sons, O Jerusalem, that have come from afar, and have lifted out of obscurity your daughters, namely Joppa, and many other places that have suffered ruin."[70]

One can make a number of observations based on these examples. First, the reference to the feminine Jerusalem was by no means universal among the first generation of chroniclers. Indeed, the oldest surviving eyewitness account of the campaign, the anonymous *Gesta Francorum* (ca. 1101), lacks any such reference and also lacks many of the scriptural allusions found in other works. Considering that a layman, a Norman knight, probably wrote it, this fact is not surprising. Second, with a few major exceptions like Robert of Rheims, most of the references to Jerusalem as woman invoke the imagery of motherhood. This development can be understood as a reflection not only of Jerusalem's role as the birthplace of Christianity, but also of ecclesiastical organization and hierarchy. Jerusalem is a mother to Tyre and Joppa precisely because of the relation of her patriarch and her church to other local bishops and churches. In effect, most of the early crusade chroniclers had an understanding of Mother Jerusalem that was as much ecclesial as it was scriptural or patristic.

Other visions of Jerusalem suggest the marriage metaphor between God and his holy city among the Old Testament prophets and in Revelation. Indeed, some authors carried this idea further, conceiving of the adulterous violation of this marriage. Baldric of Dol's account, perhaps the most theologically developed of the early chronicles, represents one of the earliest examples of this metaphor. Baldric describes the Christians' capture of Jerusalem in 1099: "Friends and sons surrounded [Jerusalem] and closed in on the interlopers and adulterers."[71] In Albert of Aachen's account of the First Crusade, written in the second quarter of the twelfth century, the Muslim occupation of the city is likewise seen in adulterous terms, with the feminized city, as the "beloved" of God and "mother" of the faithful, being defiled by their enemies. Albert writes of the holy city, "our mother Jerusalem, whom adulterous sons have seized and denied to her rightful sons."[72] The mere presence of Muslims in God's chosen city was an unacceptable outrage. They have committed "adultery" with a city that had been betrothed to God and as such, her "sons," the Christian crusaders, had a right to exact suitably bloody revenge. The first generation of chroniclers all believed that Jerusalem had been defiled by the presence of the Muslims and that their slaughter was a necessary step in ritually purifying the holy city.[73] The application of more overtly sexual themes — Jerusalem as a whore, Jerusalem as a mother who had been prostituted, the Muslims as adulterers — became a common feature of this discourse in the decades after the events of 1099. Again, it is important to remember that this understanding of the feminine Jerusalem was not in and of itself novel, but what was new was the immediacy of her defilement, that the ancient vision of Jeremiah or Ezekiel could be applicable to Jerusalem's present-day distress.

Thus even before subsequent crusades were undertaken, Jerusalem was perceived in the collective memory of the Latin West as a woman living within a whole range of what one may call "kinship" structures. She was a mother to several daughter-cities within the ecclesial hierarchy of the church; she was the mother of the Christian Church as a whole; she was also a mother to the crusaders. In the chronicle accounts, one can see the contrasting images of loving children and their mother, treacherous step-children and their stepmother. She has a husband in God and adulterous paramours in the Muslims. Thus the medieval imagination had constructed a complex world of personal relationships for Mother Jerusalem to inhabit. As additional crusades were launched in the twelfth and thirteenth centuries, this imaginary world was continually evoked in the service of the crusading enterprise.

Many of these themes were elaborated upon over the course of the twelfth century, particularly as Christian rule over Jerusalem grew more tenuous in the years before the city fell to Saladin. An excellent example of this trend can be found in William of Tyre's account of the events that took place in 1095. William, who composed his history between roughly 1167 and 1184, presents a version of the speech at Clermont that has been hailed as a brilliant exercise in scriptural quotation and also rejected as essentially fictitious.[74] Dana Munro, who undertook a thorough analysis of the different accounts of the Clermont sermon, dismissed William as having any independent value as a source on this matter.[75] However, William's account is valuable when we compare his version of the speech to those written in the first generation after 1095. The few references to Jerusalem as woman in these early accounts appear almost minimal in comparison to the role played by the feminine Jerusalem in this later version.

William imagines the holy city as a woman in several instances. God "adopted the Holy City especially as his own."[76] Jerusalem was "chosen from all eternity" (*a saeculis praeelecta*) to be the "witness" (*conscia*) of God's plan of salvation realized in Christ.[77] Consequently, God "loves her" (*diligit ergo eam*) and the fervor of his love for her has not grown cold.[78] At this point, William has Pope Urban paraphrase Isaiah 62:4: "And no more shall you be called desolate, but you shall be called 'my pleasure in her,' because the Lord has been well-pleased with you."[79] William's conception of Jerusalem echoes the marriage metaphor between masculine God and feminine city used extensively by Old Testament prophets such as Ezekiel and Isaiah.

Having described Jerusalem's relationship with God as his "beloved," William then has Urban shift to her mistreatment at the hands of "the impious race of the Saracens."[80] They "violently possess" Jerusalem, which is visualized as the "birthplace of our salvation, the homeland of the Lord, and the mother of religion."[81] William identifies the Saracens with "the son of the Egyptian bondwoman" Hagar, a common medieval reference to Mohammed. This allusion allows William to apply St. Paul's contrast in Galatians 4:25 between the bondwoman and the free mother to the supposed plight of Christians in the holy city. He has Urban claim that the Saracens are oppressing "the captive sons of the free woman," who would have been understood in this context as Mother Jerusalem, the heavenly city.[82] At another point, William quotes the opening verse of Lamentations, claiming that the city of God, "the princess of the provinces, has been made tributary."[83] This specific passage from Lamentations was to enjoy much use in the late twelfth and early thirteenth centuries, after Jerusalem was again in Muslim hands.

Even before the fall of the holy city to Saladin, Archbishop Baldwin of Canterbury stressed the necessity of coming to the rescue of Jerusalem "our mother" in a letter to his suffragans in 1185. Drawing upon the imagery of the Book of Lamentations, Baldwin describes the plight of the holy city. Because "her adversaries have become her lords and her enemies are enriched,"[84] he claims that "our mother Jerusalem cries out to you: she shows us her anguish, and for the remedy of her pain, she demands the affection due of her children [*filiales affectus*]."[85] According to the archbishop, these were children whom Mother Jerusalem had both given birth to and nursed.[86] "Because you are her sons," Baldwin urges, "pay heed to the pains of your mother [*dolores maternos excipite*] and, as Isaiah says, mourn with Jerusalem and share in her pain [*dolete cum ea*] all you who love her."[87]

The full range of the feminine Jerusalem's "social" relationships, plus the scriptural quotations to reinforce them, can likewise be found in a crusading tract by Peter of Blois, *De Hierosolymitana Peregrinatione Acceleranda*. One of the most interesting examples of crusading literature composed after the fall of Jerusalem in 1187, Peter's incendiary writing captures the many facets of Jerusalem's "womanhood." Following Lamentations, he speaks of the holy city as "the mistress of the nations, the princess of the provinces,"[88] while quoting Isaiah, he tells her to put on the garments of her glory.[89] Like earlier authors, Peter also maintains an undertone of Jerusalem's violation, referring to Lamentations 1:10: "The enemy has reached out with his hand for all her desirable things."[90] Later in this tract, he uses the image of Jerusalem as mother in Galatians 4:25 to issue a pointed challenge to his audience, partly by suggesting this theme of sexual defilement; "The Apostle speaks of Jerusalem who is our mother. If she is a mother, where then are her sons? Surely, those who allow their mother to be dishonored, trampled upon, and prostituted are not sons, but rather stepsons."[91] Moreover, Peter claims that "a mark of disgraceful betrayal" awaits those who "do not defend the patrimony of their mother and the inheritance of their Lord."[92]

These themes were also apparent in Pope Innocent III's preaching of the crusade. He explicitly linked the crusading enterprise, perhaps more so than any of his predecessors, to the issue of ecclesiastical reform.[93] Indeed, in his conception, the struggle to retake Jerusalem paralleled the work of reforming the Roman Church institutionally and spiritually. Both struggles, in turn, pointed the way to the spiritual Jerusalem, "for obtaining heavenly glory."[94] In discussing this relationship, Innocent made ample use of the feminine Jerusalem at the Fourth Lateran Council (1215). At the first session, the pope claimed Jerusalem was crying out to those present at the council through Lamentations: "O all you who pass by, look and see if there is any sorrow like mine."[95] Giving voice to Jerusalem's anguish,

Innocent then implored his audience, "Come over to me, then, all you who love me, to free me from such misery. For I who used to be mistress of the nations have been made tributary. I who used to be full of people am now deserted."[96] After denouncing Mohammed as the son of perdition, the pope then exclaimed, "O what shame! What turmoil! What disgrace, that the sons of that bondwoman, those most vile offspring of Hagar, hold captive our mother, the enslaved mother of all the faithful!"[97]

In many respects, Innocent's sermon represents the full convergence of bondwoman and mother. The Pauline distinction between the sons of the *ancilla* and the sons of the "free mother" was present and applied to Muslims and Christians respectively. However, both images were brought together with the subjugation of the holy city. Jerusalem became "*matrem nostram ancillatam.*" The most distinctive feature of Innocent's exhortation was not that he spoke *about* Jerusalem, but that he spoke *as* Jerusalem. Over a century earlier, Pope Urban may have claimed that Jerusalem was crying out for help. At Lateran IV, Jerusalem was indeed crying out for help — through Innocent. The prominence of the woman Jerusalem in this sermon, and its exegetical underpinnings, demonstrate how she was "fleshed out" over the course of the twelfth century.

Notes

1. A useful starting point of discussion for Urban's sermon has been Dana C. Munro, "The Speech of Pope Urban II at Clermont, 1095," *American Historical Review* 11, no. 2 (1906): 231–42. For additional scholarship on the various accounts of the sermon, see Carl Erdmann's comparison in *The Origin of the Idea of Crusade,* trans. Marshall W. Baldwin and Walter Goffart (Princeton: Princeton University Press, 1977), 336–42; Paul Rousset, *Les origines et les caractères de la premiére croisade* (Geneva: A. Kundig, 1945), 53–61; and Penny C. Cole, *The Preaching of the Crusades to the Holy Land, 1095–1270* (Cambridge, MA: Medieval Academy of America, 1991). See also Cole "Christians, Muslims, and the 'Liberation' of the Holy Land," *Catholic Historical Review* 84, no. 1 (1998): 1–10, and David S. Bachrach, "Conforming with the Rhetorical Tradition of Plausibility: Clerical Representation of Battlefield Orations against Muslims, 1080–1170," *International History Review* 26, no. 1 (2004):1–19. For a discussion of Robert of Rheims's account, see Luigi Russo, "Ricerche sull'*Historia Iherosolimitana* di Roberto di Reims," *Studi Medievali,* ser. 3, 43, no. 2(2002): 651–91. Translations of the most contemporaneous accounts of the sermon can be found in

The First Crusade: The Chronicle of Fulcher of Chartres and Other Source Materials, ed. Edward Peters (Philadelphia: University of Pennsylvania Press, 1998), 25–37, and in The First Crusades: A Reader, ed. S. J. Allen and Emilie Amt (Peterborough, ON: Broadview Press, 2003), 39–47.

2. Robert of Rheims, Historia Hierosolymitana, in Recueil des historiens des croisades: Historiens occidentaux, 5 vols. (Paris: Académie des Inscriptions et Belles-Lettres, 1872–1906), 3:728 (hereafter RHC Occ.): "Quid dicam de nefanda mulierum construpatione, de qua loqui deterius est quam silere?"

3. Ibid., 729: "Haec igitur civitas regalis in orbis medio posita nunc a suis hostibus captiva tenetur, et ab ignorantibus Deum ritui gentium ancillatur."

4. Ibid.: "Quaerit igitur et optat liberari, et ut ei subveniatis non cessat imprecari. A vobis quidem praecipue exigit subsidium, quoniam a Deo vobis collatum est prae cunctis nationibus, ut jam diximus, insigne decus armorum." Translation adapted from Peters, The First Crusade, 28.

5. For a fascinating discussion of the feminine vision of the city in the ancient Middle East, see Julie Galambush, Jerusalem in the Book of Ezekiel: The City as Yahweh's Wife (Atlanta: Scholar's Press, 1992), 22: "Whatever the origin of the concept, it was evidently a given in the West Semitic cultures of the ancient Near East that major cities were considered the female, divine consorts of the male gods whose temples they contained."

6. Ibid., 25.

7. Ibid., 26–27.

8. Peter S. Hawkins, ed., Civitas: Religious Interpretations of the City (Atlanta: Scholars Press, 1986), xiv: "The city is the abiding paradigm of human association, for better or worse. Personified as wife, child, murderess, and whore, it provides the collective image under which the Jews might conceive themselves in relationship with God."

9. Wilson, "The City in the Old Testament," in Hawkins, Civitas, 10: "From a theological perspective, Israel's concern for cities has been reduced to a concern for a single city. The fate of Jerusalem is now the fate of the whole of Israelite civilization."

10. Ezek. 16:6. All scriptural quotations in this paper have been adapted from the Douay-Rheims version because of its proximity to the Vulgate.

11. Ezek. 16:7–8.

12. Ezek. 16:10–13: "And I clothed you with embroidery and shod you with violet-colored shoes and I girded you with fine linen and clothed you with fine garments. I decked you also with ornaments and put bracelets on your hands and a chain around your neck. And I put a jewel upon your forehead and earrings in your ears and a beautiful crown upon your head. And you were adorned with gold,

and silver, and were clothed with fine linen and embroidered work and many colors; you ate fine flour and honey and oil and were made exceeding beautiful and were raised to be a queen."

13. Isa. 52:1: "Put on the garments of your glory, O Jerusalem, the city of the Holy One."

14. Isa. 1:21.

15. Lam. 1:8.

16. Ezek. 16:15.

17. Ezek. 16:32–33.

18. Ezek. 16:30.

19. Ezek. 23:1–4: "And the word of the Lord came to me, saying: Son of man, there were two women, daughters of one mother. And they committed fornication in Egypt, in their youth they committed fornication: there were their breasts pressed down, and the teats of their virginity were bruised. And their names were Oolla the elder, and Ooliba her younger sister: and I took them, and they bore sons and daughters. Now for their names, Samaria is Oolla, and Jerusalem is Ooliba."

20. Ezek. 23:17

21. Lam. 1:10

22. Lam. 1:1–2.

23. Ezek. 16:20: "And you have taken your sons and your daughters, whom you have borne to me, and have sacrificed them, to be devoured."

24. Isa. 66:11.

25. Isa. 47:1.

26. Lam. 2:13–15.

27. Gal. 4:25: "For Sinai is a mountain in Arabia that has affinity to that Jerusalem which now is, and is in bondage with her children." The Vulgate reads: "Sina enim mons est in Arabia qui coniunctus est ei quae nunc est Hierusalem et servit cum filiis eius."

28. Gal. 4:26.

29. Rev. 21:12–17: "And it had a wall great and high, having twelve gates, and in the gates twelve angels, and names written thereon, which are the names of the twelve tribes of the children of Israel. On the east, three gates: and on the north, three gates: and on the south, three gates: and on the west, three gates. And the wall of the city had twelve foundations, and in them, the twelve names of the twelve apostles of the Lamb. And he who spoke with me had a measure of a reed of gold to measure the city and the gates thereof and the wall. And the city lies in a foursquare, and the length thereof is as great as the breadth: and he measured the city with the golden reed for twelve thousand furlongs, and the length and the height and the breadth thereof are equal. And he measured the wall thereof an hundred and forty-four cubits, the measure of a man, which is of an angel."

30. Rev. 21:2.

31. Rev. 21:9: "And there came one of the seven angels, who had the vials full of the seven last plagues, and spoke with me, saying: Come, and I will show you the bride, the wife of the Lamb."

32. Jerome, *S. Eusebii Hieronymi Stridonensis Presbyteri Commentariam in Epistolam ad Galatas Libri Tres* (*Patrologoae cursus completus: Series Latina,* comp. J. P. Migne, 217 vols. and 4 vols. Indexes (Paris, 1841–64), 26: 390C [hereafter *PL*]): "Saram autem liberam, in Ecclesia, quae de gentibus congregata est, quae mater sanctorum sit, Paulo dicente: *Quae est mater omnium nostrum.*"

33. *PL* 26: 390D–391A: ". . . et econtrario quae sursum est Jerusalem, quae est libera materque sanctorum."

34. *PL* 26: 390C: "Haec diu non peperit, antequam Christus de Virgine nasceretur, et sterilis fuit."

35. *PL* 26: 390BC: At the very beginning of his commentary on Galatians 4:25, Jerome explicitly identifies the Jews with Hagar, and by extension, the earthly Jerusalem: "Pene cunctorum super hoc loco ista est explanatio, ut Agar ancillam, interpretentur in Lege, et in populo Judaeorum."

36. *PL* 26: 391A: ". . . et eos, qui adhuc litterae serviant, et spiritum timoris habeant in servitutem, de Agar Aegyptia velint esse generatos: eos autem qui ad superiora conscendant, et allegorice velint sentire quae scripta sunt, filios esse Sarae, quae in lingua nostra ἄρχουσα, id est, *princeps* interpretatur, genere feminino."

37. Augustine, *De Civitate Dei,* 20: 21 (*Corpus Christianorum Series Latina,* 176 vols. (Turnhout: Brepols, 1954–65), 48: 737 [hereafter *CCSL*]): "Hierusalem quoque, non illam quae seruit cum filiis suis, sed liberam matrem nostram intellegamus secundum apostolum aeternam in caelis. Ibi post labores aerumnarum curarumque mortalium consolabimur, tamquam parvuli eius in umeris genibusque portati."

38. See, e.g., Chiara Frugoni, *A Distant City: Images of Urban Experience in the Medieval World,* trans. William McCuaig (Princeton: Princeton University Press, 1991), 16–17.

39. For a well-known example, see "In Dedicatione Ecclesiae Hymnus," *Analecta Hymnica,* 51:110, in *Ein Jahrtausend lateinischer Hymnendichtung,* ed. Guido Maria Dreves (Leipzig: O. R. Reisland, 1909), 2:385: "Urbs beata Ierusalem dicta pacis visio, / quae construitur in coelis vivis ex lapidibus, / et angelis coronata ut sponsata comite. / Nova veniens a coelo, nuptiali thalamo / praeparata ut sponsata copuletur Domino."

40. *De Civitate Dei,* 20:21 (*CCSL* 48:737): ". . . sed sunt in eis quaedam, quae ad ultramque pertinere intelleguntur, ad ancillam proprie, ad liberam figurate."

41. Ibid. (*CCSL* 48:554): "Nihil enim erit illic, quod ad Hierusalem terrenam

tantum pertineat, si, quidquid ibi de illa uel propter illam dicitur atque completur significant aliquid, quod etiam ad Hierusalem caelestem allegorica praefiguratione referatur; sed erunt sola duo genera, unum quod ad Hierusalem liberam, alterum quod ad utramque pertineat."

42. Ibid.: "Haec enim et in terrena Jerusalem secundum historiam contingerunt, et caelestis Jerusalem figurae fuerunt."

43. Ibid., 17:20 (*CCSL* 48:586): "Regnauit ergo David in terrena Hierusalem, filius caelestis Hierusalem."

44. Ibid., 17:14 (*CCSL* 48:578).

45. Paschasius Radbertus, *S. Paschasii Radberti Abbatis Corbeiensis in Threnos sive Lamentationes Jeremiae Libri Quinque*, in *PL* 120 (1852): 1066D: "Sed juxta allegoriam, Christi Ecclesia scilicet illa coelestis Jerusalem, quae de coelo descendisse a Deo monilibus adornata suis legitur."

46. *PL* 120: 1063C–D: "Fitque mox vehemens exclamatio prophetae plena fletibus, plena doloribus, plena omni admiratione et stupore moerentis. In qua patenter insinuat subversionem miserae civitatis, et ruinam scelesti populi: non solum sub Chaldaeis accidisse, verum sub Tito et Vespasiano plenius omnia completa fore."

47. Hrabanus Maurus, *Beati Rabani Mauri Fuldensis Abbatis et Moguntini Archiepiscopi Commentariorum in Ezechielem Libri Viginti*, in *PL* 110 (1852): 617B: "Pro quo Septuaginta posuere: Et irrumpent in ea impii et pestilentes terrae, quae exceptis sacerdotibus soloque pontifice, nullus alius audebat intrare, quod scimus et a Babyloniis et a rege Antiocho, Cneoque Pompeio, et ad extremum factum esse sub Vespasiano et Tito, quando templum captum atque subversum est, et omnia perpetrate quae sequens prophetae sermo complectitur." For a full discussion of these two ninth-century exegetes, see E. Ann Matter, "The Lamentations Commentaries of Hrabanus Maurus and Paschasius Radbertus," *Traditio* 38 (1982): 137–63.

48. For a discussion of these issues and how the various conceptions of Jerusalem relate to them, see Sylvia Schein, *Gateway to the Heavenly City: Crusader Jerusalem and the Catholic West (1099–1187)* (Aldershot, UK: Ashgate, 2005).

49. Gregory VII, *Epistola 35: Ad Rodericum Cabilonensem Episcopum* (*PL* 148 [1853]: 317B): "Inter caeteros nostri hujus temporis principes qui Ecclesiam Dei perversa cupiditate venundando dissipaverunt, et Matrem suam, cui ex Dominico praecepto honorem et reverentiam debuerant, ancillari subjectione penitus conculcarunt."

50. Gregory VII, *Epistola 42: Ad Sicardum Aquileiensem Archiepiscopum* (*PL* 148: 322D): "Rectores enim et principes hujus mundi singuli quaerentes quae sua sunt, non quae Jesu Christi, omni reverentia conculcata, quasi vilem ancillam opprimunt."

51. Gregory VII, *Epistola 66: Ad Altmannum Episcopum Passaviensem* (PL 148): "Quia te credo sincero corde amare pro Deo sanctae Ecclesiae honorem et libertatem, volo et praecipio ut summopere cum clericis tuis vel laicis qui ad hoc apti videntur procures, ut sponsa Christi non habeatur amplius pro ancilla."

52. Paul of Bernreid, *S. Gregorii Vita* (PL 148: 065C–D): "Sic nimirum ille, majorum ascendens currum, omnem Ecclesiam superbienti calcaneo supponere, calcandamque praebere, vilem ut ancillam, pro viribus conabatur."

53. Anselm of Lucca, *Liber Contra Wibertum*, in *Libelli de Lite Imperatorum et Pontificum Saeculis XI et XII Conscripti,* ed. Ernst Bernheim (Hanover: Monumenta Germanicae Historica, 1891), 1:520: "*Ista est mater Ierusalem,* et reliqua. Adultera siquidem, quae nunc est in parte tua, olim videbatur Ierusalem, sancta videlicet ecclesia, filia regis David."

54. Ibid.: "Sed, pro dolor! Corrupta est a fratre suo et constuprata usque ad verticem. Omnis decor eius recessit ab ea, facta est quasi vidua domina gentium, quia rex Babylonis possidet eam."

55. Ibid., 520–21: "Cum enim Dominus dicat beato Petro: *Tibi dabo ecclesiam meam,* et: *Pasce oves meas,* et alibi: *Una est columba mea,* quaecunque alterius iuris usurpatione corrumpitur, non iam sponsa Christi, sed adultera, non libera, sed ancilla convincitur."

56. See, e.g., Nicholas's commentary on Revelation 17 and 18 in *Postilla super Totam "Bibliam,"* vol. 4 (1492; rpt., Frankfurt: Minerva, 1971).

57. Bernard McGinn, "Symbols of the Apocalypse in Medieval Culture," *Western Quarterly Review* 22 (1983): 215–83; reprinted in *Apocalypticism in the Western Tradition* (Aldershot, UK: Variorum, 1994).

58. Rupert of Deutz, *Monachi cuiusdam Exulis S. Laurentii de Camalitatibus Ecclesiae Leodiensis Opusculum,* in Bernheim, *Libelli de Lite,* 1:634: "Nonne vides, ubi nunc sedeat Symon, / Nerone fretus, rege simillimo, / Qui cornibus finguntur agni, / Set faciunt veluti dracones?" See John Van Engen's comments on this poem and its role in this process of scriptural actualization in *Rupert of Deutz* (Berkeley: University of California Press, 1983), 32–35. See also McGinn's comments in "Symbols of the Apocalypse in Medieval Culture," 277–79.

59. *Liber de Unitate Ecclesiae Conservanda,* in Bernheim, *Libelli de Lite,* 2:273: "Sed: *Qui acceperant characterem bestiae et adorant imaginem eius, missi sunt in stagnum ignis et sulphuris, ubi est bestia et pseudoprophetae, et cruciabuntur die ac nocte in saecula saeculorum,* sicut dicitur in Apocalypsi per Iohannem apostolum. . . . Haec sunt verba eorum, qui pertinent ad Babylonem."

60. Guibert of Nogent, *Gesta Dei per Francos, RHC Occ.* 4:38: "Et est vobis praeterea summa deliberatione pensandum, si ipsam matrem ecclesiarum Ecclesiam, vobis elaborantibus, ad Christianitatis cultum reflorere, Deo per vos agente, contigerit, ne forte contra propinqua Antichristi tempora ad fidem partes Orientis

aliquas restitui velit," in *Dei gesta per Francos et cinq autres textes,* ed. R. B. C. Huygens (Turnholt: Brepols, 1996), 113.

61. Bernard and David Bachrach suggest this date because the work is dedicated to Arnulf, Patriarch of Jerusalem, who died in 1118. See *The "Gesta Tancredi" of Ralph of Caen: A History of the Normans on the First Crusade,* ed. and trans. Bernard S. Bachrach and David S. Bachrach (Aldershot, UK: Ashgate, 2005), 4.

62. Ralph of Caen, *Gesta Tancredi in Expeditione Jerosolymitana, RHC Occ.* 3:603: "Haec mihi saepius attentiusque consideranti, occurrit felix illa peregrinatio, sudor ille gloriosus, qui matri nostrae Jerusalem haereditatem suam restituit."

63. Baldric, *Hierosolymitanae Historiae, RHC Occ.* 4:97: "Obsederunt, inquam, non tanquam novercam privigni; sed quasi matrem filii."

64. Ibid.: "Obsederunt igitur eam, non ut liberam captivarent, sed ut captivam liberarent."

65. The parts of the poem written by Gilo of Paris can be dated to before 1120. However, the editors of the text do not offer a date for the composition of those parts by the anonymous co-author. See *The "Historia Vie Hierosolymitane" of Gilo of Paris and a Second, Anonymous Author,* ed. C. W. Grocock and J. E. Siberry (Oxford: Clarendon Press, 1997), xxiv.

66. Ibid., 8: "Vrbem Hierusalem, primum caput ecclesiarum, / Matrem ac nutricem sanctorum discipulorum / Atque inspectricem signorum uiuificorum, / Sanguine sacratam primorum martyriorum."

67. Fulcher wrote his *History* throughout the first quarter of the twelfth century, circa 1101–27. See Peters, *The First Crusade,* 47.

68. Fulcher, *Historia Hierosolymitana, RHC Occ.* 3:466: "Recte mater Hierusalem gaudet de Tyro filia, cujus a dextera sedit amodo coronata." Translation adapted from *History of the Expedition to Jerusalem, 1095–1127,* trans. Frances Rita Ryan (New York: W. W. Norton, 1973), 267.

69. Ibid.: "Ubi metropolis erat, quae interpretatur *mater civitas,* metropolitani erant, qui de tribus aut quatuor civitatibus intra aliquam provinciam matri et majori aliarum civitati praesidebant."

70. Ralph, *Gesta Tancredi, Praefatio, RHC Occ.* 3:603: "Ecce filii tui, Jerusalem, de longe venerunt, et filiae tuae, Joppe videlicet; compluresque aliae ruinam pressae de latere surrexerunt."

71. Baldric, *Historia Hierosolymitana, RHC Occ.* 4:97: "Nunc ex converso circumdederunt eam amici, et filii coangustaverunt advenas et adulterinos."

72. Albert of Aachen, *Historia Hierosolymitana, RHC Occ.* 4:469: "Obsessa est autem civitas sancta, et mater nostra Iherusalem, quam adulterini filii invaserunt et legitimis filiis negaverant."

73. See Penny C. Cole, "'O God, The Heathen have Come into Your Inheri-

tance' (Ps. 78:1): The Theme of Religious Pollution in Crusade Documents, 1095–1188," in *Crusaders and Muslims in Twelfth-Century Syria,* ed. Maya Shatzmiller (Leiden: Brill, 1993), 84–111.

74. See William of Tyre, *A History of Deeds Done beyond the Sea,* trans. Emily Atwater Babcock and A. C. Krey (New York: Columbia University Press, 1943), 1:88n67.

75. See Munro, "The Speech of Pope Urban II at Clermont," 234.

76. William of Tyre, *Historia Rerum in Partibus Transmarinis Gestarum, RHC Occ.* 1:40: "Et licet totam, in partem praecipuam, sibi dedicaverit ab initio, peculiarius tamen Urbem sanctam sibi adoptavit in propriam."

77. Ibid.

78. Ibid.: "Diligit ergo eam, nec intepuit erga eam dilectionis fervor."

79. Ibid. William changed the wording of this passage: the Vulgate reads "et terra tua non vocabitur amplius desolata," while William has "et non vocaberis amplius desolata." In Isaiah, Jerusalem will no longer be called forsaken nor her land desolate; in this paraphrase, Jerusalem herself who will no longer be called desolate.

80. Ibid.: "Sarracenorum enim gens impia . . . "

81. Ibid.: "Haec igitur salutis nostrae incunabula, Domini patriam, religionis matrem, populus absque Deo, ancillae filius Aegyptiae, possidet violenter."

82. Ibid.: ". . . et captivatis liberae filiis, extremas imponit conditiones . . . "

83. Ibid.

84. Ibid.: Cf. Lam. 1:5

85. Ibid.: "Clamat itaque ad vos Jerusalem mater nostra: suas nobis exponit angustias, et in remedium sui doloris postulat filiales affectus."

86. Ibid.: "Non est qui sustentet eam ex omnibus filiis, quos genuit, et non est, qui supponat manum ex omnibus filiis quos nutrivit."

87. Ibid.: "Quia ergo filii estis, dolores maternos excipite, et, sicut dicit Isaias' tristamini cum Jerusalem, et dolete cum ea omnes qui diligitis eam." The scriptural reference is actually a paraphrase of Isaiah. 66:10: "Rejoice with Jerusalem, and be glad with her, all you that love her: rejoice for joy with her, all you that mourn for her."

88. Peter of Blois, *De Hierosolymitana Peregrinatione Acceleranda* (*PL* 207 [1855]: 1057B).

89. Ibid. (*PL* 207, 1060C).

90. Ibid. (*PL* 207; 1057B): "Manum suam misit hostis ad omnia desiderabilia ejus."

91. Ibid. (*PL* 207: 1063A–B): "Apostolus dicit: Jerusalem, quae est mater nostra. Si mater est, ubi sunt ejus filii? Sane, qui matrem suam dehonestari, conculcari et prostitui sustinent, non sunt filii, sed privigni."

92. Ibid. (*PL* 207: 1063B): "Imo quod magis est, notam ignominiosae prodi-
tionis incurrunt, si matris suae patrimonium, si sui haereditatem Domini non
defendunt."

93. For a thorough discussion of the role of the crusade in Innocent's pontifi-
cate, See John Gilchrist, "The Lord's War as the Proving Ground of Faith: Pope
Innocent III and the Propagation of Violence (1198–1216)," in Shatzmiller, *Crusaders and Muslims in Twelfth-Century Syria*, 65–83.

94. Innocent III, *Sermo 6: In Concilio Generali Lateranensi Habitus* (*PL* 217
[1899]: 675C): "Triplex autem Pascha sive Phase desidero vobiscum celebrare,
corporale, spirituale, aeternale: corporale, ut fiat transitus ad locum, pro misera-
bili Jerusalem liberanda; spirituale, ut fiat transitus de statu ad statum, pro univer-
sali Ecclesia reformanda; aeternale, ut fiat transitus de vita in vitam, pro coelesti
gloria obtinenda."

95. Ibid.: "De corporali transitu clamat ad nos miserabiliter Jerusalem in Thre-
nis per Jeremiam: 'O vos omnes, qui transitis per viam, attendite, et videte, si est
dolor similis, sicut dolor meus.'" The biblical passage is Lam. 1:12. This verse was
also used as an antiphon at Matins: see the Gregorian Antiphonary (*PL* 78: 769).

96. Ibid. (*PL* 217 [1899]: 675C–D): "Ergo transite ad me omnes qui diligitis
me, ut a tanta miseria me liberetis. Ego enim, quae solebam esse domina gentium,
modo facta sum sub tributo: quae solebam esse plena populo, modo sedeo quasi
sola."

97. Ibid. (*PL* 217: 675D): "O quantus pudor, quanta confusio, quantum op-
probrium, quod filii ancillae, vilissimi Agareni, detinent matrem nostram, matrem
universorum fidelium ancillatam!"

Part Three

Institutional Memory and Community Identity

CHAPTER EIGHT

Saladin in Sunni and Shi'a Memories

MOHAMED EL-MOCTAR

ALADIN HAD A COMPLEX personality and lived in complex times. In Western historiography, a debate is evolving about the conflicting aspects of his personality and motivations,[1] but in today's Sunni and Shi'a memories of Saladin, there is little room for complexity or ambiguity. For the Sunni Muslims, his idealism and sincerity are beyond any doubt. He was the unifier of Islam, the liberator of Jerusalem, and the ultimate example of piety, courage, and selflessness. For the Shi'a Muslims, Saladin was no more than a selfish adventurer and a traitor who compromised with the crusaders, destroyed the most meaningful empire in Islamic history (the Shi'a Fatimid Empire), and betrayed the trust of his political leaders and his people. This chapter traces the development of the image of Saladin from a holistic to a divisive, dogmatic, and simplistic one.

Muslim historians contemporary with Saladin seem to have been influenced by four factors in their assessment of his personality and achievement. The first factor was personal, reflecting close association with and loyalty to Saladin; this is the case of 'Imād al-Dīn al-Āsfahāni (hereafter al-'Imād) (1125–1200), Saladin's personal secretary; Bāhā' al-Dīn Ibn Shaddād (1145–1234), his military judge; and al-Qādi al-Fādil (1131–99), his trusted adviser for many years. These three men had, understandably, a personal attachment to and a deep admiration of Saladin. The second factor was political, such as the affiliation with another Muslim political entity that was fighting with or against Saladin. Ibn al-Athīr (1160–1234) is the best example of a historian who had a strong bias against Saladin for political reasons. He was very loyal to the Zangids of Mosul, in whose praise he wrote his celebratory book *al-Bāhir,* and he opposed Saladin's effort to include Mosul in his empire.

Regional sentiment, the deep attachment that a historian might feel toward the land of his birth, which Gibb called patriotism, was the third factor.[2] Ibn al-Athīr had such attachment to his hometown Mosul, and his negative judgment of Saladin was caused, partially at least, by his regional bias.[3] A later Egyptian historian, al-Maqrīzi (1364–1442), was also deeply influenced by this regionalism in his view of Saladin. The fourth and final factor that worked to influence contemporary representations of Saladin was the doctrinal factor surrounding the Sunni-Shi'a sectarian divisions. This factor does not seem to have had a strong impact on many historians contemporary with Saladin. The Sunni Andalusian-Moroccan traveler Ibn Djubayr (1145–1217) can be said to have admired Saladin mainly for religious and doctrinal motives, especially Saladin's support for the Muslim pilgrims to Mecca and his Sunnism.

These four factors were not mutually exclusive, and none of them alone determines the historian's views and biases; rather, there is much overlap among them. Three of the Sunni historians (al-'Imād, Ibn Shaddād, and al-Fādil) were a part of the close entourage of Saladin and had understandably been very loyal to him. All three idealized Saladin in their writing. Al-'Imād admires Saladin's firmness in faith, steadfastness, and humbleness. He also admires the Sultan's care for Muslim prisoners of war, as well as his benevolence with scholars of religion and Sufi leaders.[4] Ibn Shaddād dedicated chapters of his book, *The Rare and Excellent History of Saladin,* to discussing Saladin's "adherence to religious beliefs and observance of matters of Holy Law," "his justice," "his generosity," "his bravery," "his zeal for the cause of jihad," "his endurance," "his forbearance and clemency," and "his observance of chivalrous behaviour." Ibn Shaddād praises also Saladin's compassion toward the orphans, his pity for the elders, his graciousness toward the prisoners of war of his enemies, and his chivalrous ways in dealing with the Frankish women.[5]

Ibn Jubayr did not meet the Sultan in person, but he visited some of the regions that were under his rule, including his capital Damascus, and observed the impact of his policies and achievements, especially his tax policy.[6] He praises Saladin's fairness, generosity, and "perseverance in jihad."[7] When Ibn Jubayr visited Damascus, he reported that Saladin was absent besieging the Franks in the Kerak fortress, and he praises him for his relentlessness in fighting them,[8] and, when Saladin conquered Jerusalem, Ibn Jubayr sent him a celebratory poem in which he praised the conquest as a great victory that no Muslim king before Saladin could have achieved.[9]

A traveler and pilgrim, Ibn Jubayr was especially impressed by Saladin's decision to lift what he called "this cursed tax,"[10] imposed on Muslim pilgrims to Mecca by the rulers of Hijāz. This issue seems to have shocked Ibn Jubayr's religious feelings and become a source of suffering and a personal obsession for him. He could not stop writing about it again and again in his *Rihlah*.[11]

Ibn Jubayr was very proud of his Sunni-Maliki doctrine and North-African identity, and he judges very negatively the Shi'a of Syria and what he presents as their "deviations," "fabrications," and "strange ways" of practicing Islam.[12] He condemns specifically the Shi'a Nizaris (the Assassins) as atheists and calls their leader Sinān "a human monster."[13] These doctrinal and regional orientations explain his favorable view of Saladin.

One paragraph of Ibn Jubayr's text is especially worth mentioning here, because it is in sharp contrast with what a contemporary Shi'a scholar of his said about the sultan. Saladin's name in Arabic is composed of two words: Salāh (reform) and al-Dīn (faith), so the name means literally "Reform of the Faith." Names with a connotation of serving the faith were fashionable among the Muslim leaders of that time. For example, Saladin's father is Nadjm al-Dīn (Star of the Faith), his uncle is Asad al-Dīn (Lion of the Faith), his brother is Shams al-Dīn (Sun of the Faith) and above all, Saladin's master is Nūr al-Dīn (Light of the Faith). Ibn Djubayr commented that among all Muslim leaders of Syria, Egypt, and Andalusia with such fashionable names, none was worth his name except Saladin.[14]

This was not how the Shi'a jurist Abū Turāb (1132–1217) looked at the matter. In one of the earliest cases we have on the Shi'a negative view of Saladin, Abū Turāb, who was in Baghdad, met a man who had recently arrived in Iraq from Morocco, passing by the way of Egypt. It seems that meeting this traveler reminded Abū Turāb of the Shi'a Fatimid rule in Egypt and made him very emotional. Abū Turāb "wept and said: 'may God not be pleased with Salāh al-Dīn (Saladin). He is *fasād al-dīn* (destruction of the faith), he expelled the [Fatimid] Caliphs from Egypt,' then he started cursing him." The Moroccan traveler, who was obviously Sunni, stood up and left angrily.[15]

One can add to these historians more than fifty poets,[16] contemporaries of Saladin, who praised his victories and celebrated his generosity. Saladin's secretary, al-'Imād, quotes a great amount of this poetry in his encyclopedic collection, *Kharīda*,[17] and some modern Arab historians have provided a comprehensive survey of these poets and their poetry.[18] Any study of Saladin's image in Islamic culture needs to take the Arabic poetry written about him into account. To do justice to this poetry would require a separate study, but for my purposes here it is sufficient to make the following two observations. First, one of the frequently used metaphors in this poetry is the presentation of Saladin (whose first name is Yūsuf (the Arabic equivalent of *Joseph*) as a new Joseph, like the Joseph of the Bible and the Qur'an, who came to Egypt from the desert and saved its people from a devastating famine.[19] Second, some of the poets who met Saladin and praised him in their poetry, such as 'Arqalah al-Kalby, were Shi'a,[20] and the only two poets who attacked him, 'Umārah al-Yamany and Ibn 'Innīn,[21] were Sunnis.[22]

The view held by many historians today is that Saladin was a Sunni hero followed and supported by Sunni followers. But the sources surveyed here suggest that Saladin's good reputation in the Islamic world of his time was not limited to Sunni circles; rather, it crossed the sectarian divide between the Sunnis and the Shi'a. The sources suggest also that not all the Sunni contemporaries of Saladin perceived him positively, nor were all his Shi'a contemporaries hostile to him. Ibn Abī Ṭay (1160–1234) and Ibn al-Athīr (1160–1234) aptly demonstrate this point. Each of these historians stands an obstacle in the face of any sweeping generalization about the way Saladin was perceived and received by the Sunnis and the Shi'a of his time.

Ibn Abī Ṭay was the only Shi'a contemporary biographer of Saladin. He had a deep admiration for Saladin, but he had hated Saladin's master Nūr al-Dīn, who oppressed the Shi'a of Aleppo, including Ibn Abī Ṭay's own father, a Shi'a scholar and leader who was sent into exile by Nūr al-Dīn.[23] The extracts from his lost biography of Saladin that survived in Abū Shāmah's *Book of the Two Gardens* show Ibn Abī Ṭay to have been very loyal to Saladin.[24] He presents him as a man who "raised the flag of justice and benevolence and erased the traces of injustice and aggression."[25] He had specifically high esteem for Saladin's nobility of spirit, ability to control his anger, and willingness to forgive the petty Syrian and Mesopotamian lords who were opposing him.[26] Ibn Abī Ṭay's loyalty extended beyond Saladin to the whole Ayubid family. He writes highly of Saladin's father Nadjm al-Dīn,[27] his uncle Shīrkuh,[28] and his brothers Turan ah[29] and Farrukh Shah.[30]

Throughout his long narrative of Saladin's control of Egypt, Ibn Abī Ṭay does not express any sympathy with the Shi'a Fatimids of Egypt. To the contrary, he calls them Isma'ilis[31] and Egyptians,[32] as if he wanted to distance his brand of Shi'ism (the Twelver Imamism) from theirs (the Sevener Isma'ilism). He also approvingly quotes texts of Sunni scholars and poets accusing the Fatimids of heresy.[33] Ibn Abī Ṭay's attachment to Saladin and lack of sympathy with the Shi'a Fatimids can be seen also in the way he presented the coup d'état attempt against Saladin by a group of notables who were a part of the Fatimid political elite (though their leader 'Umārah al-Yamany was Sunni). Ibn Abī Ṭay calls them simply "a group of sympathizers with the Egyptians . . . who conspired secretly and decried the downfall of the rule of the Egyptians."[34] He then approvingly quotes a long letter from Saladin to Nūr al-Dīn describing the details of the conspiracy and condemning the conspirators as wicked apostates.[35]

More telling of the complex sectarian map is that Ibn Abī Ṭay expresses deep contempt toward the Shi'a Isma'ili community of his own city Aleppo, accusing them of "burning the markets of Aleppo" and creating much discord and confusion in the city.[36] He exhibits more contempt toward the Shi'a Nizaris (the Assassins) who tried to murder Saladin several times; he even cursed repeatedly the Assassins' leader, Sīnān.[37]

Unlike Ibn Abī Ṭay, Ibn al-Athīr was a committed Sunni in his doctrine, but he exhibited a manifest bias against Saladin, especially when the issue at hand involved Nūr al-Dīn and the Zangids of Mosul. Ibn al-Athīr implies several times that Saladin was driven by selfish ambitions and that he betrayed the Islamic cause whenever it served those ambitions. Three examples illustrate Ibn al-Athīr's view of Saladin. The first and most detrimental accusation to the Sultan's reputation is Ibn al-Athīr's affirmation that Saladin did not really want to eradicate the Frankish states on the eastern Mediterranean coast because they were a buffer that protected him from his master Nūr al-Dīn and the only guarantee of his permanent control of Egypt.[38]

Ibn al-Athīr also claims that when Saladin sent his brother to conquer Yemen, this manifested again his fear that Nūr al-Dīn might strip him of Egypt. Saladin, according to Ibn al-Athīr, was actually preparing the ground in Yemen as a potential location for his personal kingdom rather than attempting to protect Sunnism in Yemen.[39] In a third example of this vilification of Saladin, Ibn al-Athīr interprets Saladin's hesitation to omit the name of the Fatimid Caliph from the Friday's sermons, not as a wise tactic required by the shaky situation in Egypt, but as a malicious disobedience that proves Saladin's willingness to protect his realm from Nūr al-Dīn even by allying himself with the Fatimid heretics.[40] As these three examples show, Ibn al-Athīr systematically denigrated Saladin, despite their shared Sunni doctrine.

Ibn al-Athīr's negative assessment of Saladin was quickly rendered mute, however, by the synthesis of Abū Shāmah (d. 1267), in which both Nūr al-Dīn and Saladin are presented as a part of the same line of the Sunni revival and resistance to the crusades. Abū Shāmah affirms that Saladin built on the foundations of Nūr al-Dīn and completed the work that Nūr al-Dīn had started.[41] He quotes Ibn al-Athīr's claim that Nūr al-Dīn was at one point about to invade Egypt and strip it from Saladin, who "was not serious in fighting the Franks," then Abū Shāmah refutes this claim.[42] Abū Shāmah's synthesis can be seen as a desire among the Sunnis to keep the image of their two heroes intact, instead of putting one of them in opposition to the other. This way of looking at the two men was adopted by the majority of later Sunni historians and is still followed by many Arab historians today.

Abū Shāmah is also different from the previous Sunni historians in his doctrinal interpretation of history. Among the Sunni historians who preceded Abū Shāmah only Ibn Jubayr and al-Qadi al-Fādil emphasized Saladin's Sunnism. But al-Fādil's work for the Fatimids in the years before Saladin controlled Egypt may lead us to doubt his doctrinal sincerity. Moreover, a survey of al-Fādil's correspondence in the name of Saladin shows that he emphasizes Saladin's Sunnism only in the letters addressed to the Caliph of Baghdad, who was an unyielding rival of the Fatimid Caliphs.[43] Through these letters, both Saladin and al-Fādil seem to have been exercising some diplomatic maneuvering more than expressing sincere doctrinal conviction. Abū Shāmah, however, is different. He deemphasizes the differences between the two Sunni leaders, Nūr al-Dīn and Saladin, for the sake of a doctrinal harmonization within Sunnism, and he expressed high praise for Nūr al-Dīn for "humiliating the Shi'a of Aleppo and suppressing their rituals, and strengthening the Sunnis."[44]

More than a century after Saladin, regional particularism begins to reemerge again as a force shaping the historiography on Saladin in the writings of al-Maqrīzi. This Sunni Egyptian historian authenticates the Fatimid politicized lineage against the views adopted by the majority of the Sunni historians.[45] He also criticizes Saladin on major issues, accusing him implicitly of erasing the traces of the Fatimid states and dethroning and murdering al-ʿĀdid, the last Fatimid Caliph.[46] He expresses deep sympathy for the Fatimids and dramatizes their loss of the authority in Egypt, saying, for example, that "the prince among them became a mere doorkeeper in his former home, a mere handler of the horse he used to ride, or a mere agent in the fief he used to own, among other sorts of humiliations."[47] In his description of the early stage of Saladin's rule of Egypt, al-Maqrīzi writes that Saladin "managed the affairs of the state, spent its treasures and enslaved people."[48] Al-Maqrīzi's stand can only be understood within what Ulrich Haarmann calls "regional sentiment in medieval Islamic Egypt."[49]

Ever since al-Maqrīzi's time it is difficult to find a Sunni historian who criticizes Saladin and sympathizes with the Shi'a Fatimids, even when one takes regional biases into account. The doctrinal factor prevailed in the end. The purely doctrinal interpretation of Saladin's life and career based upon Sunni-Shi'a polarization began with the Salafi scholar Ibn Ṭaymiyah (1263–1328), but it would become dominant only after the death of al-Maqrīzi and the removal of his intellectual influence. Ibn Ṭaymiyah was a theologian and an apologist more than a historian, but two of his disciples, al-Dhahabi (d. 1347) and Ibn Kathīr (d. 1373), wrote extensively on the topic of Islamic history. Both scholars rewrote history in a manner congruent with their teacher's anti-Shi'a rhetoric and emphasized Saladin's role as the defender of Sunnism and destroyer of Shi'ism, not his character as a universal Muslim hero.[50]

Ibn Ṭaymiyah's legacy was revived by Muhammad Ibn ʿAbd al-Wahhāb (1703–92) the intellectual father of today's Salafism, better known (though pejoratively) as Wahhabism. This line of thinking, which reads the demise of the Fatimids as Saladin's most important achievement, is reflected in the title of the 2008 biography of Saladin, written by a Libyan Salafi historian, ʿAli Muhammad al-Sillābi — *Saladin: His Effort in Destroying the Fatimid State and Liberating Jerusalem.*[51] Competing with this Salafi revival, which started more than two centuries ago, there is today a strong movement of Shi'a revival and self-affirmation in several regions of the

Islamic world, especially in Iran, in Lebanon, and very recently in Iraq.[52] Saladin's image in the Muslim mind today seems to be caught in the crossfire of these two rival revivals.

The twentieth-century witnessed an explosion of Arabic biographies of Saladin.[53] This trend has not abated in the first decade of the twenty-first-century. In fact, two Arabic biographies of Saladin, including that by 'Awad and another by al-Sillābi (mentioned above), were published in 2007 and 2008, respectively. It is quite revealing that this modern interest in Saladin was inaugurated with a fictionalized historical novel written by a Lebanese Christian intellectual and Arab nationalist, Djurji Zaydān, published in Cairo in 1913.[54] Zaydān seems to have set the tone for a nationalistic interpretation of Saladin that deemphasizes religious characterizations while promoting the great Sultan as an Arab hero. This interpretation of Saladin is no less legitimate than the other representations. Though ethnically Kurdish, Saladin was deeply rooted in the chivalric culture of the ancient Arabs.[55] Ibn Shaddād writes that Saladin "knew by heart the genealogies of the Arabs and their [ancient] battles and was knowledgeable about their past histories and ways. He [even] knew the pedigrees of their horses."[56]

Many adopted this modern nationalistic interpretation of Saladin, not only among the Arab Christians who are disinterested in the Sunni-Shi'a divide, but also among the Sunni Arab nationalists and secularists. Even the religious Muslim intellectuals who reiterated what Ibn Shaddād and al-'Imād wrote about Saladin's character and achievements could not escape a nostalgic nationalistic tone, which reflects a need for a hero to unite the Arabs and to free the Arab lands from Israel, "the new Crusader state of the Middle East."[57]

The reemergence of the purely sectarian and argumentative presentation of Saladin that we see today started only after the Iranian Revolution of 1979 and the Iraq-Iran war of 1981–88, with their political and ideological implications. Unlike the Shi'a historian, Ibn Abī Ṭay, who deeply admired Saladin, and the Shi'a poets who praised him in his lifetime, today's Shi'a historians and intellectuals have no admiration or respect for him. In 1993, the Egyptian writer Salih al-Wardāni, published his book *The Shi'a in Egypt from Imam 'Ali to Imam Khomeini*.[58] Al-Wardāni, who converted to Shi'ism under the influence of the Iranian Revolution, dedicated a chapter of the book to "Saladin: [the man who] tolerated the

Crusaders and Oppressed Muslims" — the first systematic attack on Saladin in Arabic language as far as I know.

Al-Wardāni begins the chapter by asking Muslims to reevaluate Saladin, a man "whose deviant behavior has been overlooked by his military accomplishment."[59] He then presents his own evaluation of the Sultan, accusing him of leading a coup d'état against the Fatimids that did not serve Islam,[60] of committing war crimes against the Shi'a population of Egypt, of exercising political hypocrisy when he expressed his grief for the death of the Fatimid Caliph al-'Ādid and attended his funeral "while he was the primary cause of al-'Ādid's death."[61] As opposed to his brutality against the Shi'a, al-Wardāni argues, Saladin showed tolerance, even negligence, in his relations with "the enemies of Islam and Muslims, the crusaders,"[62] allowing them, after his conquest of Jerusalem, to leave safely with their treasures, children, and wives.[63]

In 1994 a Lebanese Shi'a historian, Hasan al-Amīn, published his book, *Saladin between the Abbasids, the Fatimids and the Crusaders*,[64] a sophisticated attempt to discredit Saladin that quickly became the normative Shi'a reference on him. Al-Amīn offers a long list of accusations against Saladin. In order to protect his personal authority, al-Amīn argues, Saladin deliberately avoided a decisive confrontation with the Franks, which would have eradicated them many years before the battle of Hattin (Hittīn),[65] when he withdrew from a concerted attack against Kerak with his Syrian master Nūr al-Dīn. Moreover, al-Amīn claims, Saladin deliberately left a part of the eastern Mediterranean coast in the hands of the Franks after Hattin,[66] and he tried to marry his brother to Richard's sister in the hope of building a strong alliance with the Franks against the Caliph of Baghdad, al-Nāsir, who was about to send an army to Palestine to complete the task that Saladin had started at Hattin.[67]

In contrast to his oppression and murder of Muslims who differed with him for theological or political reasons, Saladin, argues al-Amīn, was actually very soft and tolerant with Jews and Christians. For example, he had "suspicious" relations with the Jewish physician and theologian Mūsa Ibn Maymūn (Maimonides), whom he made his personal physician. Western historians' praises of Saladin are, for al-Amīn, a payment of the debt they owe him, because, by agreeing to a truce with King Richard I, he contributed to developments that would ultimately allow the Christians to retake Jerusalem during the reign of his nephew al-Kamil.[68]

In the last phase of his life, argues al-Amīn, Saladin "preferred rest over Jihad" and was willing to give up the Islamic lands to the Franks rather than continuing the fight.[69] While al-'Imād, followed by many historians today, presents Saladin's acceptance of the Ramla Treaty with Richard as inevitable, because of the declining morale of his armies and the longing of his military commanders for rest and for going back to their homes and fiefs, al-Amīn writes that it was Saladin himself who "wanted to rest" instead of finishing the job.

Al-Amīn's book drew strong reactions from Sunni historians. So many of them rejected his thesis outright that he felt compelled to add more than a hundred pages of counterattacks to the second edition of the book (published in 1999).[70] One of the most serious refutations of the book was made by Shakir Mustafā, an accomplished Sunni historian and former minister of culture in the Syrian government. In his book, *Saladin: The Denigrated Holy Warrior and Pious King*,[71] Mustafā focuses on the historical details related to Saladin's relations with Nūr al-Dīn in Aleppo and with the Caliphs in Baghdad.

As for al-Amīn's accusation that Saladin shielded himself from Nūr al-Dīn behind the Latin States, Mustafā argues that Saladin and Nūr al-Dīn had similar goals, but different approaches and priorities.[72] Despite some tactical disagreement, exemplified by Saladin's unilateral withdrawal from the Kerak operation, the two men understood well the common goals they shared.[73] Mustafā argues also that Saladin's letter to Nūr al-Dīn about the Fatimid conspiracy to overthrow him was written a month and a half before Nūr al-Dīn's death, proving that the relations between the two were strong until the end.[74] With regard to the accusation that Saladin rejected the military support of the Caliph al-Nāsir and preferred to compromise with the Franks, Mustafā argues that for the eighty-seven years between the First Crusade and the battle of Hattin, the Caliphs of Baghdad never sent an army to fight the Franks and that al-Nāsir himself lived thirty-three years after the death of Saladin, and he never sent or tried to send an army to fight the Frankish armies.[75]

Based on the above survey and discussion, some conclusions make themselves readily apparent. The doctrinal difference between Sunni and Shi'a Muslims was not a crucial factor in the way contemporary historians of Saladin judged his personality and achievements. This statement is in line with the broader conclusion of Gibb on the "indifference to sectarian divisions" between Sunnis and Shi'a in the Muslims' reaction to the crusades.[76] Personal, political, and regional biases seem to have had more impact on the early historians of Saladin studied here. A good illustration of this point is the striking fact that the Shi'a historian Ibn Abī Ṭay and some Shi'a poets of that time had a strong attachment to Saladin. Meanwhile, the Sunni historians Ibn al-Athīr and al-Maqrīzi, and at least two Sunni poets of the time period, were obviously opposed to him.

The personal and political factors that played a part in determining Muslim historians' views of Saladin for the most part disappeared after Saladin's generation. The regional factor continued for some time, while the doctrinal factor persists to this day. A synthesis of the Sunni views of Saladin into one ideological stream started with Abū Shāmah and was intensified by Ibn Ṭaymiyah and his disciples, but it took centuries for this development to reach the purely doctrinal image of Saladin that dominates today's Sunni writings on him. The same model can be applied for the Shi'a memories of Saladin, which were diverse and pragmatic in the past but which have evolved into the one-dimensional and dogmatic view prevailing today. The only exception to this Shi'a modern view of Saladin is to be found among the Isma'ilis, who are, ironically, the ideological descendents of the Fatimids and the Assassins who tried to kill him in his lifetime. The Syrian Isma'ilis are currently developing a self-glorifying interpretation of their history that makes them allies with Saladin at Hattin and during his conquest of Jerusalem. The works of the Isma'ili historian 'Arif Tāmir exemplify this tendency.[77]

It is also worth emphasizing here that today's Shi'a critics of Saladin base their criticisms of Saladin on the legacy of some Sunni Historians. Both al-Wardāni and al-Amīn, for example, build on the legacy of the Sunni Ibn al-Athīr, not on the legacy of the Shi'a Ibn Abī Ṭay. These two early historians of Saladin were exact contemporaries (both were born in 1160 and died in 1234). The Sunni one (Ibn al-Athīr) had never even met Saladin, while the Shi'a one (Ibn Abī Ṭay) was close to him and to the Ayubid Family in general. While most of the Western and Sunni scholars of the crusades tend to disregard as biased Ibn al-Athīr's negative characterization of Saladin, the Shi'a authors defend Ibn al-Athīr's trustworthiness and rely on him in this regard. Al-Amīn, for example, borrowed many of Ibn al-Athīr's old accusations against Saladin, especially with regards to the latter's relations with his master Nūr al-Dīn, and transferred them to the relations between Saladin and the Caliph al-Nāsir. Al-Amīn dismisses the Sunni historians, al-ʿImād, Ibn Shaddād and Abū Shāmah, and calls them simply "agents" of Saladin,[78] but the fact that he and other Shiʾa critics of Saladin rely in their argument on Ibn al-Athīr, who is another Sunni historian, proves how evolving and evasive Saladin's image has become in Sunni and Shiʾa memories.

Today's Shiʾa arguments against Saladin, as well as the counterarguments made against their deconstruction of Saladin's exemplary status, should be understood within the context of the current sectarian conflict between the two branches of Islam. Some Sunni historians present the Shiʾa as a "fifth column" for the Frankish and the Mongol invasions,[79] and the Shiʾa historians are fighting back against this denigration, upholding the reputation of their ancestors and building legitimacy for their coreligionists. In his criticism of Saladin the Egyptian Shiʾa convert, al-Wardāni, is motivated by a desire to legitimize the emerging Shiʾa minority of Egypt today. As for al-Amīn, he clearly has a strong sectarian attachment to the Fatimid Shiʾa dynasty and to the Caliph al-Nāsir of Baghdad, who was also positively inclined toward the Shiʾa doctrine despite his political problems with the Fatimids. But al-Amīn's works are much more significant: what he tried to do is no less than to rewrite the entire history of Islam in a way that legitimizes Shiʾism — a typical act of identity building. A broader look at the works of al-Amīn justifies such conclusion.[80]

It is crucial to recognize that Saladin was neither the saintly leader today's Sunni historians promote, nor the selfish adventurer Shiʾa historians portray. His "fundamental sincerity" is not difficult to establish from the historical evidence,[81] but he had his moral and practical weaknesses. Passing judgment on Saladin's personality and achievements proves extremely hard, because he combined idealism and realism, tolerance and ruthlessness, bravery and caution. In Egypt, Saladin sent his brother al-ʿĀdil to crucify three thousand Nubians who rebelled against him, but he exhibited a deep sorrow for the death of his political rival the Fatimid Caliph al-ʿĀdid;[82] in Syria, he killed the Templar and Hospitaller prisoners of war in a celebratory manner, but he was moved to tears by a Christian woman who lost her young daughter on the battlefield.[83] This mixed record does not deprive Saladin of the chivalrous status he was given by many historians. Other medieval chivalrous leaders, such as

Richard Coeur de Lion, had their own mixed record. The Middle Ages were times of "noble ideals and bloody realities,"[84] and medieval chivalry was, as Maurice Keen accurately remarks, a combination of "beauties and brutalities."[85] The chivalrous Saladin was a man of his time.

From a historical point of view, the Sunni image of Saladin today is more grounded in his medieval representations than the Shi'a argumentative and speculative attacks on him. The Sunni view is also closer to the generally positive view of Saladin in the Western literature. However, the Shi'a negative portrayal of Saladin is very important, because it is forcing the Sunnis today to reevaluate and demystify their views of this great sultan and replace it with a more historical one. The clash of the two memories is currently very tense and must be explored further by scholars should they wish a deeper understanding of the Sunni-Shi'a divide: its past roots and its future implications.

Finally, Saladin was deeply aware of the importance of a good image both for himself and for his cause. Al-'Imād related a telling story that illustrates this awareness. He writes that he saw the Patriarch of Jerusalem leaving the city after Saladin conquered it, and he told Saladin that the Patriarch was carrying with him a great treasure. In an attempt to seduce the sultan to confiscate this wealth, al-'Imād claimed that the safe-conduct the inhabitants of the city had with Muslims did not include the treasures of the churches and monasteries. Saladin, however, was not ready to compromise his oath. He told his secretary: "If we make excuses [to confiscate this wealth] they [the Franks] will accuse us of treachery . . . let us not make them accuse people of faith of breaking their oaths. Let them go. They will talk about our benevolence."[86] Eight centuries after the death of Saladin, one cannot but accept how visionary Saladin was in this regard. From William of Tyre to the Western historians of the twenty first-century, Christians are still talking and writing about Saladin's chivalry and benevolence. As long as the books of history keep such anecdotes of Saladin's life and character, his legacy will last and his image will resist vilification.

Notes

I wish to express my deep gratitude to Dr. John Howe and Dr. Saad Abi-Hamad from Texas Tech University, two serious scholars and compassionate teachers, for revising this chapter and giving their precious feedback.

1. On this debate, see H. A. R. Gibb, *Studies in the Civilization of Islam* (Princeton: Princeton University Press, 1962), and Gibb, *The Life of Saladin from the Works of Imad Ad-din and Baha' Ad-din* (Oxford: Clarendon Press, 1973); Andrew Ehrenkreutz, *Saladin* (New York: State University Press of Albany, 1972); Malcolm Lyons and D. E. P. Jackson, *Saladin: The Politics of the Holy War* (Cambridge: Cambridge University Press, 1982), 365–74; P. M. Holt, "Saladin and His Admirers: A Biographical Reassessment," *Bulletin of the School of Oriental and African Studies* 46, no. 2 (1983): 235–39; Carole Hillenbrand, *Salāh al-Dīn: Tatawwur Usturah Gharbiyah*, in *800 'Am: Hittin, Salāh al-Dīn, wa al-'Amal al-'Arabī al-Muwahhad* (Cairo: Dar al-Shuruq, 1989), 108–9; and Hillenbrand, *The Crusades: Islamic Perspectives* (New York: Routledge, 2000).

2. H. A. R. Gibb, "The Arabic Sources for the Life of Saladin" *Speculum* 25, no. 1 (1950): 63.

3. On the reasons of Ibn al-Athīr's bias against Saladin, see H. A. R. Gibb, "Notes on the Arabic Materials for the History of the Early Crusades," *Bulletin of the School of Oriental Studies* 7, no. 4 (1935): 739–54; Gibb, "The Arabic Sources," 58–72; Suhayl Zakkār, *Hittin: Masīrat al-Taharrur min Dimashq ila al-Quds* (Damascus: Dar Hassan, 1984), 13–14; and Muhammad Mu'nis 'Awad, *Salāh al-Dīn al-Ayyūbi bayna al-Tārīkh wa al-Ustūrah* (Cairo: 'Ain for Human and Social Studies, 2008), 209, 214–15.

4. 'Imād al-Dīn al-Asfahāni, a*l-Fath al-Qussi fi al-Fath al-Qudsi* (Cairo: Dar al-Manar, 2004), 93, 88 (see also 93), 73, 59, 84, 55, 82, and 100.

5. Bāhā' al-Dīn Ibn Shaddād, *The Rare and Excellent History of Saladin* (Burlington, VT: Ashgate, 2001), 18, 22, 25, 26, 28, 29, 33, 35, 38, and 36–37.

6. Ibn Djubayr, *Rihlat Ibn Djubayr* (Beirut: Dar al-Kitab al-Lubani, n.d.), 69 and 81.

7. Ibid., 172 and 207.

8. Ibid., 201.

9. See the text of this poem in Abū Shāmah, *Kitab al-RawdaTayn fi akhbari al-DawlaTayn* (Cairo: Lajnat al-Ta'lif wa-al-Tarjamah wa-al-Nashr, 1956–62).

10. Ibn Djubayr, *Rihlat*, 199.

11. See, e.g., ibid., 69, 81, 188, and 199.

12. Ibid., 188 and 196.

13. Ibid., 180.

14. Ibid., 172.

15. Ahmad al-Dhahabi, *Tārīkh al-Islam*, vol. 44, ed. Bashshar 'Awwad Ma'ruf (Beirut: Dar al-Kitab, 1988), 224; and al-Dhahabi, *Siyar 'Alam al-Nubala*, vol. 22, ed. Himzi Fayiz (Beirut: Muassat al-Risalah, 1991), 63–64.

16. 'Awad, *Salāh al-Dīn*, 21.

17. See 'Imād al-Dīn al-Asfahāni, *Kharidat al-Qasr wa Jaridat al-'Asr*, ed. Muhammad Bahjat Athari, and Jamil Sa'id (Baghdad: al-Majma' al-'Ilmi al-'Iraqi, 1955), esp. vols. 7, 8, 10, 11, and 12.

18. E.g.: Ahmad Badawi, *Salāh al-Dīn al-Ayyūbi bayna Shu'arā'i 'Asrihī wa Kuttābih* (Cairo: Dar al-Qalam, 1960).

19. Examples of the use of this metaphor are in al-'Imād, *Kharidat al-Qasr*, 11:11, and in Abd al-Rahman Ibn Isma'il Abū Shāmah, *Kitāb al-Rawdatain fī akhbāri al-DawlaTayn* (Book of Two Gardens), ed. Ibrahim Zaybaq, 5 vols. (Beirut: Muassat al-Risalah, 1997), 2:133.

20. Al-'Imād, in *Kharidat al-Qasr* (8:201) quotes al-Kalby proudly expressing his Shi'ism in this verse of his poetry:

أنا من شيعة الإمام حُسَيْنٍ   لست من سنَّة الإمام وليدِ

21. Ibn Khallikān, *Wafayāt al-A'yān wa Anbā'u Abnā'i al-Zamān*, ed. Ihsan 'Abbas, 5 vols. (Beirut, 1973–78), 14–19.

22. Ibn Aybak al-Safadi, *al-Wāfī bi al-Wafayāt*, vol. 22, ed. Ihsan 'Abbas (Beirut: Dar al-Thaqafa, 2000), 241, quotes al-Yamany in this verse of poetry praising the Fatimids for their generosity while distancing himself from their Shi'a doctrine:

مذاهبهم في الجود مذهب سنة   وإن خالفوني في اعتقاد التشيع

23. Abū Shāmah, *Kitab*, 2:118.

24. Ibn Abī Tay's lost book is entitled *Kanz al-Muwahhidīn fī Sirat al-Malik Salāh al-Dīn* [A Treasure for the Believers from the Life of King Saladin]. On this book and some speculations on the possible reasons of its loss, see Gibb, "The Arabic Sources," 59.

25. Abū Shāmah, *Kitab*, 2:344.

26. See examples of these praises in ibid., 2:345–49, 2:383–84, and 2:40–42.

27. Ibid., 1:174, 2:251–52.

28. Ibid., 1:304–5, 1:389–90, and 2:214.

29. Ibid., 3:63–64.

30. Ibid., 3:128.

31. Ibid., 2:184.

32. Ibid., 2:198 and 2:279.

33. Ibid., 2:201–2.

34. Ibid., 2:283.

35. See this document in Abū Shāmah, *Kitab*, 2:286–90.

36. Ibid., 3:54.

37. Ibid., 2:410–13 and 3:54.

38. Ibn al-Athīr, as quoted by Abū Shāmah, *Kitab*, 2:310.

39. Ibn al-Athīr, *Al-Kāmil fī al-Tārīkh* (Beirut: Dar al-Kutub al-'Ilmiyah, 1995), 10:52.

40. Ibid., 10:33.

41. Abū Shāmah, *Kitab*, 2:230–31.

42. Ibid., 2:231.

43. For a comprehensive view of al-Fādil's role in Saladin's diplomacy, see Hadia Dajani-Shakeel, *al-Qādi al-Fādil* (Beirut: Mu'assasat Al-Dirasat Al-Filastiniah, 1993).

44. Abū Shāmah, *Kitab*, 2:118 and 1:32–33.

45. To deny their Fatimid opponents the religious and political legitimacy, the Abbasid caliphs of Baghdad denied that the Fatimid Caliphs of Egypt were true descendents of the Prophet Muhammad, and they mobilized Muslim scholars to make this point. On this conflict over lineage and legitimacy, see Ayman Fuād Sayyid, *Al-Dawlah al-Fātimiyah fi Misr: Tafsīr Djadī*, (Cairo: al-Dar al-Lubnaniyya, 1992), 32–40 and 159.

46. Ahmed Ibn 'Ali al-Maqrīzi, *Itti'āzh al-Hunafā' bi Akhbār al-Aemmah al-Fātimiyyīn al-Khulafā'*, ed. Jamal al-Din Shayyal, 3 vols. (Cairo: n.p., 1996), 321.

47. Ibid., 3:321.

48. Ahmed Ibn 'Ali al-Maqrīzi, *Al-Sulūk lim'arifat Duwal al-Mulūk*, vol. 1, ed. Muhammad 'Abd al-Qadir 'aynAta' (Beirut: Dar al-Kutb al-Timiyya, 1997), 150.

49. Ulrich Haarmann, "Regional Sentiment in Medieval Islamic Egypt," *Bulletin of the School of Oriental and African Studies* 43, no. 1 (1980): 55–66.

50. See, e.g., Ahmad al-Dhahabi, *Siyar 'Alām al-Nubalā*, ed. Himzi Fayiz (Beirut: Muassat al-Risalah, 1991), 15:212. On Ibn Kathīr' anti-Shi'ism, see Henri Laoust, "Ibn Kathir historien," *Arabica* 2, no. 1 (1955): 73–74.

51. 'Ali Muhammad al-Sillābi, *Salāh al-Dīn al-Ayyūbi wa Djuhūduh fī al-Qadā' 'ala al-Dawlah al-Fātimiyyah wa Tahrir Bayt al-Maqdis* [Saladin: His Effort in Destroying the Fatimid State and Liberating Jerusalem] (Beirut: Dar al-Ma'rifah, 2008).

52. A good survey of the Salafi and Shi'a revivals in the modern time is to be found in Natana J. DeLong-Bas, *Wahhabi Islam: From Revival and Reform to Global Jihad* (New York: Oxford University Press, 2004), and Vali Nasr, *The Shia Revival: How Conflicts within Islam Will Shape the Future* (New York: W. W. Norton, 2006).

53. For an overview of the Arabic literature of the twentieth-century on Saladin's life and achievement, see 'Awad, *Salāh al-Dīn*, 26–32. A bibliographical work on the crusades by the same author contains also some titles of books and articles on Saladin. See Muhammad Mu'nis 'Awad, *Fusūl biblioghrāfiah fī Tārīkh al-Hurūb al-Salībiyyah* (Cairo: 'Ain for Human and Social Studies, 1996), 177–247.

54. Djurji Zaydān, *Salāh al-Dīn al-Ayyūbi*, 2nd ed. (Beirut: Maktabat al-Hayah, 1967).

55. The term *chivalry* is used here, not in its institutional meaning as it was

experienced in medieval Europe, but in its moral connotation, which is more abstract and open to cross-cultural extrapolation. Several medievalists argue that the chivalrous culture in this sense had deep roots in Arab societies, especially in Arabic poetry. Some even believe in certain institutional similarities, and they consider the *futuwa* orders in Arab societies during Saladin's time as "an oriental form of chivalry." On the arguments and counterarguments on this subject, see Gerard Salinger, "Was the Futuwa an Oriental Form of Chivalry?" *Proceedings of the American Philosophical Society* 94, no. 5 (1950): 481–93.

56. Ibn Shaddād, *Rare and Excellent History,* 38.

57. Hillenbrand, *The Crusades,* 600.

58. Salih al-Wardāni, *al-Shi'a fī Misr mina al-Imām 'Ali ila al-Imām al-Khumayni* (Cairo: Maktabat Madbuli al-Saghir, 1993).

59. Ibid., 53.

60. Ibid., 55.

61. Ibid., 56.

62. Ibid., 58.

63. Ibid.

64. Hasan al-Amīn, *Salāh al-Dīn al-Ayyūbi bayna al-'Abbāsiyyin wa al-Fātimiyyīn wa al- Salībiyyīn* (Beirut: Dar al-Jadid, 1994).

65. Usually spelled "Hattin" in Western references, but the spelling "Hittin" (in transliteration: "Hittīn") is more compatible with the Arabic pronunciation of the word today. This is also how the famous geographer and traveler Yāqūt al-Hamawi (1179–1229) described the pronunciation of the word in his time. He writes: حطين: بكسر أوله وثانيه وياء ساكنة ونون. See Yāqūt al-Hamawi, *Mu'jam al-Buldān,* ed. Farid al-Jundi, 6 vols. (Beirut: Dar al-kutub al-allmiyya, 2003), 4:273.

66. Hasan al-Amīn, *Salāh al-Dīn,* 121.

67. Ibid., 123, 126, and 127.

68. Ibid., 190.

69. Ibid., 160.

70. Ibid., 141–251.

71. Shākir Mustafā, *Salāh al-Dīn al-Ayyūbi: al-Fāris al-Mudjāhid wa al-Malik al-Zāhid al-Muftarā 'Alayh* [Saladin: The Denigrated Holy Warrior and Pious King] (Damascus: Dar al-Qalam, 1998).

72. Mustafā, *Salāh al-Dīn,* 144.

73. Lebanese military historian (and retired general) Yāsīn Suwayd shares Mustafā's interpretation of the Karak's event. He believes that Saladin's withdrawal was tactically sound, because time was not ripe for a decisive offensive against the Franks. See Yāsīn Suwayd, *Hurūb al-Quds fī al-Tārīkh al-Islāmi wa al-'Arabi* (Beirut: Dar al-Garb al-Islami, 1997), 84.

74. Mustafā, *Salāh al-Dīn*, 137–38, and see the full text of this letter in Abū Shāmah, *Kitab*, 2:288–89.

75. Ibid., 406.

76. Gibb, "Notes on the Arabic Materials," 745.

77. E.g., 'Arif Tamir, *Tārīkh al-Ismā'īliyah*, 4 vols. (London: Riad al-Rayyes Books, 1991), 4: 14, 16–17. See also 'Uthmān Abd al-Hamīd 'Ashri, *al-Ismā'īliyyūn fī Bilād al-Shām 'alā 'Asri al-Hurūb al-Salībiyyah* (Ph.D. diss., University of Cairo in Khartum, Sudan, 1983), 166.

78. Al-Amīn, *Salāh al-Dīn*, 126, 127, and 158.

79. Ibn al-Athīr, for example, suggests that the Shi'a Fatimids might have invited the Franks to the Islamic land in order to counter the emerging power of the Sunni Saljuqs, and al-Safadi accuses the Shi'a Vizir of Baghdad, Ibn al-'Alqami, of inviting the Mongol invasion with the intention of "destroying Islam and ruining Baghdad." See Ibn al-Athīr, *al-Kāmil*, 9:13–14; and Khalil Ibn Aibam al-Safadi, *Al-Wāfī fī al-Wafayāt*, ed. Ahmad al-Arnaut and Turki Mustafa (Beirut: Dar Ihra al-Turath, 2000), 1:151.

80. See, e.g., Hasan al-Amīn, *Itlalāt 'alā al-Tārīkh* (Beirut: Dar al-Hadi, 2000); and idem, *al-Ismā'īliyyūn waal-Mughūl wa Nasīr al-Dīn al-Tusi* (Beirut: al-Ghadeer, 1997).

81. Lyons and Jackson, *Saladin*, 374.

82. Al-'Imād quoted by Abū Shāmah, *Kitab*, 2:291.

83. On this two events, see Ibn Shaddād, *Rare and Excellent History*, 37 and 74.

84. Niall Christie and Maya Yazigi, eds., *Noble Ideals and Bloody Realities: Warfare in the Middle Ages* (Leiden: Brill, 2006).

85. Maurice Keen, *Chivalry* (New Haven: Yale University Press, 1990), 218.

86. Al-'Imād, *al-Fath al-Qussi*, 75–76.

CHAPTER NINE

Paul the Martyr and Venetian Memories
of the Fourth Crusade

DAVID M. PERRY

$\mathfrak{I}$T WAS A DARK AND stormy night. Well, it *was* both dark and stormy according to the *Translatio corporis beatissimi Pauli martyris de Constantinopoli Venetias,* a story of relic-theft that was written shortly after 1222 by an anonymous monk from the Venetian monastery of San Giorgio Maggiore. A Venetian ship on its way home from Constantinople ran into terrible weather near the Ionian island of Kefalonia. The ship lost its oars, beam, and mast. People started to panic. The captain, Pietro, suddenly guessed that he might have the body of a saint hidden in his hold. The podestà of Constantinople, the ruler of the Venetian quarter in that city, had asked Pietro to bear the merchant Giacomo Grimaldo and a precious casket to Venice, but not to inspect the cargo. When the casket had been brought to the ship, Giacomo told the captain and crew that it contained glass painted with gold (and thus it was handled very carefully), but Captain Pietro now realized, in a flash of insight that our author credits to God, that he had been duped. Surely it was a blessed body, not a bejeweled image. He had the casket brought to the deck and demanded that it be opened. Giacomo demurred, saying that he had no key and that he was escorting this casket for Prior Marcus of San Giorgio Maggiore, who was currently residing in Constantinople in order to manage the formerly Greek Monastery of the Pantepoptes. The prior, with miraculous forethought, had sent the key with a deacon on a separate ship, just in case someone like Captain Pietro tried to get inside the casket. Neither the prior nor Giacomo wanted suspicious sailors to open the container and somehow damage the secret cargo, which he now revealed was actually the body of St. Paul the Martyr.[1]

Some of the sailors grew angry at the deception. They accused the saint of being a second Jonah who had doomed them all and demanded that the body be cast into the sea. Fortunately, calmer heads prevailed, and the imperiled crew chose a more pious approach. They knelt. They prayed. They begged the saint to intercede and protect them. Within the hour, the sea calmed and all rejoiced. Of course, the ship had lost its oars, but then a divine breeze sprang up to propel the ship homeward, and the sailors marveled at the awesome power of Paul the Martyr.

The author draws three lessons from this episode — first, that one should not question the judgment of God, even when circumstances seem dreadful; second, that no matter how deep the darkness becomes, it cannot hide divine light; and third, that although enabled by deceit and marred by doubt, the presence of Paul the Martyr in Venice would bring great benefits to the city. These are not atypical lessons to draw from a story of relic theft, even though in this case no relic theft had actually occurred. Furthermore, the author links the imaginary theft to the Fourth Crusade, even though the crusade's connection to the deed was tenuous. In this chapter, I contend that these incongruities — theft where there was no theft, casting this tale as a crusade-narrative even though the war had ended almost twenty years before the "theft" — reflect the author's attempt to use the theological force of the genre of *furta sacra* to construct a new, strictly Venetian interpretation of the crusade and the crusade's significance for Venice.[2] I begin by discussing what actually happened in Constantinople in 1222, then turn to the narrative and its representation of the crusade, and finally examine the lessons that the author draws from both crusade and relic theft.

The Act of Translation

The translation of relics out of Constantinople after the Fourth Crusade is a well-known consequence of the formation of the Latin Empire, although the narrative sources recording acts of translation often gloss over both the details of the crusade and the process by which a given crusader acquired his new relics.[3] Clerical authors, most of whom resided in religious houses that received Eastern relics, seem to have tried to avoid connecting their new sacred possessions to a crusade that had not achieved its stated goal — liberating Jerusalem. In the case of Paul the Martyr, however, we find precisely the opposite; the anonymous monk of San Giorgio has added the crusade into a text where it barely belongs.

Here are actual details of the translation to the extent that the extant records permit their reconstruction. In 1220, Paolo Venier—here called Paulus—a monk of San Giorgio, returned from a stint in Constantinople, where he had been overseeing the Pantepoptes, one of Constantinople's more venerable monastic institutions, now ensconced within the expanded Venetian quarter on the Golden Horn.[4] While in Constantinople, Paulus, whose principal job may have been establishing the Latin rite in the monastery,[5] discovered the body of St. Paul the Martyr and informed his abbot, Marcus, in Venice.[6] In 1220, Marcus retired and Paulus returned to Venice to take his place as abbot. Soon thereafter he ordered his prior, also named Marcus, to acquire and send the body to Venice. The prior asked the podestà, Marino Storlato, to help, and also recruited a friend, the merchant Giacomo Grimaldo, whom we have already met.[7] The podestà found Captain Pietro and his ship, the prior gave the key to a trusted deacon (and presumably found him passage), and the saint's relics arrived in Venice in 1222. Sometime not long after, an anonymous monk produced this *translatio*.

Notice that someone from each group important in Venetian Constantinople was involved—a high-ranking monk, the chief governmental official, a merchant of means, and a ship's captain. But the author works diligently to fill the narrative with deception, intrigue, and especially suspense—will the prior be caught taking the relic? Will anyone find out that it's being smuggled aboard the ship? Will the secret be revealed? But who in Constantinople would have both cared and possessed the power to do anything about it? The Franks? While relations between the Franks and Venetians in Constantinople were not always free from tension, the 1220s were not a particularly hostile decade.[8] Other clerics? The Pantepoptes belonged to San Giorgio; canonically, they could more or less do what they wanted with their own possessions.[9] Other Venetians? The monks had Storlato, the quarter's absolute ruler, on their side. They might have worried about the privateers and pirates who frequented the Aegean and Ionian seas, but any Venetian ship was fair game anyway; concealing the relic would not have helped.[10] Regardless, no hint of that type of external danger appears in the narrative. The Greeks who venerated Paul might have been upset, but there were far more important relics leaving Constantinople in roughly the same period; besides, what could the subjugated Greeks have done about it?[11]

Little danger (brought about by a human agent) seems to have been involved in moving the relics from one site to the other; thus, the implications of peril and the need for secrecy in the narrative strongly suggest that the author shaped his story in order to address specific concerns. Otherwise, why emphasize these elements? Marcus is ordered to "abscond" with the relic, lest it "suffer great violence," but the author also insists that Marcus had no choice but to obey the orders of his superior, as he was "held by law."[12] But what violence? And why "abscond" — a word suggesting secrecy? Why mention that Marcus had to obey? Would Marcus have opted out of the "theft" if he had been given a choice? Similar questions can be asked about many other episodes in the text. Why did Grimaldo feel he had to lie to the sailors? Would they not have been honored to carry the saint? Why did the prior think he had to send the key on a second ship? These twists in the plot do lend drama to the episode, but the drama in any *translatio* comes not from deeds of men but from enabling miracles. Why, then, did the author create such an atmosphere of deception in his story? The key to understanding this text and the author's decision to write it in this way lies in the short account of the crusade with which it begins.

The Crusade

After beginning with a short account of the Fourth Crusade, the *translatio* continues with the discovery of the relic, the loading of the relic on the ship, the storm, and the ultimate arrival at Venice. In between the main events, the author often digresses into homily and parable. As for the crusade itself, the account is quite short. The author compares the Greek people (*gens*) to the Venetian *gens*. The Greeks, filled with overweening pride, were disrespectful to God, and thus all good people "in the whole world" hated them.[13] God therefore turned to the Venetians, a people who, in contrast, were wholly devoted to Him. This devotion was evidenced by their decision to join with "other counts from over the mountains" to aid the Holy Land against the Saracens and "other barbarians."

At this point, just the second paragraph of the text, the author begins to blur the objectives of the crusade. He writes that God did want the Saracens conquered, but He decided to have these "renowned nobles," the crusaders, first punish the Greeks for their pride and contempt. And so,

Prince Alexius Angelos came to Zara to meet with Duke Enrico Dandolo. Angelos recounted the sins of Alexius III, his uncle, who had blinded his brother (the emperor Isaac), stolen the throne, and "imperiled the empire" —this last piece proves important. As Dandolo and the counts loved God, to whom he, Alexius Angelos, was a devoted servant, the prince begged them to avenge these injustices.[14]

After a short account of battle that focuses on the utility of the ships as floating siege craft, the monk pauses to draw a lesson from events. It is in such moments throughout the text—when the author leaves the narrative form in order to instruct his readers—that the author turns to his central themes, themes that lie outside the narrative flow of the story. He first states that the awesome power of God handed over the Greeks on account of their contempt for Him. Then, the author suddenly changes his mode of expression from a third-person narrative ("God handed over the Greeks") to address his monastic brethren directly. He writes, "We have said these things, o my most beloved brothers, so that nobody will be prideful, even if someone is disrespectful to you: because God will hinder you if you are prideful, whereas to the humble, God gives thanks."[15] Thus, he concludes, in a critical passage, *"Grecorum imperium ex tunc in antea factum est Latinorum"*—the empire formerly of the Greeks was thus made into the empire of the Latins.[16] He returns to his third-person narrative composition with a description of the naming of a Venetian to the Patriarchate of Constantinople (Thomas Morosini),[17] the acquisition of the Greek monastery, the discovery of the relic, its translation, the storm at sea, and the eventual installation of the relic in Venice.

Analysis

This retelling of the Fourth Crusade, just a small part of the larger text, reflects a local, Venetian interpretation of the events in Constantinople. Scholars are just beginning to unravel how the Venetians understood what had happened in Constantinople, a project in which this chapter seeks to play a small role. No contemporary Venetian chronicle of the crusade exists, and the story that emerges over time, in the fourteenth-century chronicles, for example, bears a distant relationship to the facts.[18] Scholars have supposed that Venetians concocted their fables at the same time as other myths of Venice—the latter half of the thirteenth century at the earliest (after the fall of Latin Empire of Constantinople)—but new research suggests that the Venetian crusaders may have truly believed that Pope Innocent directed the fleet to divert to Constantinople in order to Catholicize the Orthodox world.[19] Returning home, such crusaders would have spread their stories, thereby allowing later artists and historians to expand on this chain of myth. In the absence of any chronicle tradition that directly records such stories, however, we must unravel the contemporary Venetian memory of the Fourth Crusade by examining secondary texts—texts such as the *Translatio corporis beatissimi Pauli martyris de Constantinopoli Venetias.*

The story as reflected in the *translatio* is not without precedent. The earliest Venetian account of the crusade is found in a letter from Dandolo to Innocent III. It, like the *translatio,* focuses on the *iniustitia* of the Greeks and asserts that the crusaders felt that they were doing God's will by trying to correct an injustice.[20] But Dandolo and others who wished to portray the crusade in a positive light had to confront an enormous problem—the Holy Land had not been liberated, and thus the expressed goal of the campaign was unfulfilled. Dandolo tried to get around the problem by arguing, like many of his contemporaries (including Innocent himself), that the fall of Constantinople would surely lead to a quick reconquest of Jerusalem. But from the perspective of our anonymous author, writing after the disaster of the Fifth Crusade, the future did not look rosy. Perhaps because of this, the anonymous monk simply avoids the problem of the Holy Land. He constructs new objectives for the Fourth Crusade, objectives that the crusaders had actually accomplished, and then claims victory. For him, it was simple—God found Greek pride objectionable. The Christian empire was therefore imperiled. God brought Angelos to Zara and diverted the crusade to Constantinople in order to punish the Greeks. The Greeks were punished and the empire was saved. God's will had been done.

But the author does more than just move the goalposts for the crusade. Throughout the narrative, he returns to the themes that appear during his account of the war—the dangers of pride, the great good that can come out of dubious circumstances, and the need to weigh results against intentions (ends against means). He locates these themes in both the critical moments of the act of translation itself and in his digressions. Brother Marcus stole the relic because he had to obey his abbot and thus had no choice.[21] Giacomo Grimaldo was asked to serve Venice and the abbot of San Giorgio, and so he lied to the sailors about the contents of the casket in order to bring St. Paul's relics home. The author explains that although Giacomo tried to deceive the sailors, he was not a deceitful man by nature. He then draws a complicated analogy between the clarity of glass and the ornate nature of gold to the purity of the saint (like glass) and the ornate nature of knowledge and virtue. Thus, although Giacomo thought he was lying, he was in fact explicating a greater truth.[22]

If the analogy proves unpersuasive, the explication of the storm is much more visceral. Using this climactic event, the author illustrates his themes by discussing both the decisions of the sailors as well as excursive examples that relate to the actions on ship. The hostile seas threatened the sailors and seemed to doom the venture but ultimately provided the opportunity for miraculous salvation. The sailors initially lacked faith, which was a sin. In choosing to pray rather than to cast the relics overboard, however, they saved their bodies and, more important, their souls. Best of all, they helped their homeland, Venice, by transporting the martyr home safely. In this episode, the author asks his readers to look beyond the superficial trappings of earthly life and to embrace the deeper meanings of events. He stresses that one must not be fooled by superficial irregularities but must instead seek true, internal light. In fact, he fills the text with metaphors of light and darkness. In a digression connected to the storm, he condemns parents who mourn that their child is born blind and those who say it happened because of parental sin. He explains that the blindness is the work of God—no mourning or blaming allowed. He then (immediately following the digression) rebukes the sailors who feared death, first for being afraid and second for their ignorance—their salvation (in the form of Paul's relics) was at hand, but they knew it not (thanks to Giacomo's subterfuge). He states that one must accept punishment of the body in order to reign with Christ and "shine" (his word) for eternity. Divine light cannot be quenched, and God sent both storm and darkness to prove this point.[23]

Such passages function as commentaries on *furta sacra*. The idea that a relic-theft might seem illicit and sinful on the surface but actually conceal an inner sanctity is a standard concept within the norms of the genre.[24] The author of this narrative, however, suggests that one can—indeed, one must—apply the same logic to the Fourth Crusade itself. At first glance, the crusade seems to be a distraction from the goal of freeing the Holy Land and ultimately a failure. Looking more deeply, the author could argue, one must see the result as a manifestation of God's will, just as parents should understand a child's blindness, and just as the sailors should have understood the storm. One is even drawn back to the description of the causes of the crusade — the blinding of the Emperor Isaac. It is unlikely to be coincidental that the author's hypothetical child was born blind or that the author litters his text with references to light, sight, and clarity on the good side and darkness, blindness, and obscurity for the sinners. Many other contemporary writers argued similarly for the providential nature of the crusade, but, as noted above, they had to deal with the Jerusalem issue.[25] This author, on the other hand, not only largely ignores the Holy Land (arguing that God cared more about the sins of the Greeks at this time) but also locates his argument in a *furta sacra* narrative. The genre of *translatio*, of which *furta sacra* is a subset, both recounts the movement of a relic from one place to another and focuses on the transformative power of the translation.[26]

The arrival of a saint in the new location, regardless of the means it took to get him there, signifies the beginning of a new phase in the saint's *acta*, a phase in which the blessings of the saint will be granted to the worshippers in the new locale. Miracles ratify the providential nature of the translation.[27] *Furta sacra* encourages the author to admit to sins, errors of judgment, or even lack of faith. It is through these human frailties — the sailors who think to cast the saint overboard, for example — that one sees the redemptive nature of God's power. What better metaphor for the Fourth Crusade than a furtive, deceptive, yet divinely ordained *translatio?*

As a regional, Venetian narrative, the metaphor could not have been more apt. *Translatio* was an interpretative tool particularly congenial to Venetian authors due to the city's long tradition of appropriating Eastern sacred objects. For Venice, relics came from the East and were acquired from Orthodox churches by force, theft, or gift, and the stories of such translations formed the foundations of Venetian civic and religious mythmaking.[28] The monk of San Giorgio explicitly invokes those prior relic thefts in several instances, the first occurring when Prior Marcus turns to the podestà for help. The author explains: "He [the prior] asked [for help] so that the precious gem [the relics] might be brought to the abbot and with its presence adorn not only the monastery, but all of Venice. For, just as innumerable men and women come from all parts to visit the blessed Mark, so too it will become the glorious custom to see the blessed Paul."[29]

The text thus explicitly compares the consequences of the translation of Paul the Martyr to the ur-myth of Venetian civic identity, the story of the ninth-century translation of the Evangelist.[30] This comparison is all the more striking because the story, in fact, better reflects narrative patterns set by the other two *translationes* so critical to medieval Venetian culture — the *translatio* of St. Stephen the Protomartyr and that of St. Nicholas of Myra. The crusade of 1100, which, according to Thomas F. Madden, "began a tradition emblazoned in the service of the faith" for elite Venetians,[31] also brought home the alleged relics of St. Nicholas.[32] The *translatio* commemorating that theft provided a template for *furta sacra* in the wake of a crusade.

The most important model for our anonymous author, however, lies in the history of the relics of St. Stephen the Protomartyr. St. Mark was housed in the ducal chapel. St. Nicholas was banished to the Lido, the better to watch over the sea and to keep him from rivaling St. Mark's glory. But St. Stephen the Protomartyr found a new home in the monastery of St. George, and for a time the institution was renamed San Giorgio Maggiore e Santo Stefano Protomartire. Unfortunately, no *translatio* contemporary to the theft survives, but later writings seem to preserve the essence of the story.

As recounted by the chronicler and Doge Andrea Dandolo, the story begins with a friendship between a Byzantine monk in Constantinople and Pietro, a monk of San Giorgio Maggiore. Pietro was in Constantinople on orders of the abbot, serving as prior of a church that San Giorgio held in the Venetian quarter in 1107 or 1108. Pietro discovered from a Greek monk (a friend) that a nearby Orthodox church held St. Stephen's relics. The two stole them and brought them back to the prior's own church. The resulting hue and cry, however, made it too unsafe to move the relics out of the sanctuary of the church. After at least a year had passed, tensions eased, and the martyr's relics were placed aboard a Venetian ship on which, by chance, seventy-two Venetian men, all from important families, were also traveling. Dandolo claims that these men did not know that St. Stephen was on board until, in peril from a storm, a voice from the heavens stopped the waves and informed the nobles of the saint's presence.[33] A document from 1109–10 confirms that major merchants did, indeed, accompany the relics. In fact, they chose to be not only St. Stephen's escorts but also promoters of his cult. Each man signed a statement, preserved in the archives of San Giorgio Maggiore, in which they pledged to support the saint's worship and venerate him worthily once back in Venice. They formed a confraternity in his honor and promised to hold an annual festival in his name.[34] The surnames on this document read like a who's who of twelfth-century Venice. Although this case of *furta sacra* began as the deed of a lone monk, it turned into a civic action, backed by this important subsection of Venice's elite.[35]

St. Paul the New Martyr's story clearly follows the same general pattern as that of St. Stephen. A lone monk of San Giorgio moves to Constantinople to run a church belonging to his home monastery and then steals a relic. He puts it on a ship in secret. He involves the mercantile elite. While being saved from peril, the ignorant sailors discover the true identity and meaning of the relic. The author even explicitly compares the arrival of St. Paul's relics to the earlier translation of St. Stephen. The final passage of the thirteenth-century text describes monks and nuns rejoicing at the arrival of St. Paul's relics, just as they had for the arrival of the relics of St. Stephen the Protomartyr, the relics of the martyrs Cosmas and Damian, Cosmas the holy confessor, and even "that most precious of all jewels, that is the wood of the particular cross, and the 'spongia,' which was placed to the blessed lord's mouth." The author adds that he could also have mentioned many other martyrs and virgins whose relics were in the treasury, but "it would take far too long to speak about each one."[36] Although Stephen was the only "stolen" martyr in that list, the relics of Cosmas and Damian were licitly translated from Byzantium in 1154,[37] and the Holy Sponge may well have been translated to Venice after 1204.[38]

The man selected to write the *translatio* for St. Paul was well-versed in Venetian narratives of *furta sacra,* especially those pertaining to his own monastery. The monk of San Giorgio deliberately places the translation of St. Paul into the well-established Venetian tradition of appropriating items of value from Byzantium and the East. But whereas once the relics of Eastern saints enabled Venice to make new claims about post-Byzantine independence and their relative status among the other cities of Italy, by 1222 Venice had fully embarked on a new enterprise — the construction of a maritime empire.[39] The meaning of *translatio* narratives would, likewise, have had to change.

Conclusion

At the climax of the story, the episode with which this chapter began, the sailors gather round the casket to pray. The author writes that the sailors, collectively, issue a powerful prayer that does not so much entreat the saint to spare them and his relics as set the stakes for success or submersion. They say: "Just as the blessed martyr Paul's brother in name and race, the master and blessed apostle Paul said to Caesar . . . that Rome would profit greatly via faith in Christ, so too the blessed martyr allowed himself to be led to Venice. And if he is escorted to Venice, it is not a prediction, but fact, that similar wonders will be made [here]."[40] The sea and winds, the story continues, became calm within the hour.

The above passage sets up the key miracle of the text. Within the genre of *furta sacra*, miracles either authenticate relics of dubious origin (here not an issue) or, even more importantly, enable the act of translation to go forward. The above lines from the text affirm that any successful translation indicates the saint's concordance with the "escort" to Venice. The miracle, the calming of the seas and the wind, demonstrates divine approbation. The eventual installation of the relics in San Giorgio finalizes the process and demonstrates manifest justification. Note that the author is asserting that this prayer is not prophetic, but it functions as an "if . . . then" statement. If, according to the praying sailors, the saint permits his relic to be translated, then Venice will reap the profit. The author, writing after the fact, uses the present tense of a dramatic narrative, rather than prediction, to press his case for the significance of this act of translation.[41] Just as Rome rose under Christianity, so now would Venice. Of course, at the time the monk wrote, it was convenient that the Rome of the East, the city of Constantine, had just fallen to Venetians (and others) and that Venice was newly proclaiming itself Lord of Three-Eighths of the Roman Empire.[42] From the perspective of a thirteenth-century Venetian monk, the apostle's prediction would now signify the imperial legacies that Venice was just beginning to appropriate.

Writing two decades after the fall of Constantinople, an anonymous monk of San Giorgio linked a relatively innocuous relic translation to the crusade of 1204. The entire *translatio* serves as a Venetian narrative of the Fourth Crusade. The war, those few paragraphs, sets the stage and introduces the reader to themes of hidden meaning and the hand of Providence in acts that might seem iniquitous or, at best, a little confusing. It is the power of *furta sacra,* a power so familiar to Venetian hagiographers, that make God's purpose clear. This story, for medieval Venetians, was far more than yet another tale of how an Eastern relic found its way to Venice. As the monk wrote, "*Grecorum imperium . . . factum est Latinorum.*"[43] The world order had been transformed to an extent not seen since Constantine built his new city in the East. St. Paul the "new" martyr, in fact, was martyred in the aftermath of the founding of the *grecorum imperium,* in an era when Arian and Orthodox battled for influence over the great emperor's heirs. In the new eastern Mediterranean world of the thirteenth century, the prior, podestà, merchant, sailors, and, indeed, the entire Venetian crusading army had done much more than enable the translation of a martyr's bones from the Bosphorus to the Rialto. Along with their secret cargo, the poor ignorant sailors had also carried with them the Christian Empire of Constantine, or at least three-eighths of it.

Notes

Research for this chapter was conducted in the Biblioteca Marciana and Archivo di Stato di Venezia. The author would like to express his gratitude to the staff of both institutions for their frequent assistance, as well as to the Gladys Krieble Delmas Foundation and Dominican University, River Forest, Illinois, for their financial support.

1. Monk of St. George, "*Translatio corporis beatissimi Pauli martyris de Constantinopoli Venetias,*" in *Exuviae Sacrae Constantinopolitanae,* ed. Paul Riant, 2 vols. (Geneva, 1877–78; rpt., Paris: Comité des travaux historiques et scientifiques, 2004), 1:141–49, is the most recent published edition of the text. For more information on manuscripts and editions, see Riant's introduction in the same volume, xcvii–viii. St. Paul the "new martyr" was the captain of the Imperial Guard and a defender of images. He was executed by Constantine V Copronymus (C.E. 741–75). The saint's full *acta,* including one edition of the *translatio,* can be found in the *Acta Sanctorum Julii, ex Latinis & Græcis, aliarumque gentium Monumentis, servata primigenia veterum Scriptorum phrasi, Collecta, Digesta, Commentariisque & Observationibus Illustrata a Conrado Janningo, Joanne*

Bapt. Sollerio, Joanne Pinio, e Societate Jesu Presbyteris Theologis, Tomus II, quo dies quartus, quintus, sextus, septimus, octavus & nonus continentur (Antwerp, 1721), 631–43. *Acta Sanctorum,* ed. Jean Bollard, Jean Carnander, et al., 70 vols. (Paris: Société des Bollardistes, 1863; rpt., Brussels: Cultures et Civilisations, 1965), July 2, pp. 631–43.

2. Patrick Geary, *Furta Sacra: Thefts of Relics in the Central Middle Ages* (Princeton: Princeton University Press, 1978), 9–27, offers a general summary of the history of relics, saints, and the genres discussing the two in the Early Middle Ages. For the genre of *translatio,* of which *furta sacra* is a subset, see Martin Heinzelmann, ed., *Translationsberichte und andere quellen des reliquienkultes* (Turnhout: Brepols, 1979).

3. Michael Angold, *The Fourth Crusade* (Harlow, UK: Longman, 2003), 227–35. Angold's volume contains the best general discussion of the translation of relics out of Constantinople in the immediate aftermath of 1204. See also Paul Riant, "Dépouilles religieuses à Constantinople au XIIIe siècle et des documents historiques nés de leur transport en Occident," *Mémoires de la Société nationale des antiquaires de France,* 4th ser., 6 (1875), 1–241. Riant published many editions of texts pertaining to the relics of Constantinople in the *Exuviae Sacrae Constantinopolitanae.* Finally, several sources translated in Alfred J. Andrea, *Contemporary Sources for the Fourth Crusade* (Leiden: Brill, 2000), pertain to the relics of 1204 (and see also Andrea's bibliography, 313–20).

4. Gino Damerini, *L'isola e il Cenobio di San Giorgio Maggiore* (Venice: Fondazione Giorgio Cini, 1969), 188–89. Paolo Venier was abbot from 1220 to 1234. For the expansion of the Venetian quarter after 1204, see David Jacoby, "The Venetian Quarter of Constantinople from 1082 to 1261: Topographical Considerations," in *Novum Millenium: Studies on Byzantine History and Culture Dedicated to Paul Speck,* ed. C. Sode and S. Takács (Aldershot, UK: Ashgate, 2001), 160–62.

5. Jean Richard, "The Latin Church in Constantinople (1204–27)," in *Latins and Greeks in the Eastern Mediterranean after 1204,* ed. Benjamin Arbel, Bernard Hamilton, and David Jacoby (London: F. Cass, 1989), 45–62. Richard provides an overview of the Latin Church in the initial aftermath of the Fourth Crusade. For the Venetian churches, more specifically, see Robert L. Wolff, "Politics in the Latin Patriarchate of Constantinople, 1204–1261," *Dumbarton Oaks Papers* 8 (1954): 234 and n24.

6. Damerini, *L'isola,* 188. Abbot Marcus was Marco Zorzi (r. 1194–1220), the sixteenth abbot. Perhaps best known for opening the monastery to nuns, he also oversaw the arrival of the first wave of relics from Constantinople after 1204. Relics of Santa Lucia were chief among these.

7. Robert Lee Wolff, "A New Document from the Period of the Latin Empire of Constantinople: The Oath of the Venedian Podestà," *Annuaire de l'institut de philologie et d'histoire orientales et slaves* 12 (1953): 561 and n3, lists Storlato as podestà from 27 August 1222 and "as late as 15 April 1223." Storlato had moved up from *iudex* (judge) in 1195 to councilor by 1219, and was alive as late as 1231. I have been unable to locate Giacomo Grimaldo, Pietro Ingosum, or the second Marcus.

8. For tensions focused on ecclesiastical matters, see Wolff, "Politics in the Latin Patriarchate," 225–303.

9. E. Dooley, "Church Law on Sacred Relics" (Ph.D. diss., Catholic University of America, 1931), 10–11 and 28–29. Although new limits on the canonical movement of relics had been imposed by Gratian's *Decretum* and the Fourth Lateran Council, it would have been difficult to make a case against transferring a relic within a monastery's own possessions.

10. For Levantine piracy and its long-term impact on Venetian trade, see Irene Katele, "Piracy and the Venetian State: The Dilemma of Maritime Defense in the Fourteenth Century," *Speculum* 63, no. 4 (1988): 865–89, esp. 866nn1–3. For the Aegean more specifically and the depredations of pirate on Venetian shipping, see Peter Charanis, "Piracy in the Aegean during the reign of Michael VIII Paleologos," *Annuaire de l'institut de philologie et d'histoire orientales et slaves* 10 (1950): 127–33.

11. No records exist of Greeks ever successfully petitioning the Latin conquerors not to translate a relic to the West. There is one account of Greeks unsuccessfully petitioning the doge of Venice for the return of a relic, but that account is not highly credible. See David Perry, "The *Translatio Symonensis* and the Seven Thieves: A Venetian Fourth Crusade Furta Sacra Narrative and the Looting of Constantinople," in *The Fourth Crusade: Event, Aftermath, and Perceptions,* ed. Thomas F. Madden (Aldershot, UK: Ashgate, 2008), 102–5.

12. Monk of St. George, *Translatio,* 143: "Abbatis Sancti Gerogii regebat . . . Marcum . . . abscondite sibi mitteret, ne tanti thesauri violentiam pateretur. Necesse habuit prior idem preceptis abbatis sui obedire: imo tenebatur de iure." All translations are mine unless otherwise noted.

13. Pride as a cause for losing God's good will is a common theme in crusading literature. See, e.g., the contemporary Oliver of Paderborn's chronicle of the Fifth Crusade, in which the author blames pride for the loss of Egypt and the chance to redeem the Holy Land. See Oliver of Paderborn, *Die Schriften des Kölner Domscholasters, späteren Bischofs von Paderborn und Kardinal-Bischofs von S. Sabina, Oliverus, Historia Damiatina,* ed. Hermann Hoogeweg (Tübingen: Litterarischer Verein in Stuttgart, 1894), 277–78.

14. Monk of St. George, *Translatio,* 141–42.

15. Ibid., 142: "Nos hec diximus, fratres mei dilectissimi, ut nemo superbire audeat, vel aliquem habere despectui: quia Deus superbis resistit, humilibus autem dat gratiam."

16. Ibid.

17. On Thomas Morosini, see Wolff, "Politics in the Latin Patriarchate," 227–44.

18. On the chronicles, see Serban Marin, "Between Justification and Glory: The Venetian Chronicles' View of the Fourth Crusade," in Madden, *The Fourth Crusade,* 113–22.

19. Thomas F. Madden suggested this interpretation in "Memory and the Diversion of the Fourth Crusade," presented at *Remembering the Crusades: Myth, Image, and Identity,* Twenty-Eighth Annual Conference of the Center for Medieval Studies, Fordham University, New York City, 29–30 March 2008. Although scholars have long been aware of the Venetian version of events, they have generally dismissed it as mere retroactive justification. The idea that the bulk of the Venetian sailors believed that the papacy had authorized the diversion is new, yet seems likely. We are well aware, thanks to the primary chronicles of the crusade, that the leaders maintained rigorous control over the information given out to the soldiers. For example, soldiers did not even know that they had been excommunicated after the diversion. The idea that the Venetians truly believed that they were obeying papal will in assaulting Constantinople requires more study.

20. This portrayal of Greek iniquity became a standard feature of anti-Greek polemic in the Crusader literature and historiography. See, e.g., Teresa Shawcross, *The Chronicle of Morea: Historiography in Crusader Greece* (Oxford: Oxford University Press, 2009), 190–202.

21. Monk of St. George, *Translatio,* 143.

22. Ibid., 144–45. The key passage is drawn from Proverbs 8:10: "Accipe disciplinam meam et non pecuniam doctrinam magis quam aurum eligite." The Venetian monk writes, "Accipe sapientiam, sicut aurum," in order to draw his analogy.

23. Monk of St. George, *Translatio,* 145–47.

24. Geary, *Furta Sacra,* 9–27.

25. For a recent overview of the contemporary sources of the Fourth Crusade and their perspectives, see Angold, *Fourth Crusade,* 3–25.

26. See above. n2.

27. Heinzelmann, *Translationsberichte.*

28. For the long history of the importance of Eastern relics in Venice, see Silvio Tramontin, "Influsso Orientale nel Culto dei Santi a Venezia fino al Secolo VX," in *Venezia e il Levante fino al secolo XV,* ed. Agostino Pertusi, 2 vols. (Florence: L. S. Olschki, 1973), 1:802–20. For the Venetian relic-cult in general, see Antonio

Niero, "Relique e corpi di santi," in *Culto dei Santi a Venezia,* ed. Silvio Tramontin (Venice: Edizione Studium Cattolico Veneziano, 1965), 181–208. For Eastern influences on Venice over time, especially in its artwork, see Deborah Howard, *Venice and the East: The Impact of the Islamic World on Venetian Architecture, 1100–1500* (New Haven: Yale University Press, 2000). For the hagiogaphical accounts of relic-translation, see Giorgio Cracco, "I testi agiografici: Religione e politica nella Venezia del Mille," in *Storia di Venezia,* vol. 1, *Origini-Età Dúcale,* ed. L. C. Ruggini, G. Cracco, and G. Ortalli (Rome: Istituto della enciclopedia Italiana, 1992), 950–52.

29. Monk of St. George, *Translatio,* 141–49: "Hunc rogavit, ut pretiosam gemmam suo abbati deferret, que non solum monasterium, sed et totam Venetiam sua presentia decoraret. Nam, sicut b. Marcum pene de universsis partibus visitare adveniunt innumerabiles viri & femine, ita beatum Paulum facta est gloriosa consuetudo videndi."

30. The best summary on the importance of the story of the theft of St. Mark to Venice, a vast subject, is still found in Otto Demus, *The Mosaics of San Marco in Venice: The Eleventh and Twelfth Centuries,* vol. 1, *Text* (Chicago: University of Chicago Press, 1984), 5–31. Cracco, "I testi agiografici," 923, describes the *translatio* of St. Mark's relics as "La prima pietra del mito di Venezia."

31. Thomas F. Madden, *Enrico Dandolo and the Rise of Venice* (Baltimore: Johns Hopkins University Press, 2003), 11.

32. Agostino Pertusi, "La contesa per le reliquie di S. Nicola tra Bari, Venezia e Genova," *Quaderni Medievali* 5 (1978): 6–56. The *translatio* is found in Monk of the Lido, "Historia de translatione Magni Nicolai," *Recueil des historiens des croisades: Historiens occidentaux,* 5 vols. (Paris: Académie des Inscriptions et Belles-Lettres, 1872–1906), 5:259–64. Citizens of Bari took the relics on the island of Myra in 1087, but the Venetians concluded, with the help of miracles, that the Bariense had stolen the wrong body. Venetians also considered invading Bari over the next few decades, but signed a peace agreement before beginning the Venetian crusade of 1122–24.

33. Andrea Dandolo, *Chronica per extensum descripta,* ed. Ester Pastroello, *Rerum Italicarum Scriptores,* vol. 12 (Bologna: N. Zanichelli, 1938), 227. The facts of the translation do not match the story. All or most of these leading Venetian citizens would have had their own ships. Aside from the desire to escort the saint's relics to Venice, there is no reason for all of these men to crowd together on a single vessel. This episode falls into the "ignorance" topos, also seen in the *translatio* of St. Paul.

34. *S. Giorgio Maggiore,* ed. Luigi Lanfranchi, 3 vols. (Venice: Comitato per la pubblicazione delle fonte relative alla storia di Venezia, 1968), 3:504n144.

35. Cracco, "I testi agiografici," 951, calls St. Stephen, "Un santo per i vinti." In Cracco's conception, St. Mark was the saint for the doges, Nicholas for the commoners (the sailors), and Stephen for the merchants. I would add that Stephen also became the key saint for the monks, most of whom were drawn from the families of Venice's mercantile elite.

36. Monk of St. George, *Translatio*, 147. One of the virgins may have been St. Lucy. Her relics, perhaps sent to Venice by Enrico Dandolo himself just after 1204, fostered a powerful and long-lasting cult in Venice that lasts through to the modern era. See Giovanni Musolino, *Santa Lucia a Venezia: Storia, culto, arte* (Venice: Stamperia di Venezia, 1987), 41.

37. Flaminio Corner, *Notizie storiche delle chiese e monastery di Venezia e di Torcello* (Padua, 1758; rpt., Venice: Sala Bolognese, 1990), 474. See also Damerini, *L'isola*, 245, for a 1362 inventory of the monastery's treasury (the oldest extant such list).

38. There is no clear record of when the Holy Sponge came to Venice, and I conjecture that San Giorgio had obtained just a small piece of it as part of the city's Fourth Crusade horde. Constantinople definitely had a large piece of the sponge as of 1204. It was among the relics acquired by Louis IX along with the Crown of Thorns and other relics of the Passion. Rome, also, had a Holy Sponge relic long before the crusades, so Venice could have acquired a fragment from Rome. I have, however, found no record of the *spongia* in Venice before the thirteenth century. Venice, in particular the treasury of San Marco, obtained many relics of Christ as a consequence of the Fourth Crusade, including the column of the flagellation, fragments of the True Cross, and, apparently, a piece of the sponge.

39. For a recent and elegant summation of the Venetian decision to pursue imperial goals, see Madden, *Enrico Dandolo,* 173–97.

40. Ibid., 147: "Beatus martyr Paulus sed sicut confors et gentium magister beatus apostolus Paulus Cesarem appellaverat, sciens per Spiritum, se Rome in fide Christi multis profuturum: ita beatus iste martyr, deduci se sinebat Venetias, et si, non predicatione, miraculis similia multis facturus." I have not been able to identify this biblical episode. Paul, of course, went to Rome after having been placed under trial in Jerusalem, and the Monk of St. George might just be referring to Acts 25:11, in which Paul says, "Caesarem appello." I suspect it refers to a medieval *vita*, but have not found the source.

41. Despite the author's claims to be avoiding prophecy, he is working within a particular medieval narrative prophetic tradition in which the author "predicts" something that has already happened (the translation of the relic) in order to lend authority to a prediction of something yet to occur (the rise of Venice). See Monika Otter, "*Prolixitas Temporum:* Futurity in Medieval History Narratives," in *Read-*

ing Medieval Culture: Essays in Honor of Robert W. Hanning, ed. Robert M. Stein and Sandra Pierson Prior (Notre Dame, IN: University of Notre Dame Press, 2005), 47–49.

42. Madden, *Enrico Dandolo*, 188, discusses the historiographical questions regarding the first use of the phrase, "*Dominator quarte parties et dimidie Imperii Romanie.*"

43. Monk of St. George, *Translatio*, 142.

CHAPTER TEN

Aspects of Hospitaller and Templar Memory

JONATHAN RILEY-SMITH

𝕴N THE 1290s Frà William of Santo Stefano, the first serious historian of the Hospital of St. John, who wrote what is still the accepted account of its beginnings, was scathing about the myth-makers who had been at work: "Our order began in the manner I have found in histories which are received and believed as authoritative by all men. It is said that there was a more ancient beginning . . . but that is not to be found in any authoritative source. . . . Now let us leave vanity and hold to the truth, for glorifying in lies is displeasing to God."[1] William was not, of course, taking into account the way visions of the past can be transmuted by emotional forces surfacing in times of crisis. I wish to draw attention to the way memory was distorted by three traumatic events. Echoes of the first, an internal dispute about the direction the Hospital of St. John was taking in the twelfth century, were to be heard for hundreds of years. The second, the loss of Jerusalem in 1187, may have had the effect of relocating in the minds of many of the Templars the scene of their foundation. The third, the catastrophic situation in which the Templars found themselves in the early fourteenth century, gave rise to speculation about the behavior of an earlier grand master.

The Militarization of the Hospital

Grants recorded in two charters dated 17 January 1126 were witnessed by men encamped with a Christian army that was advancing, or was just about to advance, into territory controlled by Muslim Damascus, because the main engagement was fought eight days later.[2] The presence among these witnesses of six Hospitallers, one of whom was a brother with the title of *Hospitalis constabularius*,[3] suggests that the Hospital of St. John, which had been established to care for poor pilgrims when they were ill, was making a contribution to Christian warfare only six years after the foundation of the Temple; not merely in a policing or protective capacity but as an element in an invasion force. The order was given its first major castle ten years later,[4] and its growing military reputation must have begun to attract richer nobles, who appear in its ranks from the 1140s.[5] Although no reference to a brother knight can be found before a doubtful one in 1148,[6] the knights must have been quite numerous by the 1160s, because a report sent to Rome suggests that they were already occupying many of the major posts in the order,[7] and because the design of the castle of Belvoir, begun at about that time, allowed for a large conventual enclosure.[8]

The near silence enveloping the growth in the order of a military wing, which reigned for forty years, masked the controversial nature of this development. In the 1160s the internal tensions, which took more than a decade to resolve, could no longer be suppressed. They were generated by unease about the relationship between nursing and warfare and by worry about resources, since the care of the sick on the scale felt to be appropriate competed with the growing costs of war. They were fueled by the way the master, Gilbert of Assailly, who energetically pursued militarization, had plunged the order into near bankruptcy.[9] Gilbert, who succumbed to what seems to have been a clinical depression, resigned the mastership in 1171 and retired to a cave to live as a hermit. In the chaos that followed, compounded by Gilbert's mood swings, most of the brothers in the central convent made demands that were to be confirmed by Pope Alexander III, including the insistence that the conventual chapter give consent to the acquisition of frontier castles and to any important agreements made on the order's behalf.[10]

The views of different factions were reflected in two papal letters of the late 1170s, which must have echoed opinions that had been transmitted to the apostolic see by the parties concerned. In *Piam admodum* Pope Alexander stated that the Hospitallers' prime obligation was to care for the poor and that they should not be diverted into military enterprises except on very special occasions, which he believed had already been defined before 1160 as those on which the relic of the True Cross was carried with the Christian army, and then only if the order's contribution was seen to be appropriate and reasonable. The Hospital, he added, had been instituted for the reception and refection of the poor and it should concentrate on those duties, "especially as it is believed that the poor are better defended by showing them love and mercy than by force of arms."[11] At almost the same time, however, his curia reissued one of the order's most important early privileges, *Quam amabilis Deo,* in which passages borrowed from an earlier charter for the Templars and describing a military function were now interpolated. It used to be thought that the letter was a forgery, but Professor Rudolf Hiestand has demonstrated that it is genuine and that with these additions the curia recognized the Hospital's military role.[12]

The Hospitaller leadership responded to the internal strains by stressing, successfully as it turned out, that the warfare in which the order was engaged had a symbiotic relationship to the care of the sick poor. For the first time the order blandly associated warfare with acts of mercy in statute, and it decreed that the bodies of the poor who died in its hospital should be draped with palls that replicated its battle standard, while insisting that even the warhorses of the brother knights should be at the disposal of the sick if they needed transportation.[13]

It is significant that the solution the order found was not to abandon one of two disparate roles but to link them more closely together. The traumatic nature of the crisis the brothers had undergone may explain why a "folk-memory" of the process of militarization survived for several centuries. It is to be found in two versions; in each, accounts of the introduction of knights into the brotherhood, echoing in their approach the divisions three centuries earlier, are embedded in a lot of nonsense, including myths of the Hospital's biblical foundation and an apparent misdating of the First Crusade. One is in a historical introduction to an edition of the statutes made by William Caoursin, the vice-chancellor on Rhodes, and published in 1496.

> Devout persons on pilgrimage dedicated themselves to the service of the holy house (the Hospital) and, induced by divine zeal, took up arms for the defence of the Catholic faith and also to protect pilgrims and the (holy) places from the incursions of the barbarians. At length these men, imitating the most famous Judas Maccabaeus and the most devout John (the Baptist), engaged with all care in hospitaller work and in the bearing of arms in defence of the divine cult and the Catholic faith.[14]

The second, written slightly later by a Hospitaller priest, survived in only one manuscript, which is now lost but was in England in the seventeenth century.

> When . . . the riches of this holy order had grown greatly, it hired knights . . . to protect its properties . . . and to drive back the pagans. For the priests themselves, occupied with the sacred mysteries and preaching, could not do what the knights practised. Then in an act of utter madness, motivated by greed, the knights were raised up . . . and the priests were disregarded. Accordingly it was decreed that the knights themselves should become members of the Hospital and defend the Christian order. Whence it was established that these men, fighting for the name of Christ, were to wear the cross on their chests.[15]

So, either secular knights, who from the First Crusade onward had been coming to the East to serve for a few years as an act of devotion, had attached themselves to the Hospital, or mercenaries, who were employed by it, had been incorporated into the order to form the class of brothers-at-arms, and the wearing of the cross had been instituted for them.

These accounts, although differing in mood and details, contain elements that ring true. I have not found any contemporary evidence for paracrusading knights serving the Hospital at an early date,[16] but it would have made sense if, like other religious institutions in Jerusalem, the order was benefiting from the attachment of secular knights serving for pay or, more likely, out of devotion. The earliest Templars seem to have been devotional soldiers of this sort. The knights would have been present in the army invading the territory of Damascus in 1126,[17] and the constable could have been the brother appointed to look after them, being perhaps the only member of the order with a military function at that time. Their needs would explain references from the 1120s to arms bearers in the West leaving their horses and weapons to the order in their wills.[18] Clause 19 of the Rule, which established the wearing of the cross throughout the order, is an accretion dating from before 1153,[19] and it may be that the story associating the adoption of the cross with the establishment of brothers-at-arms was accurate.

That accounts of militarization, whether accurate or not, should have survived for centuries is evidence of the intensity of the trauma to which I have referred. It cast a very long shadow, which arguably extends to the present day, and it marked the moment when a reconciliation between acts of mercy and of war was achieved in a religious institute, establishing a precedent for later orders with somewhat similar combined functions, such as the orders of St. Mary of the Germans, the Sword Brothers, and perhaps St. Lazarus. One of its effects, however, was the account of a miracle, which may have been circulating in the 1160s and was associated with the order's founder, Gerard.[20]

At the time of the First Crusade Gerard was the administrator of the hospice that was to metamorphose into the Hospital of St. John. The hospice was dependent on the Benedictine Abbey of St. Mary of the Latins in Jerusalem,[21] which had recently been restored and repopulated by Cassinese monks from southern Italy.[22] Gerard was probably one of them. On his death in 1120 he was buried in the Hospitaller precinct in Jerusalem, and his epitaph was recorded in an interpolation, probably inserted before 1128, in a manuscript of Fulcher of Chartres's *Historia,* which Heinrich Hagenmeyer believed may have been in Hospitaller hands:

> Here lies Gerard, the most humble man in the east, servant of the poor and devoted to the sick, meek of countenance but with a noble heart. One can see in these walls how good he was. He was provident and active. Exerting himself in all sorts of ways, he stretched forth his arms into many lands to obtain what he needed to feed his own.[23]

It has been suggested that for some reason Gerard did not come to be commemorated in the order's liturgy, although the evidence for this in the central Middle Ages is very slight.[24] It is, however, certain that his cult flourished in Jerusalem. The chronicler William of Tyre, who was not friendly toward the Hospitallers, described him as "a man of venerable life, renowned for his piety . . . who for a long time rendered devoted service to the poor."[25] His remains seem to have been sent at a later date to Europe, because by 1283 the body of a saint called Gerard was being venerated in the Hospitaller commandery of Manosque in Provence. During the 1280s all the major institutions in the East were transferring their archives, and presumably treasures, across the Mediterranean, and the appearance of Gerard's bones in the West cannot be coincidental. It looks as though they had been abstracted by the Hospitaller brothers from Jerusalem when the city was lost to Saladin in 1187. They must have been taken to the order's new headquarters in Acre before being transported to the West when the position of the Christians in the Holy Land became precarious.[26] This removal of Gerard's remains from Jerusalem — which was, after all, the preferred resting place for Christians because of its special location in the Christian geography of providence[27] — would be further evidence of the strength of his cult.

The account of a miracle that Gerard supposedly performed was added to some redactions of a *Legenda* composed by the Hospitallers in Jerusalem. The core of the *Legenda,* consisting of an attempt to give "scriptural" origins to the Hospital — or more particularly to its site — has been dated to the period 1140–60, a time when the church and crown were engaged in a major program to transform Jerusalem architecturally and to improve its facilities, with the intention of enhancing its role as a major cult center by making it more "pilgrim friendly."[28]

The story recounts how, when Jerusalem was still in Muslim hands, "a servant of Jesus Christ called Gerard had custody of the holy house and served the poor with kindness, using alms that the Muslims gave him." The First Crusade arrived before the city and besieged it, but the crusaders were on the verge of starvation. Three or four times a day, therefore, Gerard filled his mantle with bread and, pretending the loaves were stones, hurled them at the Christians. When the Muslim guards on the ramparts saw this they reported him to the garrison commander. Gerard was brought before the commander, together with his mantle and the bread, which had now miraculously lapidified. The commander therefore ordered Gerard to continue as before. For this assistance to them, the leaders of the crusade later "gave a great part of the possessions of Jerusalem to Gerard in honour of St John the Baptist."[29]

There may be some recollection in this *miraculum* of the temporary food shortage that afflicted the siege camp before Jerusalem.[30] Of more significance, however, is the evidence, which is not found elsewhere, that the Shi'ite rulers of Jerusalem allowed alms to be passed through their hands to the Christian hospice. Presumably these were the gifts of pilgrims, which Muslim officials insisted on collecting. Cooperation by the Muslim authorities in alms-gathering may explain why the hospital admitted non-Christians as patients in the twelfth century — a practice that, as far as I know, was unparalleled in the rest of Christendom[31] — but it could have been initiated before the First Crusade. The Muslim and Jewish patients must have been pilgrims to those holy places of importance to them, and respect for their special dietary requirements may have been reflected in the statutes, which laid down that the sick in the hospital were to have chicken if they could not stomach pork and were to be issued with sugar — presumably to add to water — if they did not want wine. There are also references in a contemporary description of the hospital to a second kitchen, in which the chicken was cooked.[32]

But if the *Legenda* provides us with some hitherto unknown information, it may also demonstrate how actuality can be reversed. It was known in twelfth-century Jerusalem that, far from deceiving the Muslim garrison during the siege of the summer of 1099, Gerard had aroused the suspicion of the guards, who, believing that he was hoarding money, had tortured him so badly that he was left severely disabled.[33] Even in the third quarter of the twelfth century there must have been people — perhaps in the Hospitaller convent — who had seen Gerard or had known him personally. In the *miraculum,* on the other hand, he deceives the guards and gains the commander's support. He is also shown assisting the First Crusaders — although by feeding them rather than by the use of arms — and this surely linked him to a military engagement. The story of the miracle may reflect the need some brothers felt during the crisis that enveloped the order to associate with the founder the acts of mercy, mingled with warfare, that resolved the crisis.

The Origins of the Templars

By the thirteenth century different versions of the story of the foundation of the Order of the Temple were in circulation. The one that has been generally accepted is that a small number of knights, who had come to the East for a few years as an act of devotion and had been attached to the Church of the Holy Sepulchre, formed themselves into a brotherhood under the leadership of a petty noble from either Champagne or Burgundy called Hugh of Payns, with the aim of securing the pilgrim roads to and from the holy places, which were still very unsafe.[34] If this is what really happened, the decision must have been taken during the winter of 1119–20, in the aftermath of the annihilation of a Christian army by the Muslims in northern Syria, which had left the Western settlers feeling particularly exposed. The proto-Templar knights took vows of poverty, celibacy, and obedience, and their society was approved by the patriarch of Jerusalem. They seem to have been recognized at a church council in Nablus in January 1120, which also agreed to a canon legitimating the bearing of arms by churchmen.[35] They gained the support of Count Fulk V of Anjou, who was in Palestine on crusade,[36] and of St. Bernard of Clairvaux, who persuaded a papal legate and the archbishops, bishops. and abbots attending the council of Troyes in 1129 to recognize them.[37] Meanwhile, King Baldwin II had lent them part of one of his residences, the building on the Temple esplanade that had been the al-Aqsa Mosque. The king was notoriously mean,[38] and the palace was in a ruinous state.[39]

There was, however, an alternative account, which was known to at least some of the brothers in the Levant, and also to the Hospitallers, as we shall see. It was retold in 1311 to the papal commissioners investigating the order by a lawyer called Anthony Sicci, who had served the Templars in Palestine in the 1270s.[40] According to Anthony, two Burgundian knights had been responsible for guarding the pass lying between Mount Carmel and the sea, where later the Templar castle of Chastel Pèlerin would stand. This pass, known as "The Pilgrim Way," was dangerous, and many pilgrims had been robbed and even killed there. During the nine years the two knights had custody of this road they were joined by nine companions, and as a reward for their work the pope confirmed their institution as an order and, moreover, established that they should have by right the *relevia*, the leftovers from the conventual table of the brothers of the Hospital of St. John, to provide for them and to help them assure the security and freedom of the Holy Land.[41]

In this account, therefore, the foundation of the Temple is attributed to two men, not one, and the Temple is located not in Jerusalem but further to the north on the Palestinian coast, although the cofounders being given *relevia* by the Hospitallers suggests that they were considered to be in close touch with Jerusalem. The story may reflect the fact that the Templars had indeed had a fortified road station in the Carmel district in the twelfth century.[42] But the situation in which the brothers found themselves in the later thirteenth century also helps to explain how the site of their order's origins could have been transposed in their minds from Jerusalem to the neighborhood of Mount Carmel. Jerusalem had been lost in 1187, and the Templars had established a new headquarters in Acre. Christian possession of Jerusalem was restored in 1229, but the Temple esplanade remained in Muslim hands, and the Templars could not transfer their headquarters back there. Jerusalem was finally lost in 1244 and by the 1270s would have been a distant memory, whereas the coast road round the foot of the Carmel range was still Christian, and specifically Templar, territory.[43] It would have been natural to relocate the site of the Temple's foundation to a district the brothers knew well. The story of the two knights may have benefited, moreover, from the mythic reputation that Chastel Pèlerin, which was built only in 1217–18, had quickly gained for itself. It was one of the most important of the order's castles and seems to have had a particular fascination for the last generation of brothers in the Holy Land. It was immensely strong. It was close to the headquarters in Acre; indeed, the original intention had been to move the central convent out there, away from the bustle and vice of the great port city. It was also the order's chief prison, in which were immured those brothers whose behavior had been particularly scandalous.[44]

The reference to *relevia* in this story is especially interesting. These leftovers were indeed rendered by the Hospitallers to the Templars, until they were redeemed by the master of the Hospital in the 1240s. They have attracted the attention of a number of historians,[45] but only Pierre-Vincent Claverie has provided a convincing explanation of them. He has drawn attention to two charters in the cartulary of the Holy Sepulchre, which describe how in the 1160s the canons gave the Templars three villages in place of an annual rent of 150 besants, which they had been accustomed to pay "for the defence of the land."[46] It seems, therefore, that back in the early 1120s, before the Templars had been properly endowed, there had been a whip-round in Jerusalem, and some of the religious institutions in the city, including the Holy Sepulchre and the Hospital, had committed themselves to contribute to their upkeep.

In yet another twist, however, the Hospitallers, who also knew the Levantine Templars' narrative, adapted it in a remarkable way. The author of a recension of the *Chronology of Dead Masters* written in Italian circa 1472 — which, incidentally, provides yet more evidence of the way memories of militarization still haunted the order — added to an account of the redemption of the *relevia* in the 1240s the same story of the original Templars guarding a narrow pass. In this version, however, there were twenty-five of them, and it was to Hospitaller donats that Master Roger of Moulins (1177–87) had granted the *relevia*. These donats were so successful that they were organized into a separate order by the pope.[47]

It may well be that this legend of the Templars' birth grew out of the need to justify the Hospitallers' acquisition of the Templars' estates after the latter had been suppressed. The properties had been granted to the Hospital in the bull of dissolution of 1312, but it took it a very long time for it to occupy them; indeed, in Portugal and Aragon it never succeeded in doing so. An account that purported to show that the Temple was the Hospital's daughter may have been circulating to reinforce its claims to the Templar lands.

The Introduction into the Temple of a Blasphemous Rite of Passage

What happens to memory when it is recalled in a time of acute distress? There survives a body of material from the early fourteenth century recording the responses of a large number of Templar brothers, ranging from the well-born and well-educated to the very simple, who were being asked to recall under pressure details of conversations they had had with others and of events occurring as long as fifty years earlier. Most of them were under arrest. Torture was employed extensively during the interrogations in France and in parts of Italy, and its use was at least sanctioned in England. When, in 1310, a movement of resistance, which had been growing among the prisoners for some time, came to the surface, the protests of its leaders were silenced by an episcopal tribunal under the archbishop of Sens and a provincial council under the archbishop of Rheims, which, responding to pressure from the French crown, had sixty-seven prisoners who were maintaining their innocence burnt.

Most of the Templars in France, including James of Molay, the grand master who was on a visitation from Cyprus, were arrested on 13 October 1307 on charges of blasphemy, idolatry, and immorality. Within a matter of days many of them, including the master himself and the visitor-general Hugh of Pairaud, his chief representative in northwestern Europe, acknowledged their guilt. Their formal depositions were made in the presence of the papal inquisitor William of Paris and set in train a general enquiry into the order. The Templars' responses to the accusations are to be found in the very detailed descriptions of their testimony recorded at the examinations. The first group of these comprise the investigation by the papal inquisitor in Paris[48] and surviving episcopal enquiries in Normandy,[49] Champagne,[50] and Languedoc and Provence[51] during the nine months after the arrests. This period culminated in depositions made before the pope at Poitiers and a team of cardinals at Chinon in the summer of 1308.[52] Rather later came investigations in Clermont,[53] Nîmes,[54] Mainz and Trier,[55] the papal states,[56] Tuscany,[57] Cesena,[58] Apulia,[59] Sicily,[60] Portugal and Castile,[61] Roussillon,[62] Aragon and Navarre,[63] Cyprus,[64] and Britain.[65] Meanwhile a papal commission, which was set up to consider the state of the order itself, sat in Paris from 1309 to 1311.[66]

The interrogations took the form of asking each witness to remember as much as he could about the way he had been received into the order and then of guiding him through an itemized list of the charges. Memory was here, of course, subverted by fear, by a desire to please the interrogators, and by the fact that everyone, from the interrogators to the brothers, recognized that the grand master and other leading Templars *had* confessed to heinous crimes. The case had been settled, as far as they were concerned, and they all assumed that there had been corrupt practices, even if they had not experienced them.

Sometimes witnesses recalled isolated moments from the past, almost like snapshots: domestic cats wandering about commanderies;[67] a brother sergeant holding a candle close to priests celebrating Mass to throw light on the missal on stormy early mornings in Limousin;[68] a sudden call to arms disturbing a chapter meeting in Sidon.[69] Or they remembered conversations they had had in the past with brothers who claimed to know the order's history, because some of the interrogators, and particularly those on the papal commission, had led the discussion on to the questions about when and how corrupt practices had entered the order.

Some brothers apparently believed that the evils had arisen almost as soon as the Temple was founded,[70] but these seem to have been in a small minority. A substantial body of opinion among those Templars who had been stationed in the West was that the blasphemous practice of demanding that some postulants, upon admission, deny Christ and spit, stamp, or urinate upon a cross or crucifix had originated "overseas" and reflected Muslim influence,[71] although the sergeant Bosco of Masualier also claimed to have heard talk of a "prophet" called Joshua.[72] Some were concerned with the identification of the individual who might have brought the practice into their province in Europe. The sergeant Thomas of Thoroldby was told that the errors had been introduced into England either by "Adelard" or by Hugh of Pairaud, when they were grand commanders there.[73] Others drew attention to the lack of faith of another English grand commander, Brian le Jay.[74] Geoffrey of Goneville, the grand commander of Poitou and Aquitaine, had heard word of a master Roncelin,[75] who must have been Roncelin of Fos, grand commander of Provence off and on between 1248 and 1278.[76] Rumors about Roncelin were perhaps also reflected in the sergeant Stephen of *Stapelbrugge*'s belief that the errors had spread throughout the West from the diocese of Agen.[77]

Two masters, Philip of Milly of Nablus[78] and Thomas Berard,[79] were named by witnesses as having been responsible for the introduction of the blasphemous rite of passage, although it is hard to see why they should have been credited with it. On the other hand, the well-known Dominican Peter of La Palud, who was present at many interrogations, heard that the errors had been introduced by a grand master who had been captured by a Muslim sultan and released in return for a promise to introduce the blasphemy. This story was also repeated to Geoffrey of Gonville, who had been in the East,[80] while another brother knight, Hugh of Faure, who had served in the Levant for fourteen years, was of the opinion that the errors had been introduced by a grand master who was a Burgundian.[81] Of the twenty-three grand masters of the Temple, Bertrand of Blanchefort, Eudes of St. Amand, Gerard of Ridefort, William of Beaujeu, and Armand of Peragors were taken prisoner by the Muslims, but Eudes and Armand never regained their freedom. Robert Burgundio, born in Anjou but from a family that had come fairly recently from Burgundy, Bernard of Tremelay, Andrew of Montbard, William of Beaujeu, and possibly Hugh of Payns and Everard of Barres were Burgundians.

Of these, William of Beaujeu, grand master from 1273 to 1291, may have been the individual in the minds of the witnesses, although he was never openly implicated.[82] He was a Burgundian and had been a prisoner of the Muslims, although he had been released over a decade before his election as grand master. The sergeant Hugh of Narsac, who had never been overseas but was another of those who believed that the errors had emerged in the Levant, where there were close relations with the Muslims, said that William had had frequent dealings with them and had been criticized for this; indeed, he had had some Muslims in his pay and said that they had given him greater security.[83] Hugh's testimony was supported by that of the sergeant Peter of Nobiliac, who had lived in the East before joining the Temple and who said that William was very friendly with the Muslims because otherwise the order could not have remained in Palestine.[84]

William of Beaujeu had certainly had close relations with the Egyptian Mamluks. James of Molay recalled the discontent he and many of the pugnacious young brothers serving in Acre had felt with what they considered to be William's policy of appeasement in the 1270s and 1280s.[85] William's secretary, the "Templar of Tyre," who knew Arabic, testified in his chronicle to William's friendship with a Mamluk amir called Salah, who, in return for bribes, was accustomed to warn William when a Mamluk advance was planned and who advised him of Sultan Qala'un's project to take Acre, which was only averted by the sultan's death.[86] Could it be that this Salah was Qala'un's son and designated successor Salah ad-Din Khalil, known in history as the sultan al-Ashraf, who was to take Acre in 1291? It was certainly Sultan al-Ashraf who transmitted to William his final announcement of his advance on Acre.[87]

By the early fourteenth century few Templars could remember much before 1273, when William of Beaujeu had been elected, and so would not be inclined to turn to events beyond memory. A number of them, particularly those who had served in the East, knew of the controversy over William's policy of appeasement. They were searching their minds for examples of Muslim influence and naturally lighted on his mastership.

Conclusion

Memories of the kind I have described, recalled in the course of bitter argument or in times of acute stress, are dangerous for the historian to handle, not least because the men engaged in creatively redesigning the past must have thought that they were telling the truth. In the first of the examples I offered, a miracle appears to have been deployed in support of an order's ambivalent mission; in the second, an alternative foundation story may have developed to provide the Templars with more familiar surroundings and later to justify the Hospitallers' claims to Templar lands;

and in the third, circumstantial evidence provided an answer to a question put by interrogators. Elements of reality can be identified, but of course the greatest value these inventions have is that they help us to understand the problems confronted by their inventors.

Notes

1. William of Santo Stefano, "Comment la sainte maison de l'Hospital de S. Johan de Jerusalem commença," *Recueil des historiens des croisades: Historiens occidentaux,* 5 vols. (Paris: Académie des Inscriptions et Belles-Lettres, 1872–1906), 5:424 (hereafter *RHC Occ.*). For William, see Jonathan Riley-Smith, *The Knights of St. John in Jerusalem and Cyprus, 1050–1310* (London: Macmillan, 1967), 272–73, and Anthony Luttrell, "The Hospitallers' Early Written Records," in *The Crusades and Their Sources: Essays Presented to Bernard Hamilton,* ed. John France and William G. Zajac (Aldershot, UK: Ashgate, 1998), 139–43.

2. Ibn al-Qalanisi, *The Damascus Chronicle of the Crusades,* trans. H. A. R. Gibb (London: Luzac, 1932), 175–77.

3. *Cartulaire général de l'ordre des Hospitaliers de S. Jean de Jérusalem (1100–1310),* ed. Joseph Delaville Le Roulx, 4 vols. (Paris: Ernest Leroux, 1894–1906), 1:71 (hereafter *Cart. Hosp.*).

4. See Denys Pringle, *Secular Buildings in the Crusader Kingdom of Jerusalem: An Archaeological Gazetteer* (Cambridge: Cambridge University Press, 1997), 27.

5. See Jonathan Riley-Smith, *The First Crusaders* (Cambridge: Cambridge University Press, 1997), 164.

6. "Fragment d'un cartulaire de l'ordre de Saint Lazare en Terre-Sainte," ed. Arthur de Marsy, *Archives de l'Orient Latin* 2 (1884): 127.

7. *Papsturkunden für Templer und Johanniter,* ed. Rudolf Hiestand, Vorarbeiten zum Oriens Pontificius, I-II, 2 vols. (Gôttingen: Vandenhoeck and Ruprecht, 1972–84), 2:222–30.

8. Pringle, *Secular Buildings,* 32.

9. Riley-Smith, *The Knights of St. John,* 69–73.

10. Hiestand, *Papsturkunden für Templer und Johanniter,* 2:222–30.

11. *Cart. Hosp.* 1:360–61. The "custom" defining when or not the Hospitallers should engage in warfare must have dated from before the grant of Bethgibelin in 1136, since the holding of a castle would have carried with it military obligations whether the True Cross had been taken on campaign or not.

12. Hiestand, *Papsturkunden für Templer und Johanniter,* 2:159–62. See Hiestand's commentary, 136–59, esp. 150–51.

13. *Cart. Hosp.* 1:426 and 429 and Benjamin Z. Kedar, "A Twelfth-Century

Description of the Jerusalem Hospital," in *The Military Orders: Welfare and Warfare,* vol. 2, ed. Helen Nicholson (Aldershot, UK: Ashgate, 1998), 21–22.

14. William Caoursin, "Promordium et origo sacri xenodochii atque ordinis militiae Sancti Joannis Baptistae Hospitalariorum" (*RHC Occ.* 5:431–32). Translated as "Le fondement du S. Hospital et de l'ordre de la chevalerie de S. Jehan Baptiste de Jerusalem" (*RHC Occ.* 5:435).

15. "De primordiis et inventione sacrae religionis Jerosolymitanae" (*RHC Occ.* 5:429).

16. None, indeed, until an agreement with Duke Bela III of Hungary in the 1160s, which contains a clause covering the possibility of his sons wanting to serve the order and being lent horses and arms (*Cart. Hosp.*1.222).

17. And perhaps also on a *chevauchée,* led by King Baldwin II into the lands around Ascalon in 1128, in which the Hospital's second master, Raymond of Puy, is to be found (*Cart. Hosp.* 1:78).

18. *Cart. Hosp.* 1:6–8 and 71.

19. Its wording suggests that it was an early statute (*Cart. Hosp.* 1:68).

20. See Hiestand, *Papsturkunden für Templer und Johanniter,* 2:195.

21. William of Tyre, *Chronicon,* ed. R. B. C. Huygens, in *Corpus Christianorum Continuatio Mediaevalis* 63, 2 vols. (Turnholt: Brepols, 1986), 375 and 815–17.

22. See *Papsturkunden für Kirchen im Heiligen Lande,* ed. Rudolf Hiestand, Vorarbeiten zum Oriens Pontificius III (Göttingen, 1985), 115.

23. Fulcher of Chartres, *Historia Hierosolymitana,* ed. Heinrich Hagenmeyer (Heidelberg: Carl Winters, 1913), 642. For the MS, see 102–3.

24. Anthony Luttrell, "Préface" to *Les Légendes de l'Hôpital de Saint-Jean de Jérusalem,* ed. Antoine Calvet (Paris: Presses de l'Université de Paris-Sorbonne, 2000), 8; on the basis of the rather slight material uncovered by Anne Marie Legras and Jean-Loup Lemaître, "La pratique liturgique des Templiers et Hospitaliers de Saint-Jean de Jérusalem, in *L'Ecrit dans la Société Médiévale: Divers aspects de sa pratique du XIe à XVe siècle,* ed. Caroline Bourlet and Annie Dufour (Paris: Editions du CNRS, 1991), 89–94 and 110–13.

25. William of Tyre, *Chronicon,* 63, 375 and 817.

26. When inspected in 1629 the skeleton was virtually complete, but it was destroyed during the French Revolution, although fragments of bone can still be found in some Provençal churches and, incidentally, in London as well. Gerard's skull is now in the Monasterio Santa Ursula in Valletta. It had reached Malta in 1749 from Manosque. See Anthony Luttrell, "The Skull of Blessed Gerard," *The Order's Early Legacy in Malta,* ed. John Azzopardi (Valletta: Said International, 1989), 45, and Luttrell, "The Hospitallers' Early Written Records," 138–39.

27. Benedicta Ward, *Miracles and the Medieval Mind* (London: Scolar Press, 1982), 124–25.

28. The surviving account dates from the thirteenth century. Luttrell, "Préface," 5–11. For the program to develop Jerusalem, see Jonathan Riley-Smith, "The Death and Burial of Latin Christian Pilgrims to Jerusalem and Acre, 1099–1291," *Crusades* 7 (2008): 165–80.

29. Luttrell, *Les Légendes,* 122–24, 134–36, 144–45, and 153–54.

30. See *Gesta Francorum et aliorum Hierosolimitanorum,* ed. Rosalind M. T. Hill (London: T. Nelson, 1962), 89; Peter Tudebode, *Historia de Hierosolymitano itinere,* ed. John H. and Laurita L. Hill (Paris: Librairie Orientaliste Paul Geunther, 1977), 136; Raymond of Aguilers, *Liber,* ed. John H. and Laurita L. Hill (Paris: P. Geunther, 1969), 139–40; Fulcher of Chartres, *Historia,* 294–5; and Albert of Aachen, *Historia Ierosolimitana,* ed. Susan Edgington (Oxford: Oxford University Press, 2007), 408.

31. Kedar, "A Twelfth-Century Description," 18.

32. Ibid., 20.

33. William of Tyre, *Historia,* 375.

34. See Simonetta Cerrini, *La Révolution des Templiers* (Paris: Perrin, 2007), 75–85; Pierre-Vincent Claverie, "Les débuts de l'ordre du Temple en Orient," *Le moyen âge* 111 (2005): 546–57; Malcolm Barber, *The New Knighthood: A History of the Order of the Temple* (Cambridge: Cambridge University Press, 1994), 6–10; Anthony Luttrell, "The Earliest Templars," in *Autour de la première croisade,* ed. Michel Balard (Paris: Publications de la Sorbonne, 1996), 193–202; and Kaspar Elm, "Kanoniker und Ritter vom Heiligen Grab," *Die geistlichen Ritterorden Europas,* ed. Josef Fleckenstein and Manfred Hellmann (Sigmaringen: Thorbecke, 1980), 159–65. For Hugh of Payns, see Cerrini, *Le Révolution,* 37–39.

35. See Benjamin Kedar, "On the Origins of the Earliest Laws of Frankish Jerusalem: The Canons of the Council of Nablus, 1120," *Speculum* 74 (1999): 324–25 and 334.

36. Jonathan Riley-Smith, *The First Crusaders, 1095–1131* (Cambridge: Cambridge University Press, 1997), 162–63.

37. See Rudolf Hiestand, "Kardinalbischof Matthäus von Albano, das Konzil von Troyes und die Entstehung des Templerordens," *Zeitschrift für Kirchengeschichte* 99 (1988): 295–325; Cerrini, *La Révolution,* 100–19.

38. See Riley-Smith, *The First Crusaders,* 170.

39. Denys Pringle, *The Churches of the Crusader Kingdom of Jerusalem: A Corpus,* 3 vols., to date (Cambridge: Cambridge University Press, 1993–), 3:420–22.

40. *Le procès des Templiers,* ed. Jules Michelet, 2 vols. (Paris: Imprimerie royale, 1841–51), 1.641–48 (hereafter *Procès*).

41. *Procès* 1:642–43.

42. At Le Destroit (Pringle, *Secular Buildings,* 47–48).

43. See Pierre-Vincent Claverie, *L'Ordre du Temple en Terre Sainte et à Chypre au XIIIe siècle,* 3 vols. (Nicosia: Centre de Recherche Scientifique, 2005), 1:268–71.

44. Oliver of Paderborn, *Schriften,* ed. Hermann Hoogeweg (Tübingen: Litterarischer Verein in Stuttgart, 1894), 171. See Rudolf Hiestand, "*Castrum Peregrinorum* e la fine del dominio crociato in Siria," in *Acri 1291: La fine della presenza degli ordini militari in Terra Santa e i nuovi orientamenti nel XIV secolo,* ed. Francesco Tommasi (Perugia: Quatroemme, 1996), 31–32.

45. E.g., Anthony Luttrell, "Templari e ospitalieri: alcuni confronti," in *I Templari, la guerra e la santità,* ed. Simonetta Cerrini (Rimini: Il Cercio, 2000), 143–45, and Cerrini, *La Revolution,* 76–78.

46. *Le Cartulaire du chapitre du Saint-Sépulcre de Jérusalem,* ed. Geneviève Bresc-Bautier (Paris: P. Geuthner, 1984), 157–58 and 262, and Claverie, "Les débuts," 548.

47. See Luttrell, "Templari e ospitalieri," 144–45.

48. *Procès* 2:277–420.

49. Heinrich Finke, *Papsttum und Untergang des Templerordens,* 2 vols. (Münster: Aschendorff, 1907), 2:313–16, and Hans Prutz, *Entwicklung und Untergang des Tempelherrenordens* (Berlin: Grote, 1888), 325–26 and 334–35.

50. Prutz, *Entwicklung und Untergang,* 335.

51. Finke, *Papsttum,* 2:316–24 and 342–64, and Prutz, *Entwicklung und Untergang,* 324, 326, and 338–39.

52. Konrad Schottmüller, *Der Untergang des Templer-Ordens,* 2 vols. (Berlin: Ernst Siegfried, Mittler & Son, 1887), 2:14–71, and "Inquesta dominorum Commissariorum Clementis pape V in castro de Caynone dioceses Turonensis," ed. Barbara Frale, *I Papato e il processo ai Templari: L'inedita assoluzione di Chinon alla luce della diplomatica pontificia* (Rome: Viella, 2003), 198–214.

53. *Le procès des Templiers d'Auvergne, 1310–1311,* ed. Roger Sève and Anne-Marie Chagny-Sève (Paris: Editions du CTHS, 1986), 93–244.

54. Léon Ménard, *Histoire civile, ecclésiastique et littéraire de la ville de Nismes,* vol. 1, *Preuves* (Paris: H. D. Chaubert, 1750), 166–219.

55. *Monuments historiques relatifs à la condamnation des chevaliers du Temple et à l'abolition de leur ordre,* ed. François-Just-Marie Raynouard (Paris: Egron, 1813), 268–70. These are little more than notes. The manuscripts were looted by Napoleon's troops and disappeared.

56. *The Trial of the Templars in the Papal State and the Abruzzi,* ed. Anne Gilmour-Bryson (Vatican City: Biblioteca Apostolica Vaticana, 1982), 65–262.

57. "Dei Tempieri e del loro processo in Toscana," ed. Telesforo Bini, *Atti della Reale Accademia Lucchese di Scienze, Lettere ed Arti* 13 (1845): 460–501.

58. "Interrogatorio di Templari in Cesena (1310)," ed. Francesco Tommasi, in Tommasi, *Acri 1291*, 287–98.

59. Schottmüller, *Untergang des Templer-Ordens*, 2:108–39.

60. Raynouard, *Monuments historiques*, 280–84.

61. Fragments, some quite substantial, in "L'inedito processso del Templari in Castiglia (Medina del Campo, 27 Aprile 1310)," ed. Josep Maria Sans i Travé, in Tommasi, *Acri 1291*, 249–64; Fidel Fita y Colomé, *Siete concilios españoles* (Madrid: Maroto, 1882), 78–110; and Aurea Javierre Mur, "Aportacion al estudio del proceso contra el Temple en Castilla," *Revista des Archivos, Bibliotecas y Museos* 69 (1961): 75–100.

62. *Procès* 2:424–515.

63. Finke, *Papsttum*, 2:364–79.

64. Schottmüller, *Untergang des Templer-Ordens*, 2:147–400.

65. *Conciliae Magnae Britannie et Hibernie*, ed. David Wilkins, 3 vols. (London: n.p., 1737), 2:334–400, and Schottmüller, *Untergang des Templer-Ordens*, 2:78–102. See Sève, *Le procès des Templiers d'Auvergne*, 245–63.

66. *Procès* 1:1–648, and 2:1–274.

67. Sève, *Le procès des Templiers d'Auvergne*, 144.

68. *Procès* 1:606.

69. *Procès* 2:260.

70. *Procès* 2:61, 195–96, and 236, and Bini, "Dei Tempieri e del loro processo in Toscana," 484, 498. On the other hand, the sergeant James of Troyes (*Procès* 1:258–59) and brother priest William Textoris (2:131–32) seem to have considered the introduction of the practices to have been quite recent.

71. See the evidence of the sergeants James of Troyes (*Procès* 1:258), Andrew of *Monte Laudato* (2:104), Hugh of Narsac (2:209), Bosco of Masualier (2:231), Peter Blanc (2:247), John of *Crenacon/Cranaco* (by implication, Schottmüller, *Untergang des Templer-Ordens*, 2:23) and John of Naples (Gilmout-Bryson, *The Trial of the Templars in the Papal State*, 255). For other references to friendship with Muslims, see the evidence of the Franciscan John of Donnington and the Templars William of Kilross and Thomas of Thoroldby, in Wilkins, *Conciliae Magni Britannie*, 2.363, 377, and 387.

72. *Procès* 2:229–30.

73. Wilkins, *Conciliae Magni Britannie*, 2.387. Adelard might be the Amblard, who was grand commander under Henry III: Thomas said that he had governed the province fifty or sixty years ago.

74. Schottmüller, *Untergang des Templer-Ordens*, 2.79, and Wilkins, *Conciliae Magni Britannie*, 2:383–84 and 386.

75. *Procès* 2:400

76. *Procès* 2:158, 374; Finke, *Papsttum*, 2:324, 347–48, and 356; Ménard,

Preuves, 185–86, 188, and 191–93; Marie-Lusie Bulst-Thiele, *Sacrae Domus Militiae Templi Hierosolymitani Magistri* (Göttingen: Vandenhoeck & Ruprecht, 1974), 228n235 and 228n249.

77. Wilkins, *Conciliae Magni Britannie*, 2:384.

78. Evidence of Galcerand of Teus: Raynouard, *Monuments historiques*, 283.

79. Evidence of Geoffrey of Gonneville: *Procès* 2:400.

80. *Procès* 2:196, 398, and 400.

81. *Procès* 2:222 and 224.

82. Although the brother priest William Textoris opined that the errors had been introduced after William's mastership: *Procès* 2:131–32.

83. *Procès* 2:209. So had Matthew Sauvage, a grand commander in Acre in 1260 and later commander of Sidon, whom another witness claimed had been Sultan Baybars of Egypt's blood brother, "because they had exchanged blood. See *Procès* 1:645.

84. *Procès* 2:215.

85. *Procès* 1:44–45.

86. The Templar of Tyre, *Cronaca del Templare di Tiro (1243–1314)*, ed. Laura Minervini (Naples: Ligouri, 2000), 194 and 202. For William's treaty with Qala'un of 1282, see Peter M. Holt, *Early Mamluk Diplomacy (1260–1290)* (Leiden: Brill, 1995), 66–68.

87. Minervini, *Cronaca del Templare di Tiro*, 204–6.

CHAPTER ELEVEN

Visual Self-Fashioning and the Seals of the Knights Hospitaller in England

LAURA J. WHATLEY

A S HIGHLY MOBILE AND intrinsically visual artifacts, medieval seals both embody and convey individual or institutional identity, sometimes providing the most complete record of a group's structure and self-conception. This is certainly true of the seals of the Order of the Hospital of St. John of Jerusalem in England, whose visual culture was mostly eradicated during the Reformation. Representative seals of the English order, many of which are still affixed to the original document, survive from the twelfth to sixteenth centuries, allowing the seal to be roughly dated and perhaps identifying the sealer. In this chapter, I discuss both the pictorial content and inscriptions of select Hospitaller seals from England, locating these seals in their immediate social context, both international and local. Not only can the seals used by the Hospitallers in England be understood in relation to the crusade movement and the order's central authoritative body in the Latin East, but they can also be investigated within their domestic religious, political, and social milieu.[1] They provide important and unique insight into how the Order of the Hospital of St. John identified or fashioned itself in England, as both a military order and an international monastic foundation. Importantly, this self-presentation changed most dramatically over the course of the twelfth and thirteenth centuries, following the establishment of the English order after 1128 and its subsequent independence from the Grand Priory of St. Gilles in France in the 1180s. I therefore consider the ways in which the English seals reference or break from the seals produced in the Latin East and France, analyzing changes in the iconography on the English seals as public statements of an emerging corporate autonomy in England and the desire to propagate a distinct sigillographic identity.

That the seal played a role in the formulation and expression of medieval identity has been well established by Brigitte Bedos-Rezak, who suggested that "seal users came to develop a new awareness of themselves in relation to an object, the seal, whose operational principles were categorization, replication, and verification."[2] In general, sealing was a process for establishing ownership, signing commitment, designating identity, representing authority, and of course authenticating documents.[3] Seals have two key features: (1) the pictorial symbol, which could be personalized or highly conventional, and (2) the inscription around it, which identified the author or authorial body of the document to which the seal was attached. Medieval written records refer to both the engraved matrix, also known as the *die,* and its impressions as seals, but the matrix was, without doubt, an exceptional object, which was the personal property of its owner. There is evidence that personal seal-dies were either kept among one's treasure or were worn on the body as pendants, rings, or brooches.[4] Institutional seals, like those of the Hospital of St. John of Jerusalem, are most often described in written records as being kept locked in an iron-bound chest with several locks, and most institutions strictly regulated access to their seals.[5]

The first seal instituted by the Order of the Hospital of St. John of Jerusalem was the lead *bulla* of the master, the original great, or common, seal of the order. This seal, with only slight modifications, was used for the entire history of the order (see fig. 11.1) The master's seal is circular in shape, generally with a diameter of one and one-half inches. Double-sided, it features pictures and legends on both the obverse and reverse, much like a coin. On the obverse, the master kneels in prayer before a patriarchal cross, which is usually accompanied by the sacred letters α (alpha) and ω (omega). The patriarchal, or double-beam, cross embodied the crucifixion; Christ's body was affixed to the lower crossbeam, and the upper crossbeam bore the plaque with the initials INRI, IESVS NAZARENVS REX IVDAEORVM.[6] Over the course of the thirteenth and fourteenth centuries, the seal was slightly modified. For example, on the earliest seals the master knelt to the right before the cross, whereas on later seals he faced left. Also, the patriarchal cross became larger and more defined, with a round knob or ornamental foot for the base, which gave it the appearance of an altar cross, a liturgical object. This is evident, for example, on the bulla of Roger de Molin (1177–87), a pristine example of which is attached to London,

British Library Harley Charter 43 I. 38, and the bulla of Geoffrey de Donjon, affixed to a charter dated January 1193 (fig. 11.1).[7] On the obverse of both seals, the masters kneel in prayer before the patriarchal cross surmounted on an orb or globe. In the center of the field, between the master and the cross, are the alpha and the omega.

This image type, which features the suppliant figure of the seal-user within the design, was not uncommon on both private seals and seals of office with religious iconography; such seals are referred to as seals of devotion.[8] The devotional content is ultimately Christological; the patriarchal, or Latin, cross with two crossbars, was representative of the cross of the crucifixion, while the alpha and omega refer to the Second Coming, the Last Judgment. The central image is surrounded by a legend with the master's name followed by an official designation CVSTOS, guardian or keeper of the order. For example, the legend inscribed around Roger's effigy was: + RO[GERI]VS CVSTOS. Notably, the master's name was written in the nominative case, which was also used in the later legend of Geoffrey's bulla: + GAVFRIDVS CVSTOS. Seal legends commonly referred to the sealer in the genitive, indicating his or her possession of the seal, that is, seal of Roger. In the instance of the early Hospitaller seals, however, the legend actually identified the imaged figure and reinforced his personal presence in the seal. On later seals, the legend became more specific, as the name of the master was generally preceded by the word *frater*, and the title *cvstos* was followed by the word *Pavpervum*.[9]

The reverse of the master's seal shows a body lying on a bier before a tabernacle. The body has been interpreted in three different ways. The *Catalogue of Seals of the British Museum* identifies the dead body as that of the Lord, and the tabernacle as the Church of the Holy Sepulchre; indeed, on *bullae* from the fourteenth-century, the figure has a halo, likely prompting the identification of the figure as Christ.[10] However, a halo had not always been an attribute of the figure, and the surrounding legend identifies the institution embodied in the seal: HOSPITALIS IHERVSALEM. Scholars have thus interpreted the seal as a representation of a patient in the Hospital in Jerusalem.[11] Taking the legend into account, it definitely would be fitting for the figure to represent a patient in the Hospitallers' care. Although, while the Hospital in Jerusalem no doubt restored numerous patients to health, John of Würzburg, a pilgrim who visited the infirmary in the 1160s, describes fifty dead being carried out of the Hospital

FIGURE 11.1. Seal of Geoffrey de Donjon, Grand Master of the Hospital, 1193. Document conserved in the Archives nationales, Paris, D9880. By permission of the Archives nationales, Paris. Photograph by Laura J. Whatley.

each day.[12] Hence, the reverse's image may reference the ceremonial care of the dead and, by extension, the souls of the deceased offered by the religious community, rather than the medical care of the sick.

The Hospitallers' inventory of seals from the mid-thirteenth century, *Ci dit des bulles que le maistre et les autre baillis del hospital,* recorded that the reverse of the master's seal should feature "the body of a dead man before a tabernacle," failing to identify either the figure or the location depicted on the seal.[13] The architectural framework or canopy, the so-called tabernacle, was always rendered with three domes or spires topped with crosses, a lamp suspended from the central cupola of the canopy, and a censer swinging into frame over the man's feet. All of these iconographic elements are clearly visible on Geoffrey de Donjon's late twelfth-century seal, with its bulbous Byzantine domes hovering above the tightly wrapped body of an obviously dead man (see fig. 11.1). Changes to the reverse of the seal were stylistic rather than symbolic or iconographic; over time, the rounded domes ultimately became pointed (i.e., Gothic) spires, and the funeral bier beneath the body increasingly resembled a tomb or saints' shrine. In his study of the seals, E. J. King dismissed any specific association of the architectural framework employed on the reverse of the seals with the Church of the Holy Sepulchre, no doubt based on his knowledge of *Ci dit des bulles* and perhaps his visual analysis of the later seals with the Gothicized architecture. However, Jerusalem architecture was a fundamental aspect of twelfth-century crusader seal vocabulary, including the Templum Domini, which was featured on the seals of the Knights Templar,[14] and the Tower of David, Templum Domini, and Dome of the Anastasis Rotunda, all of which appeared together on the seals of the kings of Jerusalem.[15] The domed structure on Hospitaller seal therefore must have evoked the interior of the Church of the Holy Sepulchre and consequently the tomb of Christ in the mind of the viewer.

I believe that the obverse and reverse of the master's bulla actually participated in a shared Christological dialogue, one that functioned on two distinct symbolic levels. On the one hand, the seal presented the crucifixion, entombment, and resurrection of Christ. On the other hand, it established the role of the Order of the Hospital of St. John of Jerusalem in the care of pilgrims and the holy poor, who were all identified as Christ by the brothers charged with the care of their bodies as well as their souls. Notably, the image on the seal also seems to visualize the vigil described in the Hospital's statutes for deceased brethren of the order, during which the body of the brother was laid out on a bier in the church, draped with the Hospitallers' flag and surrounded by candles.[16] It is therefore also possible that the seal's two faces worked together to present the life cycle of the master himself, who, depicted on the seal, lived as a faithful guardian of the order and died under its care. The images carried on the master's seal certainly reflected the traditional religious and spiritual duties of the Hospitallers; they did not overtly indicate the militarization of the order in the twelfth century or the individual and communal identity of the brethren as crusaders.

The only significant change to the Hospital's seal protocol occurred at the Chapter-General of 1278, with the institution of the great seal of the convent, the Conventual Bulla, which is generally referred to as the "Seal of the Master and Convent." The statute stated that the Conventual seal was to be attached to all deeds of gifts, which were made in perpetuity or for life by consent of the convent, and to charters relating to donations, sales, and transfers of property.[17] Thus, it was used on the majority of documents produced by the house. It was fashioned to closely resemble the master's bulla: it was made of lead, with a diameter of approximately one and one-half inches and two faces. In fact, only the obverse of the seal changed, as the master was no longer depicted alone but with the Conventual Bailiffs, facing left and kneeling in prayer before the patriarchal cross. The reverse of the seal maintained the image of the dead body lying beneath an architectural framework. This seal quite literally represented the corporate body of the Hospital in Jerusalem by depicting the collective authority of the members of the order through their presence on the seal. The increasing communal jurisdiction within the Hospital is also evident in the statutes, which made clear that no single officer had complete control of or access to the order's seals. For example, a statute from 1278 dictated that the seals of the convent in the Latin East be kept in boxes or in chests with the treasurer, not with the sealer, including the master's seal and those of the grand commander, marshal, and hospitaller — the order's highest-ranking officials.

The houses of the Order of St. John of Jerusalem in Western Europe, far removed from the Holy Land, had to establish themselves as a part of this international religious order, as part of the communal body, and the provincial officers had to reaffirm both their function and authority at the local level. While the Hospitallers in the Latin East were active participants on the front lines of the crusade movement, caring for the sick and poor in the Holy Land and defending important military strongholds, the Knights Hospitaller in the West were charged with channeling recruits, money, and supplies directly to the central government, which enabled the order to maintain its distinguished and costly operations in the Latin East. In Western Europe, the Hospital of St. John was gradually organized into eight provincial nations, called *langues,* or *tongues:* the *langues* of Provence, Auvergne, France, Italy, Aragon, England, Germany, and Castile. Within each of these *langues* were grouped various priories, one of which was usually the grand priory of the nation.

The first priory constituted in western Europe was the Priory of St. Gilles near Marseilles, established by 1120. The prior of St. Gilles administered the whole of France as well as the regions south across the Pyrenees into Catalonia and Aragon and north into the Low Countries.[18] He also had authority over the order's estates in England until the later twelfth century. There is a well-preserved seal from the Priory of St. Gilles attached to a charter from around the year 1140. It is a circular impression in red wax, with a diameter of two inches; it has no reverse image or counterseal. Directly quoting the iconography of the master's bulla, it depicts the prior in a suppliant pose facing right before a patriarchal cross. The legend identifies the prior by name in the nominative, "Arnaldus," along with his official title, "Prior," and the name of the institution, the "Hospital of St. Gilles." Importantly, the oldest extant seal from the Hospital in England, which is attached to a document dated 1148, employs this same iconography, depicting a figure in prayer before a patriarchal cross (fig. 11.2). Notably, however, the English seal also includes the symbolic letters alpha and omega, which are lacking on the St. Gilles seals — perhaps a direct nod to the Master's bulla — although the engraver of the English matrix did not reverse the two Greek letters, and consequently they appear backwards on the wax impression: ωA. The seal, an impression in red wax with a diameter of two inches, is surrounded by the detailed legend: "Seal of Walter, Prior of the Hospital of Jerusalem in England," with his name in the genitive (+ S WALTERI PRIORIS [HO]SPITA[L] . . . IERLM IN ANGLIA).

The earliest priors of both France and England thus chose to mirror the image of the master on the great seal on their own seals, which visually connected the provincial houses of the order to the central administrative body. Indeed, the master personally appointed the grand priors who governed over each *langue;* he invested them with their authority. The priors were then responsible for electing certain officials within their *langue* and collecting the responsions — the dues owed to the central convent.[19] For example, as the larger priories often were subdivided into smaller units

FIGURE 11.2. Seal of Walter, Prior of England, ca. 1140–42. © The British Library Board, Harley ch. 83, C. 40. Photograph courtesy of the British Library, London.

known as commanderies or preceptories, the grand prior was responsible for appointing the commander or preceptor of each house, who ruled under his authority. The master did not directly participate in the local governing of the provincial houses; rather, the priors were his connection to the West, and they were required to attend the meetings of the Chapter-General held in the Levant in order to report on the status of all of the houses in their *langue* to the central government. The image employed on the early seals of the French and English priors therefore would have identified them as close associates of the master, legitimizing their power as his appointed officials, while also promoting them as important officials in their own right within the Hospital's complex and hierarchical internal structure.[20]

The nature of Brother Walter's role in England however is difficult to gauge; he was affiliated with the Hospital of St. John of Jerusalem at Clerkenwell, founded just outside the walls of London in 1144; this institution would become the order's administrative center, the Priory of

England in the 1180s. Documentary evidence suggests, however, that all Hospitaller houses in England were under the authority of the Priory of St. Gilles until around 1185, and thus Clerkenwell likely functioned as a large preceptory until that time.[21] Was Walter actually the head chaplain of St. John Clerkenwell, a priest or perhaps the preceptor of the London estate? As Michael Gervers suggested, the terms *prior* and *preceptor* were initially interchangeable in England, especially before the Priory of England was formally established.[22] Ultimately, by using the same pictorial scheme on his seal as those found on the seal of the Prior of St. Gilles and on the obverse of the Master's bulla, Walter was tapping into the visual language of authority employed by high officers of the Hospital of St. John of Jerusalem, both in the East and West. He ambitiously fashioned himself as an official player in the administration of the English estates and fashioned the house at Clerkenwell as a grand priory, which was continued by his successors.

Indeed, the remaining twelfth-century sealers of the Hospital in England featured the same iconography of the figure kneeling before the patriarchal cross on their seals, although they had new matrices engraved, and some of their seals exhibit important changes to both the central image and the legend. Also, counterseals, which increased document security and could be tailored to the sealer through the inclusion of heraldry or a personal insignia, come into use. Richard de Turk, who occurs in written sources until 1173, used a seal with the suppliant figure before the double-beam cross, which is now presented as a liturgical implement on an altar.[23] This image figuratively transported the True Cross from Jerusalem and placed it in England. The legend includes both Richard's title of office; like Brother Walter he identifies himself as prior, and the name of the institution.[24] Most significantly, Richard instituted the use of a counterseal, which is both pictorially and textually compelling: a small oval with a Roman bust facing right, probably from an intaglio gem, accompanied by the legend CAPVD IOH[ANNIS] BAPTISTE, "the Head of John the Baptist."[25] This is the first instance of a Hospitaller seal referencing the order's patron saint, introducing the head of St. John as a sacred image well suited to a seal.[26]

The next seal of the English Hospital, used by Brother Ralph de Dive on a charter dated 1178, features the same iconography of the kneeling prior before a patriarchal cross (fig. 11.3). Here, a Latin inscription

FIGURE 11.3. Seal of Ralph de Dive, Prior of England, ca. 1178. By permission of the National Archives, UK, DL 25/320. Photograph by Laura J. Whatley.

accompanies the cross — *"salve crux sancta arbor digna"* — which is from the hymn for the feast of the Invention of the Cross. This reinforces the symbolism of the patriarchal cross represented on the seal as the True Cross, an emblem of the crusade movement, and certainly reflects the increasing role of liturgy in the promotion of the crusade by religious foundations in the West.[27] Importantly, this seal does not include the name of the prior in the legend, simply identifying the sealer as the "Prior of the Brethren of the Hospital in England."[28]

This is the first time an English Hospitaller seal references the conventual body and, to some degree, institutional rather than individual authority, which would have been an important step in the formation of a corporate identity. While I would not classify this seal as a great or common seal, the English brethren were certainly beginning to fashion their seals in that way; a common seal was a desirable and prestigious object in medieval England, after all, because with it an institution like the Hospital of St. John could claim the rights that individuals had as owners of property and in a court of law.[29]

The growing communal authority within the provincial houses of the Hospital was also reflected in the statutes. During the Chapter-General of 1270, it was decided that every priory seal should be kept in a locked chest with four keys; the prior was in possession of one key, while three different high-ranking officers of the priory kept the other three keys. This protocol prevented the prior from sealing anything without the advice of the collective body, as all four men had to assemble with their keys before the matrix could be removed from the chest.[30] This statute reveals that the central government of the Hospital was concerned with regulating seal usage in all provincial houses, and it also indicates that the priors in Western Europe required new restrictions by the end of the thirteenth century regarding their personal authority in relation to communal authority. In other words, there was a diffusion of power, at least in terms of the authentication of documents.

Brother Ralph's successor, Garnier of Nablus (1184–90), used the same matrix for the obverse of his seal, indicating that it was, indeed, engraved for the deathless corporate body of the Hospital in England rather than for an individual officer. Granted, by 1189, Garnier was also using a personalized counterseal, which includes both his name and official title in the legend, "Seal of Garnier, Prior of the Hospital in England," and featured, in high relief, the head of a man with wild hair and a long beard, certainly the head of the Hospitallers' patron saint, John the Baptist (fig. 11.4). This impression may have been made by a signet ring worn by Garnier, even before he became the prior of England; perhaps it was an image always associated with this particular individual knight Hospitaller.[31] Like a personal badge of membership and authority, the image on his counterseal clearly, *visually,* identified Garnier as a brother of the Order of St. John the Baptist. The appearance of St. John in this image accords well with the graphic description of the saint in a sermon by Philagathos, a Greek monk of the twelfth century: "He was shaggy and wild in appearance. . . . His head was squalid, filthy, and covered with flowing locks. He was shaded by a mass of his own hair. His beard was thick."[32]

The design of Garnier's hagiographic counterseal was so compelling that by at least the second decade of the thirteenth century it had been adapted as the common seal of the English order, impressions of which appear on documents from roughly 1215 to 1385. The seal depicts the head of John the Baptist, always frontal with long hair and beard, within a

FIGURE 11.4. Counterseal of Garnier of Nablus, Prior of England, 1189. By permission of the National Archives, UK, E 40/6708. Photograph by Laura J. Whatley.

border of pellets that form a halo, or charger (fig. 11.5). Through this image, the Hospitallers in England were endowing their seal the sacred personality of Saint John. While it is desirable to locate an English model for this seal, the iconography of the seal was not drawn from western European depictions of Saint John that were common in the twelfth and thirteenth centuries. Usually rendered as a half- or full-length figure, John the Baptist was most often portrayed with standardized attributes beyond his shaggy hair and beard: he was frequently shown wearing animal skin robes and holding the *Agnus Dei*—the standard iconography for representing John on a seal. Also, the majority of images of John the Baptist found in western art are narrative, in particular depicting the saint baptizing Christ in the Jordan.[33] Although the image on the English Hospitaller seal is redolent of the story of John's decollation, it is not narrative. In fact, the face of John the Baptist on the English seal is markedly similar to depictions of his face on Byzantine icons, devotional portraits of holy persons. These wax impressions thus carried the visual weight of a sacred object, a relic, sanctifying both the order and its written records. The appearance of the seal, specifically, its Byzantinizing portrayal of the Baptist, was perhaps not a mere illusion to the East but was in fact a product of it. Before becoming prior of England, Garnier of Nablus served as the castellan of Bethgibelin in Palestine, from 1173 until 1176, and was then appointed grand commander of the Hospital in Jerusalem.[34] Hence, he could have imported this iconic image of St. John from the eastern Mediterranean—his home for over a decade—to England, quite literally on his body.

Scholarship on medieval seals stresses their "essential uniformity"; patrons wanted an image that was readily understandable in terms of a preexisting local vocabulary, iconography.[35] However, the English Hospitallers fashioned a great seal that seems to have had no direct model in England. In terms of ecclesiastical institutions, the majority of church dignitaries preferred a seal engraved with their own effigy, holding the attributes of their office, more similar to the first seals of the English Hospital with the image of the kneeling prior; very few used hagiographic imagery.[36] However, there are numerous monastic seals of the twelfth and thirteenth centuries that do feature the figure of the patron saint of the house, usually as a full-length standing figure. For instance, other institutions in England dedicated to John the Baptist, mostly hospitals, included his image on their seals, but he is always depicted as a standing figure holding a plaque engraved with the *Agnus Dei*.[37] Hagiographic seals were also used by the papacy from the eleventh century onward, and they may have provided a more direct model for the iconography of the English common seal. Traditionally, papal *bullae* featured the heads of SS. Peter and Paul encircled by a cordon of pellets—a ubiquitous sigillographic image in the Middle Ages that the military orders undoubtedly knew well, as they were ultimately under papal authority.[38]

While the primary audience for these seals was English, documents from the Priory of England circulated in France, Italy, and the Latin East. As an international foundation, the English Hospitallers had the task of fashioning a seal that was easy to read, regardless of the nationality or social standing of the viewer. In the thirteenth century, the English Hospitallers also required an image that would differentiate them from the Priory of St. Gilles, the English orders' former administrator, and they may have wanted to distance themselves visually from the authority of the central government in the Latin East and from the eastern standard seal types, especially after the devastating crusader losses of the late twelfth

FIGURE 11.5. Seal of the Hospital in England. William de Tothale, Prior of England, ca. 1297–1315. By permission of the National Archives, UK, E 329/55. Photograph by Laura J. Whatley.

century. In the thirteenth century, the English Hospitallers crafted a seal that referenced a very specific authority. Rather than displaying the body of the mortal prior on the seal, they chose instead to promote themselves as a deathless corporation embodied in the image of a saint. Both iconic and devotional, the seal of the Priory of England is a clear statement of its institutional identity, as part of the Order of St. John. Offering a bold departure from the iconography employed on Hospitaller seals in the Latin East and in France, the seal for the English brethren fashioned a public image that was distinctly international and that presented their patron saint as the true authority behind the order.

Notes

1. Select bibliography of the seals of the Knight Hospitallers: Sebastiano Pauli, *Codice diplimatico del sacro militare Ordine gerosolimitano, oggi di Malta,* 2 vols. (Luca: Salvatore e Giandomenico Marescandoli, 1733–37); Gustave Schlumberg, "Deux sceuax et une monnaie des Grands Maîtres de Hôpital," *Revue archéologique* 1 (1876): 55–57; Gustave Schlumberg, "Sceaux et bulles de l'Orient latin au Moyen Age," *Le Musée archéologique* 2 (1877): 294–343; J. Delaville Le Roulx, "Note sur les sceaux de l'ordre de Saint Jean de Jérusalem," *Mémoires de la Société nationale des Antiquaires de France,* 5th ser., 1 (1880): 52–87; Delaville Le Roulx, "Les sceaux des archives de l'ordre de Saint-Jean de Jérusalem à Malte," *Mémoires de la Société nationale des antiquaires de France* 47 (1886): 225–47; and Edwin James King, *The Seals of the Order of St. John of Jerusalem* (London: Methuen, 1932).

2. Brigitte Miriam Bedos-Rezak, "Medieval Identity: A Sign and a Concept," *American Historical Review* 105, no. 5 (2000): 1491, and Bedos-Rezak, "Replica: Images of Identity and the Identity of Images in Prescholastic France," in *The Mind's Eye: Art and Theological Argument in the Middle Ages,* ed. Jeffrey F. Hamburger and Anne-Marie Bouché (Princeton: Princeton University Press, 2006), 55.

3. Bedos-Rezak, "Medieval Identity," 1511.

4. Brigitte Miriam Bedos-Rezak, "Medieval Seals and the Structure of Chivalric Society," in *The Study of Chivalry: Resources and Approaches,* ed. Howell Chickering and Thomas H. Seiler (Kalamazoo, MI: Medieval Institute Publications, 1988), 314.

5. M. T. Clanchy, *From Memory to Written Record, England 1066–1307,* 2nd ed. (Oxford: Blackwell, 1993), 317, and T. A. Heslop, "English Seals in the Thirteenth and Fourteenth Centuries," in *Age of Chivalry,* ed. Jonathan Alexander and Paul Binski (London: Weidenfeld & Nicolson, 1987), 114.

6. John 19:19.

7. Seal of Geoffrey de Donjon, Grand Master of the Hospital, 1193 (Paris, Archives nationales, D 9880).

8. Elizabeth A. New, "Christological Personal Seals and Christocentric Devotion in Later Medieval England and Wales," *Antiquaries Journal* 82 (2002): 50.

9. King, *Seals,* 14–15.

10. Walter de Gray Birch, *Catalogue of Seals in the Department of Manuscripts in the British Museum,* 6 vols. (London: British Museum, 1887–1900), 6:848–57.

11. Jonathan Riley-Smith, *Hospitallers: The History of the Order of St. John* (London: Hambledon, 1999), 25, and Bedos-Rezak, "Medieval Seals," 324.

12. John of Würzburg, "Description of the Holy Land," in *Palestine Pilgrims'*

Text Society, vol. 4, ed. Aubrey Stewart (London: Committee of the Palestine Exploration Fund, 1896), 44. See also Edgar Erskine Hume, *Medical Work of the Knights Hospitallers of Saint John of Jerusalem* (Baltimore: Johns Hopkins University Press, 1940), 14–15, and Helen Nicholson, *The Knights Hospitaller* (Woodbridge, UK: Boydell & Brewer, 2001), 89.

13. King, *Seals*, app. A, 127. This document was included in a manuscript of the Statues of the Order dated to the end of the thirteenth century, probably before the institution of the Conventual Bulla in 1278, since it makes no mention of it. The text in its original Old French is published in J. Delaville le Roulx, "Note sur les sceaux"; reprinted in *Mélanges sur l'ordre de S. Jean de Jérusalem* (Paris: Alphonse Picard, 1910), ix.

14. The seal of the Order of the Temple carried an abbreviated image of the Temple—a large ribbed dome atop a drum supported by a circular arcade of columns—and the inscription "Sigillum Militum de Templo Christi" (see Paris, Archives nationales, D 9858 and D 9862). See also Sylvia Schein, "Between Mount Moriah and the Holy Sepulchre: The Changing Traditions of the Temple Mount in the Central Middle Ages," *Traditio* 40 (1984): 191.

15. Jaroslav Folda, *The Art of the Crusaders in the Holy Land, 1098–1187* (Cambridge: Cambridge University Press, 1995), 46–47 and 195n6.

16. Jonathan Riley-Smith, *Knights of St. John in Jerusalem and Cyprus c. 1050–1310* (London: Macmillan, 1967), 251, and E. J. King, *The Rule, Statutes, and Customs of the Hospitallers, 1099–1310* (London: Methuen, 1934), 182, 199.

17. King, *Rule, Statutes, and Customs*, 79. For the statues, see also J. Delaville Le Roulx, "Les statuts de l'ordre de l'Hôpital," *Bibliothèque de l'Ecole des chartes* 48 (1887): 341–56, and Marie Rose Bonnet and Ricardo Cierbide, *Les statuts de l'ordre de Saint-Jean de Jérusalem: Edition critique des manuscrits en langue d'oc* (Bilbao: Universidad del Paiìs Vasco, 2006).

18. Riley-Smith, *Knights of St. John*, 353.

19. Nicholson, *Knights Hospitaller*, 78.

20. For more on the Hospital's structure, see Nicholson, *Knights Hospitaller*, ch. 4; Riley-Smith, *Knights of St. John*, ch. 2; and J. Delaville Le Roulx, *Les Hospitaliers en Terre Sainte et à Chypre, 1100–1310* (Paris: E. Leroux, 1904), 285–309.

21. Michael Gervers, "Donations to the Hospitallers in England in the Wake of the Second Crusade," in *The Second Crusade and the Cistercians*, ed. Michael Gervers (New York: St. Martin's Press, 1992), 155–56, and Barney Sloane and Gordon Malcolm, *Excavations at the Priory of the Order of the Hospital of St. John of Jerusalem, Clerkenwell, London* (London: Museum of London Archeology Service, 2004), 27.

22. Michael Gervers, ed., *The Cartulary of the Knights of St. John of Jerusalem in England: Part 2, prima camera: Essex,* British Academy Records in Social and Economic History, n.s. 23 (Oxford: Oxford University Press, 1996), lxxi, and Sloane and Malcolm, *Excavations,* 42.

23. King, *Seals,* 95–97.

24. It is worth noting that in the document itself, which is a lease of land in Baybrooke, Northampton, to Pipewell Abbey (London, British Library [hereafater BL] Additional Charter 21643), Richard de Turk, who attached his seal in witness of the transaction, is referred to as "Magister . . . in Anglia," not prior. See Henry John Ellis, ed., *Index to the Charters and Rolls in the Department of Manuscripts, British Museum,* 2 vols. (London: Trustees of the British Museum, 1912), 2:652.

25. King, *Seals,* 96–97.

26. The only comparative seal is a thirteenth-century matrix for a counterseal from the Benedictine Abbey of St. Mary and St. John the Baptist, Godstow, in Oxfordshire, which depicts the head of a bearded man [John the Baptist] on a charger with the legend CAPVT IOHIS IN DISCO (London, BL cast lxx.74).

27. See Simon Lloyd, *English Society and the Crusades, 1216–1307* (Oxford: Oxford University Press, 1988), 51; Christoph T. Maier, *Crusade Propaganda and Ideology: Model Sermons for the Preaching of the Cross* (Cambridge: Cambridge University Press, 2000); Christoph T. Maier, "Crisis, Liturgy, and the Crusade in the Twelfth and Thirteenth Centuries," *Journal of Ecclesiastical History* 84 (1997): 628–57; and David Marcombe, "The Confraternity Seals of Burton Lazars Hospital and a Newly Discovered Matrix from Robertsbridge, Sussex," *Transactions of the Leicestershire Archaeological and Historical Society* 76 (2002): 48.

28. See Seal of Ralph de Dive, ca. 1178, London, BL Harley Charter 44 H. 53.

29. P. D. A. Harvey and Andrew McGuinness, *A Guide to British Medieval Seals* (Toronto: University of Toronto Press, 1996), 95, and Clanchy, *From Memory,* 315.

30. King, *Rule, Statutes, and Customs,* 78.

31. I must thank Brigitte Bedos-Rezak, who suggested to me that Garnier's counterseal was perhaps an impression from a signet ring or personal intaglio gem.

32. Philagathos, *Homilia* 34.4; cited in Henry Maguire, *The Icons of Their Bodies: Saints and Their Images in Byzantium* (Princeton: Princeton University Press, 1996), 72.

33. See Emile Mâle, *Religious Art in France: The Twelfth Century; A Study of the Origins of Iconography* (Princeton: Princeton University Press, 1978), 72–76, 128–29, and 332.

34. Riley-Smith, *Knights of St. John,* 107.

35. Heslop, "English Seals," 116.

36. Bedos-Rezak, "Medieval Seals," 323–24.

37. Cf. the common seal of the Hospital of St. John, Abingdon (London, BL cast lviii.50; the seal of the Priory of St. John Baptist, Bridgewater, in Somerset (London, BL cast lxxi.56; London, National Archives E 322/30 and E25/16); the common seal of the Hospital of St. John Baptist, Chester (London, BL cast lx.83); the common seal of the Hospital of St. John Baptist, Coventry (London, BL cast lxi.92; London, National Archives E 322/64); the master's seal of the Hospital of St. John Baptist, Exeter (London, BL cast lxi.83); and the common seal of the Hospital of St. John Baptist, Wells (London, National Archives E 322/257).

38. Bedos-Rezak, "Medieval Seals," 324.

CONTRIBUTORS

SUZANNE CONKLIN AKBARI, professor of English and medieval studies at the University of Toronto, was educated at Johns Hopkins and Columbia. Her research focuses on the intersection of English and comparative literature with intellectual history and philosophy, ranging from Neoplatonism and science in the twelfth century to national identity and religious conflict in the fourteenth. Akbari's books are on optics and allegory (*Seeing Through the Veil*, 2004), European views of Islam and the Orient (*Idols in the East*, 2009), and travel literature (*Marco Polo*, 2008); she is currently at work on "Small Change: Metaphor and Metamorphosis in Chaucer and Christine de Pizan." The volume editor for the *Norton Anthology of World Literature, Volume B: 100–1500*, and co-editor of the *Norton Anthology of Western Literature*, Akbari is at work on "The Oxford Handbook to Chaucer." She is cross-appointed to the Centre for Medieval Studies, Centre for Comparative Literature, Centre for Jewish Studies, Department of Near and Middle Eastern Civilizations, and Centre for Reformation and Renaissance Studies.

CHRISTINE CHISM joined the faculty of UCLA in 2009, after holding positions at Rutgers University and Allegheny College. Since completing her first book, *Alliterative Revivals* (2002) on late medieval alliterative romance, she has been working on several projects. The first, "Mortal Friends: The Politics of Friendship in Medieval England," explores the social force of friendship as it is tested in a range of late medieval texts, from romances, to court-poems, to Chaucer's *Canterbury Tales*, to Robin Hood ballads. The second project, "Strange Knowledge: Translation and Cultural Transmission in the Arabic and English Middle Ages," draws upon skills acquired between 2003 and 2005 while working on a Mellon New Directions Fellowship to learn Arabic and study

Islamic cultures. "Strange Knowledge" juxtaposes the great eighth-through tenth-century 'Abbasid translation movement of Greek, Byzantine, and Pahlavi texts into Arabic with the equally avid post-twelfth-century translation of Arabic texts into Latin and English. Chism has also been working on the medieval Arabic and European travel narratives of Ibn Battuta, Ibn Jubayr, John Mandeville, and Marco Polo and on the Middle English and Arabic Alexander romances.

JERRILYNN DODDS is dean of the College of Sarah Lawrence College. Her scholarly work has centered on issues of artistic interchange and on how groups form identities through art and architecture. Her most recent book is *Arts of Intimacy: Christians, Jews, and Muslims in the Making of Castilian Culture,* coauthored with Maria Menocal and Abigail Krasner Balbale. She is also the author of *Architecture and Ideology of Early Medieval Spain* (1990), *Al Andalus: The Arts of Islamic Spain* (1992), and coauthor of *Convivencia: The Arts of Jews, Christians, and Muslims in Medieval Iberia* (co-ed., with Thomas Glick and Vivian Mann, 1992), *The Arts of Medieval Spain* (ed., with Charles Little and John Williams, 1993), and *Crowning Glory, Images of the Virgin in the Arts of Portugal* (ed., with Edward Sullivan, 1997). She has brought this work to the modern day in "A Short History of Architecture in Mostar" and *New York Masjid: The Mosques of New York* (2002). Dodds has also curated and co-curated a number of exhibitions and has written and directed films about cultural interaction as seen through art and architecture.

MOHAMED EL-MOCTAR is a research coordinator at the Faculty of Islamic Studies in the Qatar Foundation (Doha, Qatar) and a PhD candidate in history at Texas Tech University, with a dissertation project entitled "The Crusades' Impact on the Sunni-Shi'a Relations," under the supervision of John Howe. El-Moctar writes extensively on Islamic political thought, sectarianism in Muslim societies, contemporary Islamic movements, Muslim minorities in the West, and Islamic-American relations. His books (in Arabic) include *The Islamic Movement in Sudan* (2002), *Political Discords among the Prophet's Companions* (2004), *Political Fatwas: Conversations on Religion and Politics* (2006), *The Prophetic Guidance on Political Legitimacy and Performance* (2009),

Standards of Organizational Success (2009), and *Wounds of the Soul* (a poetic collection, in print). All his published books, except the first, were translated and published in Turkish (2006 and 2009). He is a regular contributor at the Website of Al-Jazeera TV channel, where he has published some two hundred analytical articles in Arabic and English, many of which focus on American policies and politics.

JAROSLAV FOLDA is the N. Ferebee Taylor Professor Emeritus of the History of Art at the University of North Carolina. He has been a visiting scholar at the W. F. Albright Institute in Jerusalem, the Getty Museum in Los Angeles, and a fellow at the National Humanities Center in North Carolina. His interests include medieval manuscript illumination, medieval icon and panel painting, and sculpture from the eleventh to the fifteenth century, including the art of the crusaders in the Holy Land, 1098–1291. His recent publications include *Crusader Art, The Art of the Crusaders in the Holy Land, 1000–1291* (2008), *Crusader Art in the Holy Land, from the Third Crusade to the Fall of Acre: 1187–1291* (2005), *The Art of the Crusaders in the Holy Land, 1098–1187* (1995), and various articles on the medieval figural arts, including two recent articles, "Icon to Altarpiece in the Frankish East: Images of the Virgin and Child Enthroned" and "Byzantine Chrysography in Crusader Art and Italian Maniera Greca Painting." Folda's current research focuses on chrysography, with regard to its origins, development, concept, technique, and distinctive characteristics in Byzantine and Crusader icon painting and with regard to Italian panel painting of the *maniera greca,* from circa 1225 to 1311.

CHAVIVA LEVIN is a visiting assistant professor of Jewish History at Yeshiva College, Yeshiva University. She received her doctorate in Jewish studies and history from New York University and holds bachelor's and master's degrees from Yeshiva University, where she was a fellow of the Wexner Graduate Fellowship Program. Her research interests center on the experiences of medieval Ashkenazic (Northern European) Jewry and on medieval Jewish-Christian relations, with specific focus on her dissertation topic, Jewish conversion to Christianity in medieval Northern Europe, and on medieval Jewish historiography. Her current work concentrates on *Sefer Zekhira,* Ephraim of Bonn's twelfth-century Hebrew narrative of the Second Crusade. She is a member of the steering committee for the proposed Program Unit for the Study of Religious Conversions at the American Academy of Religion.

DAVID MORRIS is a PhD candidate in medieval history at the University of Notre Dame. He holds a master's degree in medieval history from the University of St. Andrews in Scotland. His doctoral dissertation explores the relationship between historical thought, hermeneutics, and biblical exegesis in the thirteenth century, especially among Franciscans such as St. Bonaventure, Peter John Olivi, and Nicholas of Lyra. Specializing in the cultural, intellectual, and religious history of the high and late Middle Ages, his research interests include scriptural exegesis, heresy, apocalypticism, and the rise of the mendicant orders.

NICHOLAS PAUL is an assistant professor of history at Fordham University, where he has taught since 2006 on a variety of topics relating to the crusades, medieval political history, and the social and cultural history of the nobility. His articles, which have appeared in *Speculum,* the *Journal of Medieval History,* and the *Haskins Society Journal,* explore questions of dynastic politics, commemoration, and literacy. His first book, which examines how experiences of crusading were memorialized within family environments and how the crusading movement influenced the development of noble cultural identity more broadly, will appear in 2012.

DAVID M. PERRY is an assistant professor of history at Dominican University, in River Forest, Illinois. He received his PhD degree from the University of Minnesota in 2006. He has received grants to study in Venice from the University of Minnesota, Dominican University, and the Gladys Krieble Delmas Foundation. Perry is currently developing a monograph on Venice and the translation of relics out of Constantinople in the aftermath to the Fourth Crusade.

JONATHAN RILEY-SMITH is Dixie Professor Emeritus of Ecclesiastical History at the University of Cambridge. His research has surveyed a wide variety of crusade-related topics, including the institutional history of the military orders (*The Knights of St. John of Jerusalem and Cyprus,* 1967), the feudal society of the Latin Kingdom of Jerusalem (*The Feudal Nobility and the Kingdom of Jerusalem, 1174–1277,*

1973), the early development of the crusade movement (*The First Cru-sade and the Idea of Crusading,* 1991), and the participants in the early crusades (*The First Crusaders, 1095–1137,* 1997). He has also pub-lished general histories of the crusade movement, such as *Crusades: Idea and Reality* (1981), *Atlas of the Crusades* (1990), *The Oxford Illustrated History of the Crusades* (1995), *The Crusades: A History* (2nd ed., 2005), and *What Were the Crusades?* (1992; 4th ed., 2009).

JAY RUBENSTEIN, associate professor of history and medieval studies at the University of Tennessee, Knoxville, has published widely in the field of medieval intellectual history, including the book *Guibert of Nogent: Portrait of a Medieval Mind* (2002) and the essay collection, co-edited with Sally N. Vaughn, *Teaching and Learning in Northern Europe, 1000–1200* (2006). His most recent work has centered on European intellectual and cultural responses to the First Crusade, particularly in the first half of the twelfth century, including the article, "Putting His-tory to Use: Three Crusade Chronicles in Context" (2004) and the book *Armies of Heaven: The First Crusade and the Quest for Apocalypse* (2011).

LAURA J. WHATLEY is an associate professor at Kendall College of Art and Design at Ferris State University, Grand Rapids, Michigan. Before holding this post, she was a visiting assistant professor in the Depart-ment of Art History at the University of Tennessee, Knoxville. She received her doctorate in art history in December 2010, completing the doctoral dissertation "Localizing the Holy Land: The Visual Culture of Crusade in England, c. 1140–1400," in the Department of Art History at the University of Illinois Urbana Champaign. Her research interests include the impact of the crusade movement on visual and chivalric culture in late medieval Europe, crusader iconography, virtual crusade and pilgrimage, and the replication of the tomb of Christ in medieval art and architecture.

SUZANNE YEAGER is an associate professor of English and medieval stud-ies at Fordham University, where she has taught since 2005, after hold-ing a visiting assistant professorship at Cornell University. Her recent monograph, *Jerusalem in Medieval Narrative* (2008), identifies the vir-tual crusade as a feature of premodern affective piety and complement to virtual pilgrimage; the former interior exercise was represented in a range of medieval sources in which crusade was both promoted and remembered. Her recent articles have examined the exegetical place of the Jews within medieval Christian apocalypticism, representations of self-awareness in premodern pilgrim accounts, as well as audience receptions of Sir John Mandeville's *Travels* and the work of Marco Polo. Her new project, entitled "Lives on the Move," explores the roles of memory, violence, and interiority as they shaped the identity of the medieval traveler; this new book draws from medieval drama, Chaucer's *Canterbury Tales*, and work composed by late-medieval pilgrims and crusaders.

Page numbers in italics indicate illustrations.

bodies (*cont.*)
44–45; of saints, translation of, 215–16, 217, 224, 225; Six Ages model and, 83; suspended, 164–70. *See also* male body
Boethius, philosophy of, 152
Bohemond of Taranto, 70, 88–89, 133, 134–35
The Book of John Mandeville, 151
Book of Lamentations, 176, 184, 185
Book of Revelation, 177
Bordeaux, alternating voussoirs of, 104–5
boundaries, invisible and visible, 33–40, 42–44
buildings. *See* architecture; voussoirs, alternating; *and specific buildings*

Caiphas, 158–59
Caoursin, William, 235
Capystranus, 164, 166–67, 168
Carruthers, Mary, 9
cemeteries of fallen crusaders, visits to, 126–27
Charlemagne, 4, 105, 164, 165
Chastel Pèlerin, 240, 241
Chazan, Robert, 59–60, 62–63n4, 65n15, 66n20
Children's Crusade, 2–3
chivalry, 212–13n55
Christians: filth of, 37, 41, 45; monasticism of, 44; Saladin and, 205; seduction of Muslims by, 36–38, 39; in Sicily, 38–40
Chronology of the Dead Masters, 241–42
Church of the Holy Sepulchre, Jerusalem: commemoration of missals from, 125–27; dedication of, 127; in First Crusade, 114; knights attached to, 239; medieval seals and, 256; Peter the Hermit at, 132, 133; polychrome masonry of, 116–17
El Cid, 111
Ci dit des bulles que le maistre et las autre baillis del hospital, 255–56
cities: biblical allusions to, 174–77; bodies as metonym of, 166; identified as female, 151; openness of, postcrusade, 41; siege and fall of, 146–47;

translatio imperii and, 150. *See also* specific cities
The City of God (Augustine), 71, 156, 177–78
Claverie, Pierre-Vincent, 241
Clermont, council of, 3
Cluny, monks of, 110–11
commemoration: burden of, 7; calls for, 1–2; of conquest of Jerusalem by First Crusade, 125–32, 138–40, 140, 141, 142; of crusades, 8–9; for Jerusalem, 128, 131, 132; in Jerusalem, 116–17; of July 15, 125–27, 132, 137; purpose of, 131
communities: bodily suffering on behalf of, 164, 165; erasure of, 159; poetic lament for, 57–58; variety of memories within, 10–11. *See also* Ashkenazic Jews
Constantinople, 42–44, 129, 134, 166, 216, 217–18
conversion, to Christianity, 58
crusades: Alfonso VII and, 111; apocalyptic, 70–71, 88–89; in architecture, 100, 102; Children's, 2–3; definitions of, 2–5; Fifth, 129, 130; German, 129; Gregorian Reform and, 180; as identity machines, 7–9; to recapture Jerusalem, 130–31; Seventh, 10–11; Shepherds', 2–3; tactical multiplicity of, 33. *See also* First Crusade; Fourth Crusade; Second Crusade; Third Crusade
crusading, "affective," 3, 5

Damascus, 106, 107
Daniel, book of, 77–78, 84, 87, 89
Derbes, Ann, 100, 117
desire, in travel narrative, 29–30, 39–40, 42, 44
devotion, seals of, 253–54, 255
al-Dhahabi, 203
Diego Gelmirez (archbishop), 3–4
Dome of the Rock, 106, 114–16, 115, 118. *See also* Templum Domini
Dupront, Alphonse, 71

Eliezer bar Natan ("Raban"), 50–51, 54
Ellenblum, Ronnie, 33
Enrico Dandolo, 219, 220

King, E. J., 256
knights, secular, attached to Hospital of
St. John, 236
Knights Templar, 18, 256
Kuhnel, Gustav, 116

Lambert of Saint-Omer: apocalyptic
speculations of, 70, 71, 72, 73, 79, 82,
85, 87; mathematical calculations of,
76, 79–81, 84, 85; prophetic history
and, 87–88; "The Years of Our Lord,
the Sixth Age," 69. See also *Liber
floridus*
lament, commemoration of crusader
Jerusalem as, 128, 132
landscape, postcrusade, 40–46
Late Antique style, 105–6, 109, 110
Legenda of Hospital of Jerusalem, 238,
239
Léonard of Noblat, 88
Le Puy, cathedral of, 100, *109*, 112–14,
117–18
Liber floridus (Lambert of Saint-Omer):
First Crusade as theme of, 69–70, 84–
85; human events in, 75–76; Nebuchadnezzar diagram, 81, *82*, 83–85;
"On the Ages of the World" diagram,
87; "The Order of the Chief Ruling
Kingdoms," 73, *74*, *75*; organizational
system of, 69; prophecies of Adso, 78–
79; prophecies of Pseudo-Methodius,
78; on siege of Jerusalem by Chris-
tians, 157–58; Six Ages model, 71, 72,
73, *73*, 79–81, *80*, 83–84; Three Ages
of History, 84
Life of Antichrist (Adso of Montier-en-
Der), 77, 79
liturgical commemorations of fall of
Jerusalem, 125–32
Louis VII (king of France), 99
Louis IX (king of France), 4, 131
Louis Philippe (king of France), 5

Madden, Thomas F., 223
"Magdeburg charter," 3–4
"Mainz Anonymous," 50
Mâle, Emile, 112–13, 114
male body: liminal status of *imperium*
and, 151–52; as "matter of time,"

169–70; narratives of fall of Thebes
and, 161; phenomenon of siege and,
152–53; *Roman de Troie*, 153–55;
"scene of suffering" and, 157, 163–64;
in *The Siege of Jerusalem*, 161
al-Maqrīzi, 198, 203, 207
marble revetment, 105, 106
Marco Polo, 31, 32
Marino Sanudo, 138
martyrdom: as failure, 61; in Hebrew
narratives of First Crusade, 51–53;
Jewish attitudes toward, 51; in prose
and poetry, 57–59; resistance and, 56,
57; sacrificial, 52, 53, 58, 60; in *Sefer
Zekhira*, 53–56; similarities of Hebrew
narratives of, 59–61
Matthew Paris, *Flores historiarum*, 156
Mayo, Penelope, 85
McGinn, Bernard, 180
Meir of Rothenburg, 53
memorialization of martyrs in *Sefer
Zekhira*, 57–59
memorials: of crusading experience, 1–2;
of First Crusade, 4; by Ibn Jubayr, 31.
See also commemoration
memory: architecture as evoking, 113–
14; buildings as evoking, 117–18; concept of, 5–6; confectional, 32; construction of, in Hebrew narratives of
crusade, 60–61; crusade, mobilization
of, 19; as dynamic, 40; as gender specific, 7; genres of, 30–33; of Hospitaller process of militarization, 235–
39; intimacy of, 29; in medieval world,
study of, 5; passage of time and, 45; in
practice, 7–11; as recapitulation of
journey ongoing, 31; sacred, invocation of, in calls for crusades, 3–4; of
Saladin, 197, 202, 204–6, 207–8; in
theory, 5–7; travel as mode of, 45;
Venetian, of Fourth Crusade, 219–25;
wonder and, 29–30, 32. *See also* seals;
trauma and memory
miracles: *'aja'ib* account of, 32; associated with Gerard, 237; of St. Léonard
of Noblat, 88; translation of relics and,
222, 225
mnemonic practice, historical sociology
of, 7–11

Mohammed, medieval reference to, 184
Mount Carmel, 240–41
Munro, Dana, 183
Muslims, 38–40, 182–83, 242–45. *See also* Shi'a Muslims; Sunni Muslims
Mustafā, Shakir, 206

Nadjm al-Dīn, 199, 200
al-Nāsir, 205, 206
Nebuchadnezzar: dream of, 77–78, 81, 88–89; images of, in *Liber floridus*, 81, 82, 83–85, 86
Nicaea, conquest of, 133–34
Nicholas IV (pope), 138
Nicholas of Lyra, 180
Nora, Pierre, 6
Notre Dame du Port, *108*, 112–14
Nūr al-Dīn, 200, 201, 205, 206

Oedipus, 153, 160
Olick, Jeffrey K., 7
opus sectile decoration, 106
Order of the Hospital of St. John of Jerusalem in England: earliest seals of, 258–59, *259*; iconography of seals of, 260–61, *261*, 262–65, *263*, *265*; Reformation and, 252; role of Brother Walter, 259–60. *See also* Hospital of St. John of Jerusalem
Order of the Hospital of St. John of Jerusalem in Western Europe, 257–59, *259*, 262
Order of the Temple. *See* Knights Templar
Orosius, Paulus, 81, 84, 149–50, 155, 156, 157

Paris, 153, 154, 169
Partner, Nancy, 146
Paschasius Radbertus, 178
past: perception and interpretation of, in understanding crusades, 4–5; poetry as "re-membering," 151; sculpting of depictions of, in service to goals, 60–61; transfer of knowledge of, 8. *See also* memory
Patterson, Lee, 150
Paul (apostle), 176–77, 178
Paul of Bernreid, 179
Paul the Martyr, 215–16, 217, 224–25

Peter the Hermit, 71, 132–33, *133*
Peter the Venerable, 110, 111–12
Philagathos, 262
Philip II Augustus (king of France), 100, 102
Piam admodum (Pope Alexander III), 234–35
Pierre Dubois, 138
piyyut, 58
poetics: crystallization of temporal shift through, 146–47, 169–70; of siege, 149–55
Poetics (Aristotle), 152–53
Polyneices, 160–61
Prawer, Joshua, 126
Priam, 151, 152, 153, 154, 155, 157, 166
processions: in Jerusalem, 116–17; wedding procession described by Ibn Jubayr, 36–37
Pseudo-Methodius, 71, 78

al-Qādi al-Fādil, 197, 202
Quia major (Innocent III), 129–30

Ralph de Dive, seal of, 260–61, *261*
Ralph of Caen, 181, 182
Raymond of Aguilers, 100
recovery treatises, 138
relevia, 240, 241–42
relics: of St. Stephen the Protomartyr, 223–24; theft of, 221–23, 224–25; True Cross, 128, 234–35. See also *furta sacra;* translation of relics
reliquaries, 159–60
remembering: as shaping new forms and nuanced memories, 9; as social process, 6–7. *See also* memory
Remensnyder, Amy, 7
responses. *See* apocalypticism and crusade; martyrdom; travel narrative: desire in; wonder in cultural encounter
"Revelations of Pseudo-Methodius," 71
Reynauld of Chatillon, 48n15
Rhineland Jews. *See* Ashkenazic Jews
Riccardiana Psalter, 127, 130
Richard de Turk, 260
Richard I Coeur de Lion (king of England), 100, 102, 205, 206, 209
Richard of Cornwall, 130

Robbins, Joyce, 7
Robert of Flanders, 70, 73, 75–76
Robert of Ketton, 110
Robert of Rheims, 174, 182
Roger of Moulins, 242, 253–54
Roman Church, plight of, as *ancilla*, 179–80
Roman de Thebes, 160–61, 163
Roman de Troie (Benoît de Saint-Maure), 151, 153–55, 156, 159, 163, 169
Romanesque architecture, 100, 104–5, 112–14, 115–16
Rupert of Deutz, 180
Russo, Luigi, 88

Saladin: Abū Shāmah on, 202; defeat of crusader army by, 127–29; Ibn Abī Tay and, 200–201; Ibn al-Athīr on, 201–2; Ibn Jubayr on, 35, 198–99; Jerusalem and, 41; mixed record of, 208–9; name of, 199; nationalistic interpretation of, 204; regional particularism and historiography on, 202–3; sectarian and argumentative presentation of, 197, 204–6, 207–8; siege of Kerak by, 34; twentieth-century biographies of, 204–6; views of contemporaries of, 197–99, 206–7; views of poets on, 199–200, 207
Salafism, 203
"sanctification of God's name" in *Sefer Kekhira*, 57
San Giorgio Maggiore, 215, 224
San Pedro de Cardeña, 110–12
seals: bodies on biers on, 254–56, 255; common, 261; Conventual Bulla, 257; counterseals, 260, 262, 263; essential uniformity of, 264; features of, 253; of Geoffrey de Donjon, 253–54, 255, 256; with head of John the Baptist, 262–65, 263, 265; identity and, 252–53; of Order of the Hospital of St. John in Western Europe, 258–59, 259; of Ralph de Dive, 260–61, 261; shared Christological dialogue of, 256–57; storage and safekeeping of, 253, 257, 262
Second Crusade, 3, 50, 53–56, 99–100
Sefer Zekhira (Ephraim of Bonn): date of

composition of, 59–60; martyrdom as portrayed in, 51, 53–56; memorialization of martyrs in, 57–59; objectives of, 56–57, 60, 61
Sege of Melayne, 164–67
Seidel, Linda, 100, 112
Senra, Jose Luis, 110
Sephardic Jews, 53
Seventh Crusade, 10–11
Shepherds' Crusades, 2–3
Shepkaru, Shmuel, 53–54
Shi'a Muslims: alms-gathering in Jerusalem and, 238–39; Fatimids of Egypt, 201; Ibn Abī Tay as, 200–201; Ibn Jubayr on, 199; revival and self-affirmation among, 203–4; Saladin and, 204–5; views of Saladin, 197, 204–6, 207–8
The Siege (Kadare), 148–49, 167–69
siege literature: double chronology of, 162; examples of, 164–70; narrations of, 147–48; of Jerusalem, 156–64; poetry, 146–55; 167; tradition of, 164
The Siege of Jerusalem (fifteenth-century work), 147, 162–64, 167, 169–70
The Siege of Jerusalem (fourteenth-century alliterative poem), 147, 158–60, 162, 163, 169
The Siege of Jerusalem (vernacular texts), 158
al-Sillābi, 'Ali Muhammad, 203, 204
Simon the Pious of Trier, 55
Sīnān, 199, 201
Six Ages model: images of, 72, 73, 80, 83; overview of, 71, 73, 79–81, 83–84
"Solomon bar Samson," 50
Spiegel, Gabrielle, 146, 150–51
Statius, *Thebaid*, 161
St. Demetrios, 105
Stein, Robert, 146
Ste. Madeleine de Vézelay: alternating voussoirs of, 103, 104, 108–9, 112–14; church fabric of, 100, 101, 102; launch of Second Crusade in, 99–100; tympanum of, 100, 101, 102–3
Stephen the Protomartyr, 223–24
St. Gilles, Hospitaller priory of, 258, 260, 264
St. Gilles-du-Gard, 102, 118